The Road Ahead for America's Colleges and Universities

The Road Ahead for America's Colleges and Universities

ROBERT B. ARCHIBALD

DAVID H. FELDMAN

OXFORD
UNIVERSITY PRESS

Oxford University Press is a department of the University of Oxford. It furthers
the University's objective of excellence in research, scholarship, and education
by publishing worldwide. Oxford is a registered trade mark of Oxford University
Press in the UK and certain other countries.

Published in the United States of America by Oxford University Press
198 Madison Avenue, New York, NY 10016, United States of America.

© Oxford University Press 2017

Library of Congress Cataloging-in-Publication Data
Names: Archibald, Robert B., 1946– author. | Feldman, David H., author.
Title: The Road Ahead for America's Colleges and Universities /
Robert B. Archibald, David H. Feldman.
Description: New York, NY : Oxford University Press, 2017.
Identifiers: LCCN 2016041671 | ISBN 9780190251918 (hardback)
Subjects: LCSH: Education, Higher—Aims and objectives—United States. |
College costs—United States. | Universities and colleges—United States—Finance. |
Education, Higher—Effect of technological innovations on—United States. |
Nontraditional college students—United States. |
BISAC: BUSINESS & ECONOMICS / Education. | EDUCATION / Higher.
Classification: LCC LA227.4 .A74 2017 | DDC 378.73—dc23
LC record available at https://lccn.loc.gov/2016041671

9 8 7 6 5 4 3 2 1

Printed by Sheridan Books, Inc., United States of America

To

Ginger Archibald
Henry Paradise
Walter Paradise

and

Susan Lontkowski
Anthony Feldman
Aidan Feldman

Contents

Preface

WE CAN TRACE the origins of this book to two factors. First, our 2011 book, *Why Does College Cost So Much?*, generally was well received. That book explored the long trajectory of rising cost and price in the US higher education industry. In our story, the driving forces of rising cost are broader economic forces rippling through the entire global economy, not growing inefficiency and bad decision making on campus. As we expected, some observers of higher education took issue with our analysis and our conclusions. Those disagreements largely were confined to print.

On the other hand, the publication of the book led to a substantial number of speaking invitations from a wide variety of colleges, universities, and organizations. One or both of us gave presentations to many associations representing the diverse spectrum of American higher education institutions. A partial list includes the Annapolis Group, the National Association of Independent Colleges and Universities (NAICU), the Association of Public and Land Grant Universities (APLU), the Association of Communicators in Education, the National Association of Student Financial Aid Administrators (NASFAA), and the Minnesota Private College Council. We were also invited to speak to various groups on college campuses, and we spent many days talking to college governing boards. The list includes everything from small private colleges and universities like Bates, Bucknell, Fairfield, Kings, Macalester, Oberlin, and Pitzer to larger and more research-oriented universities like Rensselaer Polytechnic Institute, Rice, Wake Forest, Yale, and our own William and Mary.

Our presentations usually stimulated a lively conversation and we often got very good feedback. But on almost every occasion most of the questions were not about our book. They were about the future of higher education. This was especially true of board members, some of whom wanted to know if their institution could continue to thrive, while others were concerned if theirs could even survive the particular challenges they faced. The questions were very diverse. Some wanted to discuss the risks and rewards of embracing distance education options. Others wanted to know if the pricing model of ever-increasing tuition discount rates could persist for long. All wanted to know more about the value of education and if students would continue to come. Our analysis of the past drivers of cost and price was an eye opener for many, but most were far more interested in the future than in our detailed account of how we got to where we are.

The second factor pushing us to continue our story is the tone of many recent books and popular articles about the future of higher education. In part, our first work was a call to calm the exaggerated rhetoric of crisis. We didn't succeed. Instead, apocalyptic narratives have proliferated and this has sucked much of the air out of constructive debate. Examples include PayPal cofounder Peter Thiel's declaration that college debt is the next bubble, potentially laying waste to the economy more thoroughly than the financial meltdown of 2008. In 2012, Sebastian Thrun, who developed the first massively open online course (MOOC), famously suggested that the future world of higher education might have only ten providers. We have also seen a spate of books based on the overused business school jargon of "disruption" that forecast the coming demise of higher education as we know it.

These books are uniformly caustic in their condemnation of the current state of affairs at America's colleges and universities. At the same time, they are all surprisingly optimistic in their visions of the future of higher education. In some versions, breakthroughs in artificial intelligence will break the hold of brick-and-mortar institutions, allowing high-quality Internet-based programming to bankrupt a substantial portion of today's colleges and universities. Others contend that the college degree itself will wither away, replaced by a collection of badges and certificates. Alternatively, no-frills schools stripped of their athletics infrastructure and their inefficient research mission supposedly will outcompete existing schools, not because they're better, but because traditional colleges have taken their eye off the ball by trying to be bigger, better, and more Harvard-like than students want or need. The current system will be burned clean, and what replaces it will offer students a leaner, less expensive, and more focused training in the skills they supposedly really value.

We hold the opposite opinion. We're quite realistic about the serious problems facing American higher education institutions, and we'll dig into those problems in detail throughout this book. But our reading of the evidence and our understanding of how the higher education market works lead us to think that the current campus-based educational system likely will survive. Technology will continue to change the campus experience, but the bundle of services that most American colleges offer their students will retain great value for the bulk of the students of traditional college age. In plain language, the apocalypse isn't upon us. In that limited sense, we're rather more optimistic about the near-term future of the American higher education system. But we are not particularly optimistic about the longer-term future. American colleges and universities do face severe threats. The higher education waters are turbulent indeed. And we see little evidence that technological advances will ride in cavalry-like to save the day.

To understand the possible futures of higher education in the United States, we have to understand the structure of the system facing those threats. American colleges and universities constitute perhaps the most diverse system in the world today. They are public and private, big and small, almost unimaginably selective and completely open enrollment. Some focus exclusively on the traditional liberal arts. Others are heavily skewed toward professional fields. Some are highly endowed, while others are almost completely dependent on tuition. Some are in states with growing populations, and others must plan for demographic decline. The challenges facing our higher education system will play out differently as a consequence.

We're gloomier about the future of higher education because the institutions facing the biggest stresses are those that serve great numbers of students who most need the resource-intensive traditional campus experience. Our current higher education system is not a well-functioning engine of social mobility. Absent far-reaching changes, we risk a future in which higher education reinforces inequality instead of diminishing it. The future, however, isn't written. As a nation, we have options that can restore the capacity of our higher education system to promote social mobility. In our final chapter we suggest a diverse set of policy options that could change the trajectory of our system. The nation's policy machinery, however, is deadlocked in a partisan strife reinforced by mostly fact-light ideology. We need a new national dialogue, and this book is our modest contribution to that national conversation.

This book was written before the 2016 election that elevated Donald J. Trump to the presidency. His administration seems more likely to work on the nation's physical capital than on the system that produces its human capital. We're not optimistic that proposals to improve social mobility, especially if they come with a price tag, are likely to advance in the next four years. Nonetheless, we offer our analysis and our suggestions in a spirit of cooperation. Progress on improving our higher education system depends on depoliticizing many of the issues and seeking pragmatic solutions.

Our colleagues at the College of William and Mary have been very supportive of our efforts, and we would like to thank them, as well as the many board members, faculty, and administrators who attended the presentations we mentioned earlier. Our coauthor Peter McHenry deserves special thanks.

Peter's help with the paper we wrote as a threesome was invaluable, and his insights have helped us on numerous occasions. Finally, David benefited from a Faculty Research Assignment provided by the College, and Bob benefited from support as a Plumeri Faculty Fellow. These two awards allowed us to focus on writing this book.

PART ONE

Introduction

1

The Rhetoric of Higher Education in Crisis

AMERICA'S COLLEGES AND universities have sailed into turbulent waters, and revolution is in the air! For many commentators the only question is how fast the crisis will develop and how many of the nation's traditional higher education institutions will founder. In a 1997 interview in *Forbes Magazine*, Peter Drucker said, "Thirty years from now the big university campuses will be relics. Universities won't survive. It's as large a change as when we first got the printed book."[1] More recently, at a symposium in May 2014, Clayton Christensen predicted that "half of all colleges could be in some form of bankruptcy or reorganization within 10 to 15 years."[2]

A quick check of recent book titles or a glance at the opinion pages of major news outlets portrays an inefficient system ripe for disruptive change. Runaway tuition growth threatens to price out all but the wealthiest Americans from acquiring the educational ticket to prosperity. Easy federal loan availability fuels rising student debt that is rapidly becoming the next financial bubble. In Kevin Carey's words, "The modern American university has endured for this long only because almost as soon as it was created, it began an epic run of good luck that is only now coming to an end."[3]

Yet at the same time, the educational ticket is increasingly debased by the poor quality of undergraduate teaching and increasingly lax demands placed on students.[4] Schools have focused more effort on faculty research and bloated administrative staff while shifting the burden of teaching to an increasing number of adjuncts and graduate students in large and impersonal courses. Cost is also rising because schools supposedly spend too much on lavish amenities and on prestige investments in research centers and superstar faculty who educate few students. And tenure supposedly saps the vitality of our universities.[5] The value of the traditional liberal arts curriculum is also under the microscope since it doesn't train students in specific job skills.

In this environment, many claim that technological innovations in online learning will help transform the landscape of higher education, freeing students from the high cost of traditional face-to-face instruction while sharpening the focus and quality of the training available to the average American. This trio of rising cost, declining value, and technological breakthroughs will combine to reshape higher education in ways that leave large numbers of traditional institutions in reorganization or bankruptcy. Their luck will have run out.

What will the American higher education system actually look like in twenty-five years? The apocalyptic outcomes we just outlined are indeed plausible. But it's not a future we find particularly likely. The higher education system today does face a set of significant stresses and challenges, and we will outline how those challenges arose and how they may affect the extraordinarily diverse set of institutions that make up the US higher education system. Yet when today's graduates return for their twenty-fifth reunions, we think that most of them will recognize their alma mater. The returning alumni will indeed see changes, some of them quite substantial, just as the graduates of the 1970s and 1980s have seen significant developments in the time since they left school. And the schools that will change the most are the ones facing the greatest stresses today.

We will focus our attention on the nonprofit institutions, public and private, that offer the bulk of the traditional four-year bachelor's degree programs and most of the graduate and professional degrees. These are the schools seemingly in the cross hairs of disruptive forces. This is a very diverse set of institutions that includes everything from small private liberal arts colleges to immense public research universities, from tuition-driven colleges with no meaningful endowment to Harvard with financial resources well in excess of $30 billion. The higher education sector includes other actors, such as community colleges that offer certificate programs and two-year associate's degrees, and the growing for-profit sector that caters to large numbers of older nontraditional students. We will weave these other actors into our story where doing so helps us advance our understanding of how universities respond to stresses and incentives. But our goal in this short volume isn't to explore the entire terrain of the American higher education system.

Although this is a work of nonfiction, a few fictional stories about the future of colleges and universities facing today's stresses will help us to set the stage. Imagine with us the experiences of three returning alumni who have been out of touch with developments on the campuses they left twenty or twenty-five years ago, and who are shocked at what they see.

Story 1: Pradhi Gupta

Pradhi Gupta was anxious to see the campus of North Central State again. He had not been a faithful alumnus since he left with his BA in 2017. He returned to India after finishing and then moved several times without sending forwarding addresses to North Central. He had no interest in getting annual requests for donations that he would simply discard. As a result, he knew very little about what had transpired at the school. In the late summer of 2042, he found himself in the Midwest for business, and he decided to pay a midlife nostalgia visit to his alma mater.

Pradhi hadn't been thrilled with his education in the United States. North Central wasn't a very demanding school. Though he remembers liking the easy classes at the time, he felt even then that they weren't preparing him particularly well for his return to India. The best part was that he got to practice his English and hone his social skills. Also, he resented paying much higher tuition than the in-state students sitting beside him. Still, he had some fond memories of North Central, and he wanted to see what the school was like now.

As he walked down the main street of the small city where the school was located, he recognized the landscape. But despite the warm September day, he did not see the normal bustle of a college campus. He saw no students chatting as they walked to class, no pick-up football games on the green, and none of the co-eds tanning themselves in their tiny swimsuits that had so shocked him when he first arrived, only one older gentleman walking with the aid of a cane. With relief, he did see that the iconic main administration building was still flying a purple and yellow North Central banner.

Pradhi entered the lobby and took a look at the office directory. He saw a listing for the college's president and several other administrators, but he couldn't find a dean of students or a foreign student advisor. He would have been lost without Sally Mitchell, the foreign student advisor who had taken him under her wing. He introduced himself at the information desk and asked if he might speak with the dean of students. The answer shocked him. North Central had no dean of students and no foreign student advisor because they did not have any students on campus. All of North Central's courses were online.

Pradhi explained that he was a long-lost alum, and the woman at the desk suggested he talk to an enrollment counselor who could fill him in on the

recent history of North Central. He took a seat while he waited for the enrollment counselor, whatever that was. As he waited he examined the posters
on the walls. He saw advertisements for an online MBA, online engineering
degrees, online nursing degrees, and online education degrees. The glossy
posters showed pictures of happy people staring into computer screens or
walking along looking down at various digital devices. None included the campus life that Pradhi remembered.

Mr. Samuel McClain, the jovial and welcoming enrollment counselor,
came into the lobby a moment later and introduced himself. He told Pradhi
that he too was a product of the old North Central, so he understood Pradhi's
questions. The North Central story was very simple and quite similar to the
path taken by a large number of state-supported institutions. Long before
Pradhi arrived, he said, the state appropriation for public institutions had
begun to decline, and this had put upward pressure on tuition. At the same
time, that decision helped spur North Central to seek more out-of-state students, and especially foreign students like him.

To cut costs, North Central started to rely increasingly on online delivery
of courses, while adjunct teachers began to replace permanent faculty. During
the last recession a decade ago, the state finally eliminated general support
altogether, opting for a fully tuition-driven model of education. Students sud-
denly had to pay the full cost of their education. On-campus enrollment fell
dramatically, while online enrollment surged. Almost overnight, campus
facilities were dramatically underused and most departments were hopelessly
overstaffed. At first North Central fought to preserve its campus and its traditions, but it was a losing battle. Five years ago most of the campus was sold
to a large retirement home. The dorms, the dining halls, everything except
for the administration building and one information technology building that
housed the servers and the support staff for the online courses had been sold
off. Mr. McClain was quick to assure Pradhi that North Central was thriving
in its new incarnation. Enrollments in the online courses were growing steadily, and some of the courses had won national awards for the effective use of
artificial intelligence.

After listening to this explanation, Pradhi had one question. What happened to the professors? Mr. McClain responded that North Central didn't
employ many. A few were retained to design online modules to reflect North
Central's vision and to interact by email with students in some of the more specialized courses at the graduate level. For the most part they relied on courses
produced by textbook publishers and courses designed by professors at other
institutions. Mr. McClain explained that the undergraduate education at all
of the surviving state campuses was very similar. Most of the undergraduate

curriculum came from the same providers. North Central's distinctiveness came from some of its own graduate programs and from how thoroughly it had integrated artificial intelligence into its courses. As a result, North Central needed very few faculty members.

Pradhi decided to walk around the old campus after he left McClain's office, but he gave up after twenty minutes. Though the buildings were familiar, the feel just wasn't the same. Although his education had been far from ideal, he wondered if the online students were getting the same package of experiences he remembered. He had his doubts, but from what Mr. McClain had said, most American public institutions had switched their entire curriculum to online delivery. Campuses like the one he remembered were mostly gone. Mr. McClain had told him that the old style of education was now reserved for a small group of elite students, and for families of great wealth who could afford to indulge their children with the traditional four years of personal growth.

Story 2: Bertram Williams

Bert Williams was anxious to see what his old college campus was like. Given his last name, he had endured a large amount of teasing for attending Ben Williams College. As a native of Bath in England, he had endured even more teasing for studying British literature. Still, he had enjoyed his college years in the United States, and he was embarrassed that he had not kept up with events at BW in the twenty years since he finished in 2017.

As he drove through the campus gates he immediately felt at home. The buildings on the main quad were unchanged. Bert walked over to Founders Hall, which had housed the English department when he was a student. The directory in the building showed him that things had changed. Founders Hall now housed the offices and laboratories of the computer engineering department. This struck Bert as odd. Ben Williams had a computer science department when he was a student, but it did not have computer engineering, or any kind of engineering for that matter. He poked his head in what seemed to be the main office and asked where he could find the English department. The person at the desk—receptionist, secretary, or administrator, Bert couldn't really tell which—looked it up on his computer and told Bert that English was in McCorker Hall on the west edge of campus. Bert had never heard of McCorker, so he took a look at a campus map.

This change of buildings seemed very strange. Founders Hall was big. In his time, the building had housed philosophy and modern languages, as well as English. Now computer engineering occupied the whole building. If the map was to scale, McCorker Hall was much smaller. Bert was also surprised that anyone on campus would not know off the top of their head where the English department was located. Perhaps he had run into a new employee.

Bert found McCorker Hall and took a look at the directory. The same departments that had occupied Founders Hall in his day were now in McCorker, and there were two more departments: political science and sociology. He was shocked to see only five professors listed in the English department. One of them, a certain Dr. Holmes, had taught one of Bert's introductory nineteenth-century literature courses.

Dr. Holmes was in his office, and he welcomed Bert to sit down for a chat. Holmes apologized for not remembering him. Even though the literature classes had been small sections of twenty-five, that was a lot of students ago. But he was happy to talk to alumni who were visiting. Some people still showed up for homecoming and other events, but the school had changed so much that it was hard for the older alums to relate to the place.

According to Dr. Holmes the changes started right around the time Bert left. Two factors were important. First, a drumbeat of information had come out tying the economic returns from a college education to the specific major a student studied. All of this information suggested that the STEM fields (science, technology, engineering, and mathematics) and a few others, like economics and business, had dramatically higher career earnings than other majors. The careers available to liberal arts majors just did not command salaries that justified spending a lot or borrowing a lot to go to a high-tuition private school like BW. Second, fairly good online courses were cropping up in social science and humanities fields, but the online courses in the sciences, particularly in the advanced classes, were not as good. They couldn't replicate the hands-on laboratory experiences offered face to face.

Applications to Ben Williams had begun to decline, and the students who did apply were increasingly attracted to physics, computer science, biology, chemistry, and even geology. If Ben Williams was to survive in this brave new world, it had to change. The president and trustees decided on a bold new strategy. They built new science buildings, retrofitted old buildings to house science departments and their laboratories, added engineering to the curriculum, and shrank the rest of the departments.

Bert suggested that Ben Williams College had morphed into Ben-Tech. Dr. Holmes said that was a fair characterization. Bert then asked if there were any English majors in the new Ben Williams. Holmes answered that the English major disappeared five years ago. There was still a major in "liberal studies," which did include some English courses, and which still drew some students. Holmes added that most of the liberal studies students were people who found they couldn't succeed in the basic science courses all entering students had to take. Like most of the other humanities and social science departments, Holmes said that English had become a service department for the school. The current department's primary task was staffing the writing course required of every student. One of the newer professors also taught technical writing for some of the engineering departments.

Bert was shocked, but he could see why the English department now only needed five professors. BW had fourteen English professors when he graduated. And he was one of fifty English majors in his graduating class. As a last question, Bert asked Dr. Holmes if he liked working at the new Ben Williams. Holmes thought for a moment and then replied, "I am happy to have a job actually teaching students face to face." He explained that few English PhDs had jobs like this anymore. Most English courses were offered online at other universities. Also, other departments actually had taken larger hits than the English department. "At least we can teach writing," he quipped. He also said that some of the science and engineering students were very good and very interesting, and he enjoyed teaching them. Another group, however, desperately needed to learn how to communicate. "Some of them are just plain terrible writers when they get here," Holmes said, and he got some satisfaction from improving their writing. He sighed and said that this was not what he had signed up for when he came to BW. Early in his career he was a scholar of American literature who got to teach subjects he loved to students who were genuinely interested in the same things. That was gone now. A humanities education was just not something people were willing to pay for today.

Bert thanked Dr. Holmes for talking to him and said he wanted to walk around campus to reflect on the changes. The more he wandered, the more differences he noted. All of the new or renovated buildings he saw housed some kind of science or engineering laboratory, and most had prominent placards showing the sponsorship of some high-tech company. The playing fields were still there, but the football stadium (he never really understood that game) was gone. He did not overhear one student conversation about anything cultural, political, or metaphysical. The physical surroundings, things like the quad and most of the dorms, made Ben Williams look like the BW that he had known, but the soul of the school had changed in profound ways. Broad inquiry and personal growth weren't really on the academic menu anymore.

Story 3: Ramona Martinez

Ramona Martinez wanted to make one last stop during her trip to the United States. Although she was here primarily on business for her consulting firm, she had scheduled extra time to pay a visit to her undergraduate college.

She was glad of the timing. October was beautiful in Ohio, and she would be happily home in Buenos Aires before the cold and cloudy winter arrived in the northern hemisphere. As she drove up the hill onto the grounds of Lackey College, she immediately felt a warm glow of remembrance wash over her. The sugar maples that lined the gravel paths, the vast expanses of green grass, and the stately buildings lovingly constructed over almost two hundred years all looked the same or better. She felt as though no time had passed since her graduation twenty years earlier. Nostalgia wasn't her only motive for the trip. She wanted to reconnect with Lackey to see if it might be a good place for her fifteen-year-old son Galeno to consider for school. She headed first to the admissions office and picked up a glossy brochure that described the school and its very personalized programs. She didn't think she could talk Galeno into anything, but she wanted to put the information casually under his nose.

She left the admissions office and sat down on the lawn in front of the campus chapel. This was a place where she had enjoyed sitting and chatting with friends about coursework, and about her deepest thoughts and feelings. The brochure was very informative. Lackey's enrollment was unchanged from the 1,500 of her years. The listing of the academic departments also seemed much the same. She noted a few more interdisciplinary programs with interesting titles. She also saw more emphasis on research teaming between students and professors, and among students from different disciplines. She thought that emphasis was quite appropriate, given the way interdisciplinary team analysis had shaped her career in consulting for a firm with offices across the western hemisphere. She nodded approvingly at the colorful photos of happy students and faculty working together with state-of-the-art equipment in everything from science labs to music performance. And Lackey still offered the same rich set of student activities. The brochure included a dramatic picture of the Lackey symphony, as well as one of the football team.

On the last page she found the difference. The list-price tuition at Lackey sent an electric shock through her. Ramona and her husband both had very good jobs in Argentina, and both of them came from well-off families, but the cost of tuition, fees, and room and board at Lackey was at the outer limits of what Ramona would consider. She realized that she had been out of touch with college pricing in the United States. Everything else on her brief working trips to the United States over the years was always quite reasonable, subject to the usual swings in the value of the US dollar to the peso. The sticker price of going to Lackey was another matter. She went back to the admissions office to ask a few questions about aid. She remembered that many of her classmates had received financial aid that had helped them pay what even at the time seemed to be a high price for their Lackey education. She wondered if aid had expanded along with tuition.

The director of financial aid happened to be free, and she beckoned Ramona into her office. Yes, Lackey had a considerable amount of financial aid to disburse, and a large percentage of students received some. Lackey's own internal grants, however, went primarily to students with special abilities in academics, the arts, and athletics. Grant aid was a tool to help Lackey construct the best incoming class, and economic diversity was only one of many attributes they sought. And as a tuition-driven school with a modest endowment, grant aid couldn't meet all the need. This was especially true for students from families that had good incomes, even if they considered themselves middle class. Lackey students could also qualify for federal financial aid that was given strictly on the basis of financial need, but that aid went to Americans, and it was designed for very low-income students. That sort of aid covered the cost of a year at a community college, not a private four-year school like Lackey that lavished attention and resources on its students.

Ramona then told the director about Galeno, and a little about her and her husband's finances. The director told Ramona that as a legacy, Galeno's chances of being admitted were good, as long as he was a decent student. But given their income, his chances of getting any significant cut in his tuition would depend on his special talents and achievements. Ramona said that Galeno was crazy about soccer, but he had yet to demonstrate any World Cup ability. He was a good student, and his mother was sure that he could hold his own at a place like Lackey, but she didn't think he was on the path to a Nobel Prize either. Ramona was frustrated at this point. Perhaps more sharply than she intended, she suggested that students who could pay a king's ransom or who were supremely talented must fill Lackey. The director said that her summary was just about right. She wished they could attract more students from middle-class families, but that kind of tuition cutting would require double the current aid budget. Big-time philanthropy could do the job, but Lackey would need to get a nine-figure gift on top of existing fundraising targeted at other needs and priorities. Unfortunately that kind of donor had not yet appeared.

Ramona had maintained contact with several American friends from her college days, and when she got back to her hotel she made a few calls. Her friends were not at all surprised by what she had learned on her return visit to Lackey. If your children were merely very bright, and you wanted them to have the college experiences available at a small private residential program like Lackey, you had to have saved quite a lot, or you needed to be a really high-income family. The other option was debt, but American students increasingly couldn't use that to finance an expensive place like Lackey. Ramona learned that the kind of education she received was reserved for a few. Most other students went to big state universities or studied online. Perhaps Galeno would stay home in Argentina.

Linear Forecasts and Predictions of Radical Change

Take a trend and assume it continues. In each of these three stories, we took a recent trend in the higher education environment and presumed that it continued apace for twenty or more years. The results are caricatures with a message. We did this to get the discussion started, not because we think this is a good forecasting method. Linear extrapolation is almost always a poor strategy. Random "black swan" events change the historical path. Higher education has witnessed a number of those game-changing events in the past, from the Morrill Act, which inaugurated the spectacular rise of public land grant universities, to the GI Bill, which helped make mass higher education thinkable and politically salient. Purposive decisions on campus also deflect and alter the way institutions and the whole industry behave. Those decisions often are taken in response to certain trends, and they bend the trend.

Yet the language of dramatic changes and even impending doom increasingly dominates the public discourse about the higher education system. As of this writing, Google reports over 300,000 hits just for the phrase "crisis in higher education." Peter Thiel, the cofounder of PayPal, likens the condition to the final phases of a financial bubble potentially more catastrophic than the real estate bubble of recent memory.[6] This rhetoric of doom is complemented by a sense that a radical technology-driven transformation of this vital national industry is just around the corner. As the quotations we took from Peter Drucker and Clayton Christensen suggest, people who are taken very seriously think that the higher education landscape will soon be littered with the wreckage of a substantial fraction of America's colleges and universities. Drucker and Christensen are certainly not alone in suggesting that the traditional American college experience is headed toward the scrapheap of history.[7]

Like our three stories, most narratives of radical change begin from a set of disturbing trends. The narratives also share many notions of causality. Tuition increases are generated by rapidly (and often irresponsibly) rising costs within institutions that have lost sight of their core mission. These universities produce reams of largely useless faculty research and engage in unproductive prestige and amenity competitions. Tuition increases also are fueled by easy access to state and federal grants and loans that pump up demand. As a consequence, fewer students can afford the traditional college experience without taking on massive debt.

The narrative continues by suggesting that the coming disruption might be avoidable if traditional nonprofit colleges and universities were nimble and adaptable, but in apocalyptic scenarios they are anything but flexible. Faculty self-interest preserves the status quo just at the time when radical change is most needed. This process works in part through the long-standing commitment to faculty governance at most academic institutions. The tenure system also is supposedly a drag on productivity and innovation. In this view, traditional colleges and universities are prisoners of a pernicious special interest politics that ossifies decision making and eliminates administrative flexibility. More and more of a university's costs become fixed instead of controllable, and institutions lose the ability to respond to changes in their economic environment.

The storyline then shifts to technological changes that will ultimately overwhelm most institutions and complete the makeover of this important economic sector. The revolutionary stories almost all share a striking optimism about the new online horizons. Over time, Internet-based content delivery platforms will drive down the costs of providing higher education, signaling the start of the disruption. Quality will rapidly improve, so students will learn as easily, or perhaps even better, on their tablets and laptops as they do today on traditional college campuses. As a result, many of the schools that offer face-to-face classes and a residential campus experience won't be able to compete. They will wither away financially and pass into history. Like the slow and dimwitted dinosaurs in a 1960s cartoon, a substantial portion of the nation's traditional colleges and universities will face an extinction crisis as the environment around them changes.

In these disruption-inspired narratives of the American higher education system, the decline and fall of the prestige-obsessed university is very near. This bloated institution is a contemporary Babylon in the corrupt twilight of its splendor. And just as Belshazzar and his court could not conceive that the rabble army outside would breach their strong walls, so the presidents and deans of the modern university cannot comprehend the technological storm that is coming to destroy them and their extravagantly wasteful cathedrals of learning. University administrators see the excessive spending on staff, program proliferation, and amenities and say they are just meeting a demand. They see the excessive reward for research and say that it is the price of excellence. Yet far-sighted change agents in the private sector, and from within the academy, are busily building the software platforms and nimble corporations that will revolutionize how people learn. These people propel the inexorable march of artificial intelligence and the logic of disruption. Theirs is the writing on the wall that university administrators cannot or will not decipher. Some observers, however, claim they can read the signs. They think they are the Daniels of this age.

Threats We Face

Like our linear extrapolation stories, the dystopian images of the future of higher education are based on trends quite evident to most observers of American colleges and universities. Any analysis of the future of American higher education has to explore the causes, the true magnitude, and the likely consequences of these trends. We also believe that any analysis of higher education has to recognize the considerable diversity of the colleges and universities in the four-year sector. These trends will have very different effects on different types of institutions. The next two chapters describe the four-year institutions we wish to study, highlighting the things that make them different, as well as what makes them similar. The chapters that follow focus on the threats these institutions face. This is the meat of our story. We will divide these threats into three broad categories.

Internal Threats

We classify internal threats as those that come from conducting business as usual in the traditional model of producing a college education. As economists, we divide the threats into those that affect the supply of educational opportunities and those that affect the demand for higher education.

The supply-side threat is the rapid growth in costs that some fear will price many or most traditional colleges and universities out of the market. If the cost of supplying the bundle of services that make up a traditional four-year education grows without bound, many colleges will indeed face survival problems. These concerns echo most strongly in the Lackey College tale. To evaluate the severity of this threat, we will review the debates about the important drivers of college costs. This topic has generated a lot of discussion and disagreement, so there is considerable ground to cover. As part of this discussion, we will be very careful to make the distinction between college costs and college prices. Rising price is not always an indication of rising costs. College pricing is very complicated. First, colleges receive subsidies from state appropriations and/ or from endowment earnings, and these subsidies allow the average student to pay less, and often far less, than the average cost of the education he or she receives. Second, many students receive a grant or scholarship directly from the university they attend, so the net price they pay is very different from the list-price tuition printed in the catalog.

On the demand side, perhaps large numbers of students in the typical college-going age range will stop going to traditional colleges and universities. To evaluate this possibility, we will review two factors: demography and the economic return to education. Forecasts of the number of new high school graduates indicate that rapid expansions are a thing of the past except in the South. In the West, the Midwest, and the Northeast, projections are flat or declining. Some institutions in the hardest-hit regions will have to work hard to stay out of economic trouble, but demographic collapse isn't in the cards. Also, the demographic makeup of high school graduates is changing rapidly, and these trends will change the ethnic and economic composition of the pool of potential college students. The percentage of the pool composed of minorities (and especially Hispanics) will grow rapidly and the white non-Hispanic share will decline. The message is that nationally there will be enough students, but the location and background of those students will be very different. Universities must adjust, and the ones that do so effectively will see real opportunities.

The evidence on the value of acquiring a college degree paints a more reassuring picture. On average, the economic returns that flow from a college degree are substantial, and there is no evidence that these returns are shrinking. Although the average return is high, there is a distribution around this average. This variance comes from the schools attended, the choice of academic concentration, and individual differences. Given this variance, a college education does not guarantee economic success. In an era of rising list price it's only natural to wonder if the value proposition remains high. Using anecdotal accounts, reporters and editorialists can easily find examples of students who are in financial difficulty despite their college education. Tales of new graduates moving back in with mom and dad support this view, as does first-time employment of college graduates in occupations that seemingly do not require a degree. These stories paint a very unrealistic picture about the economic return to education. We recognize that a well-crafted anecdote often trumps a good theory and its supporting data, so we will spend some quality time reviewing the evidence about the individual and social benefits of higher education.

Environmental Threats

These are broader economic changes in the world outside of higher education that make the current financial model for colleges and universities more challenging. Over the last decade the real value (corrected for inflation) of median family income has decreased in the United States. Almost all of the gains in family income have accrued to the very top of the income distribution. If this trend continues, much of the potential student population will find the "business as usual" model of college education increasingly difficult to afford. Something will have to change. In our narrative, changes in the national distribution of income over the past forty years offer up some of the most significant challenges the American higher education system faces for the foreseeable future.

Rising student debt is due in no small part to broad trends in family income, though recessions like the significant downturn that began in 2008 have contributed much to current woes. And while student loan debt problems are often overhyped in the media, many students face real hardships. Although colleges are only partially responsible for this problem, they must adapt to it. One form of adaptation is long-standing—the rising discount rate that schools have used to fill seats and to preserve mission-driven socioeconomic diversity. This adaptation itself is a trend that may be difficult for many schools to sustain.

Another external challenge reflects fears that the revenue model of the typical college will become unsustainable. There are two important parts of this threat. The first comes from state governments, long the most ardent supporters of higher education. They have ratcheted back the share of the bill they will pay. Our fictitious Pradhi Gupta found that the state had finally abandoned its support for his alma mater North Central State. That was a useful exaggeration for our story, but the nation has indeed experienced a sea change in state spending away from higher education and toward other priorities. It began over thirty-five years ago and now seems a permanent part of the higher education landscape. There is scant evidence that most states have any appetite to restore funding percentages of the past. Indeed, those who would push states to spend more have to fight the headwinds generated by the contemporary narrative of wasteful university spending, change-resistant faculty, and elitist administrative leadership. Why should states pump money into a hidebound set of institutions when smart investment in online technologies—the magic bullets of higher education reform—will produce a better outcome at a much lower price? To many in state government, raising the levels of state subsidy would amount to a bailout of a failing industry.

This leaves state-supported colleges and universities in the same position as most private institutions. They have to depend on tuition and philanthropy for an increasing share of their revenue. But the current tuition model of higher education may be at its limit. Colleges and universities have eagerly sought out students who could afford to pay. Selective schools have pushed up list-price tuition quite rapidly, while discounting it for lower-income families or for students who help bring desirable traits to the first-year class. These desirable traits include everything from regional and ethnic diversity to a good jump shot or high SAT scores. As state support has waned, public institutions have begun to move in the same direction. But this model works less well for less selective institutions, whether public or private. These institutions are highly dependent on full classes to pay their bills. Because less selective colleges are often a student's third-choice safety school, they have less leverage to extract large amounts of tuition revenue. And for all universities there aren't large amounts of potential extra tuition waiting to be collected by ever-slicker discounting strategies in an era of flat family incomes for 95% of the population.

Philanthropy offers the other way to pay the bills, and colleges and universities have ratcheted up their fundraising efforts to persuade donors to give generously. Success in this effort differs considerably across institutions. As one might expect, the haves are generally much better at fundraising than the have-nots, though the have-nots have the greater need.

Those who are pessimistic about the future of America's existing institutions argue that these internal challenges are exacerbated by the cumbersome nature of higher education decision making. While there is some truth to the notion that colleges and universities are not the most nimble firms, there is considerable evidence that they have readily adapted to changing circumstances. The college curriculum of today is substantially different from the college curriculum of forty years ago. Whole departments and schools have appeared and disappeared. Teaching methods have changed too. Many colleges and universities have instituted freshman seminars, have placed more emphasis on undergraduate research, and have experimented with online modules and courses. We will discuss this academic ferment and assess the potential for universities to find new best practices in a changing world.

Technological Threats

Even if families were financially healthy and colleges were quite nimble enterprises, the current model could fall prey to new technologies. The digital world may revolutionize the way colleges and universities operate. Expansions of online education play a role in many forecasts of the future of colleges. It was featured in two of our stories. Pradhi Gupta found that his alma mater had morphed into a completely online institution, and Bert Williams found that Ben Williams College had to make a radical change in its curriculum to survive in a world dominated by online providers.

Currently, the basic teaching model at the typical American college relies on face-to-face interaction between students and professors. Some of these face-to-face interactions happen in large impersonal groups, while others occur in small and highly interactive sessions. New digital technologies offer many potential advantages over face-to-face coursework. Class size can grow beyond the artificial room-size limitations of face-to-face interactions. In the ideal world imagined by computer science optimists, this could allow education to be delivered at a dramatically lower cost. The experiments with massively open online courses (MOOCs) showed this potential quite nicely. Class size can be enormous, and the costs of delivering an online course are not much different than the costs of delivering the same course to the relatively few students who register for the course on campus. In 2012, Professor Sebastian Thrun's initial artificial intelligence class "enrolled" 160,000 online students in addition to the Stanford students who took it in person, and 23,000 earned "certificates of completion."

There are other possible advantages to college courses offered over the Internet. Many can be taken asynchronously (though this was not the case for Thrun's 160,000-student artificial intelligence class). The student does not have to show up for class at a particular place and at a particular time. This has made distance education very popular with nontraditional students who may have a full-time job and a family to manage. Also, online courses offer students many chances to repeat lessons. In a traditional course on a residential campus, a student who misses a lecture can get another student's notes, but the experience is not the same. Finally, cleverly constructed online courses can have exercises that provide students instant feedback on the material.

There are already numerous online degrees offered both by stand-alone online institutions and by universities that also offer traditional degrees. For the most part these degrees have not attracted traditional-aged college students. Most of their success is with older students who are picking up the undergraduate degree they skipped in the past or with students interested in acquiring some specific knowledge or job-related skill. We are still fairly early in the evolution of this technology. The quality of online courseware is improving, and given the potential cost advantages of these courses and programs, they have the potential to grow dramatically.

Those who forecast a technologically driven overhaul of the traditional college or university suggest that the new technology may bring more than a different mode of educational delivery. In a world in which lots of online providers are offering courses, there may be no reason to enroll in any college. A student could pick and choose a set of connected courses, and agencies would develop to certify that the program of study was worthy of a degree. This represents an unbundling of the traditional university. Global competition to provide the best coursework could conceivably lead to a large set of course providers catering to a vast audience that can customize their own degrees. In such a world, why would a student want to be bound to one university's offerings and one department's faculty in creating the academic concentration that is at the heart of the traditional degree?

There are even more radical proposals floating around. Perhaps the traditional degree has outlived its usefulness. All a person needs to navigate the modern world is a set of specific skills. Courses that teach these skills will be available on the Internet, and badges or certificates will be awarded to students who demonstrate they have mastered the skills. The correct set of badges would then make an applicant very attractive to an employer.

The Way Forward

Which will it be, revolution or evolution? Clear claims like the ones offered by Peter Drucker and Clayton Christensen are the territory of futurists. For the most part we are inclined to characterize futurists as people who are happy if you don't read their twenty-year-old books. We will shy away from making sweeping forecasts about what the future has in store. Instead, we will examine the viability of the American higher education system from a number of perspectives.

The answers to this question will depend on a complex course of economic events whose path at present can be but dimly discerned. The road ahead is not foreordained. This future also will be driven by a set of choices made in Washington, in state capitols, in meetings on university campuses and between college administrations and their boards of trustees, and lastly in family kitchens across the United States. We don't presume to know the outcome of all of these future choices, but we think we can see the outline of likely evolutionary pathways toward a recognizable higher education system of the future. We also think we can understand better and worse policy options for the nation as we wrestle with how best to achieve wide access to educational opportunity within clear financial constraints.

While generally we will shy away from making forecasts, there is one that we are very comfortable making. The future will not produce a single model of a successful college or university. The higher education system is composed of many different kinds of institutions filling many different market niches. In the future some of those institutions will thrive, and others will not survive. But we are quite certain that the diversity we currently see will continue. We are not headed to a one-size-fits-all system of higher education.

Our "bottom line" is hopeful but realistic. The future is not inevitable. Because cost has risen rapidly in the past does not mean it must rise inexorably. Because schools have used tuition discounting in the past to respond to certain needs and opportunities does not mean that discount rates will forever rise. As Herbert Stein, the former head of the Council of Economic Advisors, once quipped, "Things that can't continue, won't." Our job is to identify the forces and the decisions that will change these fundamental trends. And technology is not economic predestination. The wholesale transformation of the American higher education system strikes us as a highly unlikely outcome of the set of decisions people and institutions will make over the next several decades.

For all its faults, the existing system offers great value both to the people who buy its services and to society more broadly. Billions of dollars of public and private money flow through this complex industry. Its many "outputs" include educated (and credentialed) undergraduates, research and graduate education, and public service. Each of these can play a vital role in raising labor productivity and living standards, improving social mobility, and influencing a nation's international standing both politically and economically. Evolution within this complex system is far more likely than revolution. The greatest risks we see are to the social mobility function of higher education. The threats we will examine have the potential to reinforce our higher education system's existing division into high-quality programming for the wealthy and the supremely talented and second- or third-class options for most of the disadvantaged.

A Note on Method: Human Agency Versus Economic Forces

In this book we will treat readers to engaging stories about incentives, and we will rely on a small mountain of empirical evidence to support our narrative about the likely evolutionary path of American higher education. You will hear much less about individuals and individual institutions. When we talk about specific colleges and universities, the case is meant to exemplify broader forces that constrain or affect the choices that schools and their students can make.

Here is an example that highlights the importance of incentives, and which shows the risks of personalizing complex processes. Many higher education narratives focus on the active decisions of people whose great or terrible deeds push the story forward. On the "good" or "hero" side are people whose insights about the flaws of the modern university were seemingly prescient, or people whose ingenuity will sweep away the old rot. In techno-optimistic versions of the narrative, this includes the computer scientists and entrepreneurs whose new understanding of education—linked to the profit motive—will disrupt the hidebound and inefficient universities that have stood for centuries. All good narratives of this sort also need villains. These are the people whose choices represent the worst of the current system. Personalizing complex processes often makes for a simpler and more exciting narrative, but characterizing the higher education system's development in this way risks missing, or misunderstanding, the bigger forces that shape the choices that agents can make.

The rise of George Washington University under its aggressively entrepreneurial president Joel Trachtenberg is a case in point. Kevin Carey uses this example as a cautionary tale about the prestige game that has supposedly driven up cost and paved the way for the downfall of the wasteful modern university.[8] A generation ago, George Washington University in Washington, DC, was a minimally selective commuter school in the shadow of nearby Georgetown University. After a multi-million-dollar makeover, George Washington is much more selective and much more expensive. Its facilities have been enlarged and upgraded, and it competes for faculty it could not have hired before its makeover. Does this story, driven by the oversized personality of one man, exemplify the failures and the wrong values of an entire system?

To many critics of contemporary higher education, the services of elite institutions are a perfect example of a Veblen good. A Veblen good is something people desire more as its price goes up. The idea is associated with prestige, where a high and rising price both signals and fuels the sense of exclusivity that is supposedly the trait in demand. The actual quality of the product or service is of secondary importance at best. To critics, the world simply does not need another example of a bloated "Rolex" university on the Harvard model. This narrative makes for fun reading, but one can look at the makeover of George Washington from a very different and less personalized perspective. In our view the rise of a school like George Washington reflects a growing niche, not a harbinger of destruction to come.

What is the definition of elite? In one sense the term is comparative or relative. There are, after all, only ten spots in *US News and World Report*'s list of the top ten national universities.[9] Fewer than 16,000 students make up the entering first-year class on this list of prestigious schools. Forty years ago, the list of the top ten would have included some different names, but the lists then and now are all composed of recognizable blue-blood universities. It's a very stable group at the top. Forty years ago, the number of students in the entering class of this group accommodated at most a few hundred less than the current total. Over the same time span the number of students going to four-year schools has risen by over six million, and the average annual income of families at the ninety-fifth percentile of the income distribution has *risen* by $78,000 in 2014 dollars. Why should anyone be surprised if the number of schools with elite-level programming grows? The incentives all point toward expanding the number of elite institutions. This is true independent of the value judgments people make about the wisdom of paying for an elite-level education.

The top 100 national universities and the most elite 100 liberal arts colleges all have seen substantial increases in their applicant pools, in their selectivity, and in the quality of the average enrolled student. Likewise, the quality of the faculty, facilities, and programming at a university ranked fifty-fifth today is probably better than it was forty years ago. The fifty-fifth-ranked school today may be better, or more elite in an absolute sense, than the twenty-fifth-ranked school forty years ago. In a growing nation that educates an increasing number of students, the absolute number of elite institutions can grow as well. The fact that George Washington University, under the leadership of a charismatic individual, tried to become more "elite" is neither a shock nor a harbinger. The demand for eliteness has risen, and an institution in the nation's capital, only a few blocks from the White House, has certain locational advantages. The George Washington example is hardly unique. A number of institutions have experienced significant quality improvements over the past thirty years, and some have also moved up the relative rankings as a result. The University of Miami, Boston University, and Northeastern University are three additional examples. Boston University offers another "charismatic president" story under the leadership of John Silber. It's not an accident that all three are located in major urban areas with some locational advantages. Miami, for instance, is at the crossroad of growing commercial and cultural links between North and South America.

Whenever a university upgrades its faculty and facilities in a way that stands out, any good writer can craft a story of change built on the energy or ego of the "great men and women" who push the process forward. People do have to seize the moment and make the risky decisions to invest resources in changing the trajectory of their institution. In hindsight, other factors like location and changes in the regional or global economy also explain much of the rise of any particular institution. Yet all of this institution-specific story-telling misses a broader point. The growing demand for high-quality under-graduate programming has created incentives for more schools to invest in that quality. Some have even succeeded in climbing the greasy pole of the rankings.[10]

Human agency remains vital. Things don't happen by themselves. But broader economic and political forces condition the decisions that have changed the trajectory of individual institutions, and of the industry as a whole. These broader forces are the primary focus of this book. We under-stand that our type of narrative lacks the sexiness of more personalized tales of virtue and vice. That's a price we willingly pay. Our "story" ratchets down the rhetoric of crisis and blame, and we believe that is a virtue if we are to find policy remedies to the real problems that the US higher education system faces today and is likely to confront over the next generation.

2

The Diverse US Higher Education System

MANY NARRATIVES ABOUT the precarious condition of the US higher education system are built around statements like "The typical college or university ... " or they presume that all schools are trying to emulate a particular model of prestige or excellence, often named Harvard. It's certainly easier to describe the flaws in a supposedly homogeneous university template than to explore a diverse system in which different types of schools face very different circumstances, tradeoffs, and incentives. The next two chapters are an antidote to this form of argument. Higher education is delivered in an astonishingly wide variety of settings, and there is no single aspirational model toward which all schools have converged. With apologies to Ecclesiastes, there is a time to generalize, and a time to recognize important differences. This is the time to dig into the complexity of America's four-year nonprofit colleges and universities to show their variety. These differences lead us to tread very warily in issuing general statements about the future of "American colleges and universities." These differences also form the necessary backstory that helps motivate our picture of the turbulence that is buffeting the US higher education system.

Table 2.1 gives a picture of this diversity for five particular four-year institutions. We didn't select these schools scientifically, but they are good representatives of the major types of four-year institutions that are often lumped together when people talk about "colleges and universities" in the United States.[1] The data come from the 2013–14 Common Data Sets posted on the institutions' websites. The entries give the number of students (undergraduate and graduate), the percentage of applicants who were admitted, the percentage of admitted students who enrolled (this is called the "yield"), the percentage of enrolled students whose high school grade point average (GPA) is greater than or equal to 3.75 on a 4-point scale, the student-to-faculty ratio, the

Table 2.1 **Selected Statistics on Five American Colleges and Universities**

Institution	Undergraduate Enrollment	Graduate Enrollment	Percent Admitted	Yield	GPA >3.75	Student/ Faculty	Tuition	Liberal Arts DegVrees
Selective liberal arts	1,694	0	38.4%	30.9%	64%	10/1	$45,500	100%
Less selective liberal arts	1,424	13	66.5%	11.3%	41%	11.5/1	$40,385	86%
Selective private university	6,908	8,572	5.7%	76%	95%	5/1	$42,690	78.2%
Flagship state	32,489	8,467	77.6%	33.5%	23%	22/1	$9,388 $26,070	53.8%
Nonflagship state	15,780	2,385	92.0%	41.6%	22%	18/1	$8,722 $22,248	44.8%

list-price tuition (both in-state and out-of-state for the state-supported institutions), and the fraction of the degrees that were in traditional "liberal arts" fields.[2]

The institutional differences captured in this snapshot of five schools are quite dramatic. The two liberal arts colleges are much smaller than the three universities. The state-supported institutions have much lower list-price tuitions than the private schools, even for out-of-state students. They also have much higher admission rates and grant a much lower percentage of their degrees in the traditional liberal arts fields. Despite the fact that their list prices are quite close to one another, the three private institutions are quite different in size, selectivity, and focus on undergraduate education. The ratio of students to faculty varies by more than a factor of four.

The American higher education system currently comprises over 4,700 degree-granting institutions educating more than twenty-one million students. The four-year nonprofit programs that are the main focus of this chapter serve more than twelve million students at over 2,300 colleges and universities. Over 700 for-profit schools enroll almost two million students, and this number is up from 200,000 only twenty-five years ago. Table 2.2 shows this steady growth in the number of four-year institutions since 1980. The most remarkable change is the striking rise in the number of for-profit institutions since 2000. Yet the number of traditional nonprofits (both public and private) also has grown. Despite the occasional college bankruptcy and arguments about the earthquake to come, these data do not immediately suggest that this vital industry is approaching the edge of an existential cliff. Given the recent high-profile collapse of major for-profits like Corinthian Colleges and ITT Tech, and the 200,000-student decline in enrollment at the University of Phoenix,[3] the for-profit segment of the higher education industry may be the most prone to suffer a significant retrenchment in upcoming years.

Table 2.2 Growth in the Number of Four-Year Colleges and Universities

	1980–81	1990–91	2000–01	2005–06	2011–12
Four-year colleges	1,957	2,141	2,450	2,582	2,968
Public	552	595	622	640	682
Private	1,405	1,546	1,828	1,942	2,286
Nonprofit	1,387	1,482	1,551	1,534	1,553
For-profit	18	64	277	408	733

The Evidence of Diversity

As Table 2.1 suggests, generalizing about colleges and universities in the United States is a dangerous business. Yet much of the national conversation about higher education is based on generalizations. The first is extrapolation from personal experience. Perceptions of the strengths and weaknesses of the higher education system often are based on what people have observed at the universities they have attended, the colleges where they have sent their children, or the institutions where they work. The financial problems of an elite small college, however, can be quite unlike the economic tradeoffs facing administrators at a midsized minimally selective private university or a large state-supported university. The authors of this book aren't immune to this temptation. One of us attended Kenyon College as an undergraduate and the other studied at the University of Arizona. These schools were part of our "unscientific" sample in Table 2.1. And we are not shy about using our experiences later in the book. Yet we understand that the practices or problems at our alma maters or our employer (the College of William and Mary) may or may not be typical of the broader higher education system. We must search for patterns to understand the stresses buffeting higher education.

A related form of generalization is the "anecdote as example" inherent in case studies. At its best, case analysis can help us think about possible best practices. But because an idea works well in one context does not automatically mean that it will easily transfer to institutions that face very different circumstances or that have walked a very different historical road. The successful makeover of a small college with a powerful religious organization behind it may not offer a useful model to improve cost effectiveness at a nonselective branch campus of a state university. What is done at Harvard or Princeton may not always work at universities less focused on research output or less well endowed. Again, one antidote to overgeneralization is found in careful analysis of broader data.

The second form of generalization starts from averages and, often implicitly, assumes that "average" means "typical." Often data are about averages, and average values can indeed be very useful. The average level of published tuition and fees for an in-state student at a public four-year institution was $8,893 for the 2013–14 school year. In the same 2013 dollars, published tuition and fees averaged only $5,900 ten years earlier.[4] That is a real growth rate of slightly larger than 4% per year at a particular kind of university (public four-year). This average information is very useful because it forces us to think about the causes of a potentially system-wide problem inside public higher education.

Averages can tell you a lot if the underlying data are clustered reasonably close to the average. In that case the average really is "typical." If the underlying data about universities are more spread out, then most of the schools will not be close to the computed average. In the next few pages, we will show in detail how the idea of "the typical college" can be quite misleading. For many of the important characteristics that describe American colleges and universities, the data are quite spread out. Generalizing about our system of higher education from data averages often is a mistake.

This is especially true for any discussion about survival. Imagine for a moment that a melt-off of a large Antarctic ice sheet raises the average sea level by four feet. If the average elevation above sea level in a coastal county is only five feet, you might forecast catastrophe as the tides overwhelm the county. This is a real worry for the Republic of Maldives in the Indian Ocean, whose highest point is only 2.4 meters above sea level. In the Maldives, flat is indeed typical. On the other hand, suppose our coastal county comprises 1,000 square miles, and 80% of those square miles are at least ten feet above sea level. Well inland there is a substantial depression where the land sinks to eighty or more feet below sea level, and this is why the "average" county elevation comes in at just five feet. In this county, the average height above sea level is not the typical height. The rise in sea level will have a significant effect, and people will have to adjust, but the entire county is not about to drown.

In the remainder of this chapter we will walk through six different ways of looking at the nonprofit four-year segment of the US higher education industry. Unlike the Maldives, where most of the elevations are quite typical, the search for a typical college or university is fraught. Much of the story about the future of America's four-year higher education institutions is found in their differences, not their similarities.

Enrollment

Enrollment patterns at public and private four-year institutions are quite distinct. Figure 2.1 presents the distribution of full-time-equivalent enrollment using Delta Cost Project data from 2010.[5] The solid bars represent private nonprofit four-year institutions, and the cross-hatched bars represent public four-year institutions. These bars represent the fraction of the student population enrolled in an institution within a particular size range. For example, the bottom bar for >50,000 shows that over 13% of students enrolled in a public four-year institution go to a school with more than 50,000 students. We see

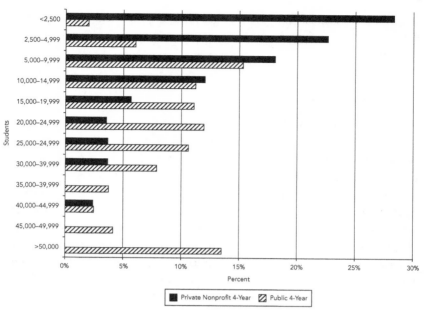

FIGURE 2.1 Distribution of students by size of institution.

a considerable variance in the distribution of enrollments across institution size in both the public and private sectors. A lot of students attend small private colleges. Twenty-eight percent of students enrolled in private nonprofit institutions go to schools with fewer than 2,500 full-time-equivalent students. In fact, if you break down that category, a full 7% of the students at private colleges attend schools with fewer than 1,000 students. A majority of private college students attend schools with fewer than 5,000 students. On the other hand, only slightly more than 10% of the students at private nonprofit four-year schools attend large institutions with more than 20,000 students. The distribution of public four-year enrollments has a much larger dispersion. Although a hefty chunk (45%) of the attendance at public four-year institutions takes place at schools that enroll 10,000 to 30,000 students, a majority goes to schools that are larger (32%) or smaller (23%).

If you take the number of students enrolled and divide by the number of schools, you will get an average full-time-equivalent enrollment number for public four-year institutions of 12,172 and for private four-year institutions of 2,319. Most students do *not* attend a school that is defined by the characteristics of schools with that average size. In addition, these averages don't really tell you about the middle of the data. The bins for larger institutions account for much more than one half of the students. The median student at a public university attends an institution larger than 20,000, and the median student at a private college or university attends a school of right around 5,000 students.

Tuition and Fees

We just saw that school size at public four-year institutions is widely dispersed, while private school enrollment is more bunched toward smaller schools. The pattern for pricing is very different. Figure 2.2 gives the distributions of published tuition and fees.[6] The solid bars again represent private four-year institutions, and the cross-hatched bars represent public four-year institutions. The vast majority (89%) of students attending public four-year schools face a published tuition and fees of less than $15,000. Over half see a list price of less than $10,000. Some public university students do pay a high list price, and this captures the high prices charged to out-of-state students. The story is very different at private institutions. That list-price distribution is spread out almost uniformly. There is very little bunching in the middle. Lastly, published tuition and fees are generally much higher at private institutions than they are at public institutions. Nonetheless, there is some overlap between the two distributions.

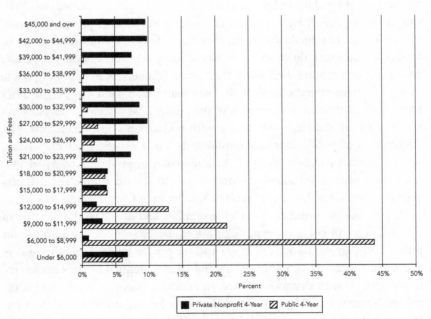

FIGURE 2.2 Distribution of published tuition and fees.

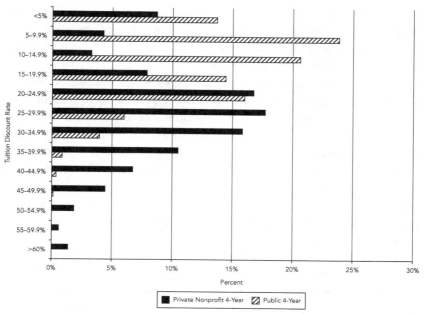

FIGURE 2.3 Distribution of tuition discount rates.

Published tuition and fees represent the prices listed in the college catalog. Most students pay less than this published price, and in many cases much less. Students receive discounts from the institution, and they may get federal or state grants as part of their financial aid package. They and their families also may receive federal tuition tax credits that further reduce the price of a year in college. Loans, however, do not reduce the price paid.

Figure 2.3 shows how much institutional discounting takes place.[7] Internal discounts from schools represent the largest amount of grant aid available to students. Tuition discounts also limit the amount of revenue available to institutions, and some schools are quite concerned that their tuition discount rates are unsustainably high. The bars show the percentages of the student population at private (solid) and public (cross-hatched) institutions that receive tuition discounts in the indicated range.

Tuition discounting is much more pronounced in the private nonprofit four-year sector than at public four-year schools. The average discount of 28.2% at private institutions is almost double the average of 14.2% at public institutions. Almost 60% of students at public four-year institutions receive a discount of 15% or less. By contrast, at private schools almost 70% see tuition discounted by 15% to 40%. Despite this broad difference, there are some public institutions with discount rates above the private average and some private institutions with discount rates below the public average. Once again, talk of a typical program is misleading. Most students attend schools whose discount rate is quite different from the national average.

Our final figure (Figure 2.4) in this section shows the relationship between tuition discount rates and published tuition and fees for private nonprofit four-year institutions.[8] The average discount rate clearly rises with published tuition and fees. Schools that charge a list price between $10,000 and $15,000, for instance, only discount by 16%, while schools charging more than $40,000 discount an average of 36%. Students who attended schools with a list price above $30,000 in 2010 paid less than 70% of the listed tuition because of tuition discounts. Because higher list prices tend to get discounted more heavily, the net tuition actually collected from students is not as variable as Figure 2.2 would suggest.

The prevalence of tuition discounts makes college pricing difficult to understand. Most private nonprofit schools, as well as many public institutions, have adopted a high price–high discount strategy. The discounts are usually called scholarships, and they are often given fancy names. This is a natural marketing strategy, and its appeal is many-faceted. The use of scholarships for talented students has a long history in athletics. Increasingly it

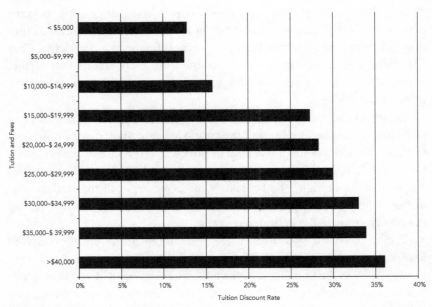

FIGURE 2.4 Tuition discount rates by tuition levels, private nonprofit four-year institutions.

is now used to attract students who will add to the quality and diversity of the student body, or simply to fill seats that otherwise might go empty. Some schools actually give scholarships to 100% of the entering class! A school that gives the biggest scholarship may sway some students, even if another school with a lower net price would have been just as good a fit. We will return to the discounting issue in chapters 6 and 7.

Selectivity

We have all heard the stories of very good students who don't get into their first-choice college. These stories are real, and they lead to considerable family angst every spring. But making good matches with schools actually is not difficult, once you set your sights below the super-elite. Figure 2.5 displays the fraction of applicants admitted to public four-year and private nonprofit four-year institutions.[9]

You have to read selectivity data very carefully. The advent of the common application submitted online makes it very easy to apply to a large number of institutions. This means that a good but not great student who has outsized ambitions can apply to every Ivy League school quite easily, even if his or her chances of being admitted are exceedingly low at all of

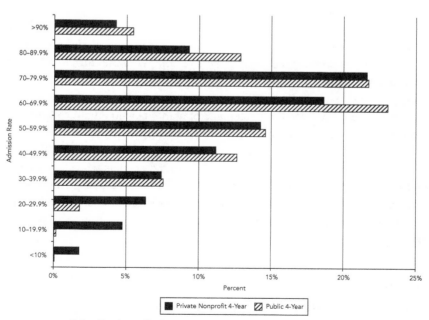

FIGURE 2.5 Distribution of admission rates.

them. The number of applications has surged by leaps and bounds. In 1990, only 9% of high school students applied to at least seven institutions. By 2012 that percentage had increased to 32%.[10] This tends to make selective programs seemingly more selective, and this effect might well be important even for schools that are not very exclusive. Despite this change in application behavior, the figure shows that a large number of students attend institutions that are not hyperselective. Almost 78% of the students enrolled in public colleges and universities attend institutions where the chances of getting in are higher than a coin toss. The figure for private colleges is 66%.

Graduation Rates

In 1970, 46.5% of the students who completed high school moved on to some sort of postsecondary schooling. Of that group who sought more schooling, 46.7% earned a BA by age twenty-five. Rolling the clock forward to 1990, 60% of high school graduates pushed on for more schooling, but only 40.4% completed a BA by age twenty-five. This evidence of falling completion led to a great debate about causes. Had the academy failed at educating, or did the failure occur earlier during the K-12 years? Declines in public funding could have reduced the quality of public higher education. We might have experienced simple diminishing returns as a greater fraction of high school students wound up in college. More recent census data from 2009–11 tells us that attendance has continued to climb (it's now 72%), while completion has largely returned to rates seen in the 1970s (45%).[11] We will return to this question of completion rates later, but for now we note that the national average completion rate masks wide differences among schools.

In Figure 2.6 we see the percentage of students who attend colleges and universities with six-year completion rates ranging from under 10% to over 80%.[12] The distributions for public and private institutions substantially overlap, but 63% of public university students attend schools whose graduation rates lie between 40% and 70%. By contrast, almost 60% of private college students attend schools whose graduation rates exceed 60%. There is nothing particularly typical about having a graduation rate that is at the national average.

Finances

Colleges and universities receive revenue from tuition, state appropriations, gifts and endowment earnings, the sale of educational services to other

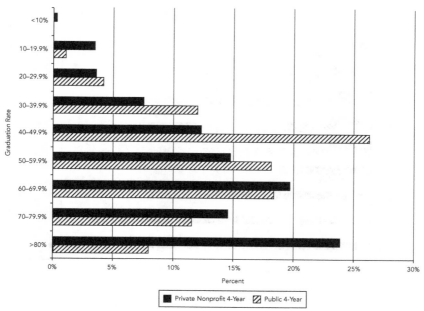

FIGURE 2.6 Distribution of six-year graduation rates.

groups, and research grants and contracts. There is considerable variation among colleges in the share of revenue they get from these different sources. This means that opportunities and vulnerabilities often are quite different among identifiable types of schools.

Figure 2.7 tells the story of tuition reliance. This is the percentage of institutional revenue that comes from net tuition.[13] For example, the bottom bars show that over 30% of the students attending private nonprofit four-year institutions go to schools that receive 90% or more of their revenue from net tuition. As one might expect, high tuition reliance is much more common for private nonprofit institutions than for public institutions. And many of the highly tuition-dependent institutions are small colleges that lack large endowment resources or the backing of a church. Despite cutbacks that we will examine in detail in chapter 7, many public institutions still receive large appropriations from their state's coffers, and this reduces tuition dependence.

Tuition payments don't all come from the students and their families, so tuition reliance is not telling us what percentage of the college's revenue comes from the student. If a student receives a Pell Grant or a scholarship

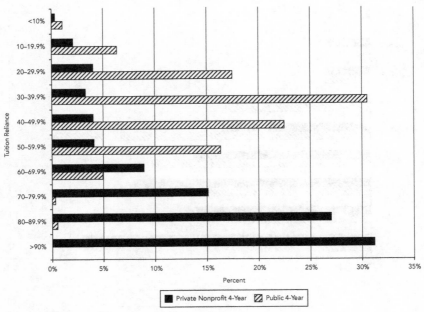

FIGURE 2.7 Distribution of tuition reliance.

from some source other than the college, the proceeds from those grants and scholarships will be used to pay some portion of the tuition. Likewise, many students take out loans to finance some fraction of the tuition bill. The source of the tuition payments is important, but so is the overall dependence of the institution on annual tuition revenue.

Institutions with heavy reliance on tuition are much more vulnerable to a variety of economic shocks. This is particularly true for small colleges. Schools do their best to forecast the yield, which is the fraction of their admissions offers that are accepted. If a school's forecast of the yield is too high and a higher than expected number of students turn the institution down, then its freshman class will be smaller than expected. Schools use waiting lists if this happens, but waiting lists work much better at highly selective institutions, where wait-listed applicants often are overjoyed to get in. Schools also have to forecast the retention rate, which measures the fraction of its current students who will return for the following year. This forecast also may be too high. Both types of error can leave an institution with fewer students than expected. Thirty fewer students out of 1,000 can wreak havoc on the budget of a small school. If an institution is very large, or if it has the cushion of a large flow of endowment funds or annual giving, small forecasting errors will have less dire consequences.

Governments remain an important source of higher education revenue, particularly for public institutions. While state appropriations for higher education have been declining in many states, public institutions still receive a significant fraction of their revenues from the state. Figure 2.8 gives the state share of the operating budget for public four-year institutions. The vast majority of students (82%) attend public institutions that receive between 20% and 50% of their revenue from state appropriations. In some ways these public institutions are in a similar position to private colleges with high tuition reliance. Instead of the vagaries of the market, public universities are exposed to the vagaries of politics. When the state is responsible for a large share of an institution's budget, a new governor with different priorities, or a fall in state revenues because of economic difficulties, can mean a large and sudden reduction in revenues. State revenue shortfalls sometimes occur midyear and state institutions are asked to give back some of the money they had received from the state. In theory, state revenues could provide a cushion for students from the ups and downs of the market. In practice, the revenue stream of public higher education has been more volatile than for private institutions.

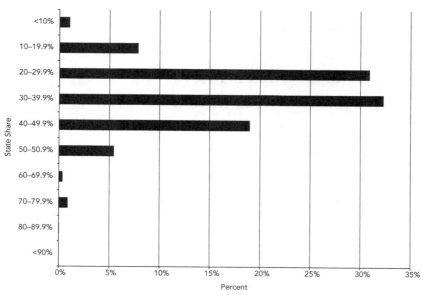

FIGURE 2.8 Distribution of share of state budget, public four-year institutions.

Curriculum

The set of courses taught at colleges and universities are by no means uniform. The Department of Education uses a system called the Classification of Instructional Programs (CIP) to classify courses and degrees. There are only forty-seven CIP codes, so the categories are quite broad. For example, *CIP Code 45—Social Science* includes anthropology, archeology, criminology, economics, geography, international relations, political science, and sociology, while *CIP Code 40—Physical Science* includes astronomy, atmospheric science and meteorology, chemistry, geology, physics, and materials science. To get a sense of the dispersion of offerings at four-year colleges and universities, we computed the percentage of degrees awarded in liberal arts, or, more precisely, arts and sciences departments. The list of departments is the same list we used for Table 2.1 and is designed to capture the set of departments in the typical "liberal arts college."

Our two types of institutions awarded roughly the same percentage of their bachelor's degrees in arts and sciences fields, 48% at public four-year institutions and 50.5% at private nonprofit four-year institutions. Figure 2.9 demonstrates that relatively few students graduate from institutions in which the degrees are predominantly from departments on our arts and sciences

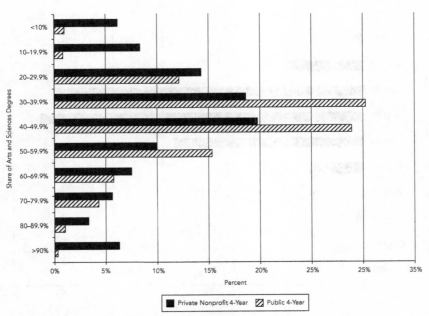

FIGURE 2.9 Distribution of share of arts and sciences degrees.

list. But the distribution for private institutions is much more spread out than for public institutions. Public colleges and universities lack the extremes like Kenyon from Table 2.1, which awarded 100% of its degrees in liberal arts, or Stevens Institute of Technology, which awarded only 18.2% of its degrees in liberal arts.

The Typical College?

Removing complexity does help in constructing a clear and satisfying story that can quickly and easily segue into a deconstruction of the typical institution's inefficiencies and intractable problems. Many recent books and articles about higher education's coming demise use a two-step process based on oversimplification. First they describe the higher education system's birth and identify the people whose decisions seemingly moved us down the road of trouble and into the cul-de-sac where US colleges and universities are now supposedly stuck. In the next step, they show how those decisions brought about fundamental flaws—high costs, inflexible decision making, and near-total disregard for educational quality—that become fatal in today's new technological environment. In many stories, little or no attention is paid to counterarguments, contrary evidence, or complexities that get in the way of the straight-line narrative. In what follows we will continue to reinsert complexity into the discussion to show why narratives that begin from "the typical college" are usually wrong about most of them.

This does not mean that all broad descriptive statements about American higher education are unfounded. Colleges and universities do share many common features and behaviors, and that is the focus of the next chapter.

3

The College Bundle

IN CHAPTER 2 WE highlighted the diversity of the institutions that populate the traditional four-year higher education system. That diversity stands as a caution against easy generalizations about typical institutions or about how the system may change in response to economic shocks and policy changes. Yet Harvard, Florida State, and Holy Cross are all higher education institutions. As such, they share certain features that differentiate them from the "firms" that populate other industries. Traditional colleges and universities offer students a bundle of services that are packaged together. This bundle does vary somewhat across the wide spectrum of US higher education institutions. Yet most of the bundle is on offer at all schools. There are sound reasons why the bundle has taken its current shape.

What Is in the Bundle?

At some risk of being arbitrary, we will divide the bundle that most schools provide into primary, secondary, and tertiary components. The primary activity of a university is to expand knowledge, both by creating it anew and by spreading it widely through teaching and collaborative research. For undergraduates, the primary service is indeed traditional classroom instruction, augmented by a variety of assignments of varying levels of interactivity. These include problem solving, paper writing, oral presentations, and team projects. Another important component of the face-to-face experience is individualized or small group mentoring. This often happens during office conversations with the faculty, and the work at these meetings runs the gamut from help with classwork and course concepts to career advice and counseling on broader life questions. Mentorship also can go well beyond occasional conversations or office-hour visits. Many students develop ongoing relationships with faculty advisors.

Independent study is one example, and it allows students to work on a topic of their choosing that is not necessarily found in the regular curriculum offered by a department or a program. The impetus for a course of independent study usually comes from the student. The process often begins when the student's work in one class stimulates an interest in digging more deeply into a particular topic or line of thought. This work is usually done under the guidance of a faculty member whose training encompasses the student's proposed topic of study. Although we call the work "independent," it usually involves regular meetings with a faculty mentor to talk about assigned readings or about the student's written analysis based on those readings. This kind of tutorial is a prime example of "the ideal college as Mark Hopkins on one end of a log and a student on the other."[1]

In a traditional university, some instruction can be offered online.[2] Online components also can be combined with face-to-face instruction in what is called a blended classroom setting. There are limits to the effectiveness, or the range, of fully online delivery. Close mentoring is inherently difficult in an all-online setting. Discussions are poorly replicated online. Peer interaction and close work with an instructor is much more likely to happen in a campus setting where proximity encourages frequent and often accidental interaction. We will spend some quality time on the costs and benefits of online coursework in chapter 8.

There are fundamental reasons to include research among the primary activities of a college or university. Colleges and universities should be engaged in creating knowledge in every field they offer. This effort is built into the way colleges and universities operate. To get a faculty position at the vast majority of colleges and universities, professors have to earn a PhD, which requires a substantial original research project. To keep a tenure track position and win promotion up the faculty ranks, a professor must continue to produce original research. The research carried out on college campuses has helped expand productivity and improve the standard of living. Many of the most important technological discoveries that are the backbone of the modern economy originated in, or were perfected in, university laboratories. And the way we understand, measure, and appreciate the world has been changed and deepened through the work of academic researchers in a great number of fields.

While most people recognize the value of this research, especially in STEM (science, technology, engineering, and mathematics) fields, some are deeply skeptical of the value of combining research and teaching. To the skeptics, faculty time spent on research takes time away from teaching. In this view, teaching and research are pure substitutes. In addition, the rewards from successful scholarship are much greater than the rewards for excellent teaching, so the contemporary professoriate is much too focused on research. In this skeptical view, teaching and research should be kept separate and research outside of STEM is of little value. Colleges should hire teaching specialists to work with undergraduates and research specialists to produce knowledge and work with industry. In our view, this would lead to an impoverished higher education for undergraduates.

Everyone recognizes the importance of research in the training of doctoral students. To complete a PhD, a student has to produce original research, and only a research-oriented faculty that is up to date can guide students who are developing and carrying out research projects at the boundary of their discipline. In many ways the training of PhDs follows the master–apprentice model. The major professor and the student work together on the research project, and when ready the student takes the lead. This only works and produces useful results if the major professor is a successful scholar.

What about undergraduate education? In a good undergraduate program the line between the upper-division courses offered to the undergraduates and the first-year graduate curriculum often is hazy. And many undergraduates at research universities wind up taking graduate classes. Introductory courses in many fields could be, and often are, handled by teaching specialists. Beginning Spanish offers a good example. But this approach works less well in upper-division courses that introduce students to current thinking in their field. Again, we note that research-oriented professors teach undergraduates in many university systems outside of the United States. This is not an approach that is specific to the American historical trajectory. Teaching and research may be quite complementary in higher education.

A faculty that is scholarly active is well positioned to instill in students an appreciation for discovery, especially if the university's incentives link them with students. In considerable part, good teachers teach by example. A faculty that is producing knowledge can help students understand the methods of research that they may need in working lives that carry them through a variety of employers in a wide range of fields. The mission statement of many institutions speaks directly about lifelong learning. This is easier to accomplish if those who teach and mentor are working at the boundaries of knowledge in their respective disciplines. Parents who pay the bill sometimes question the idea that discovery and lifelong learning should be a primary objective of a college education, but there is no inherent contradiction between broad liberal learning and the development of marketable skills that last a working lifetime. And this is the kind of education that can be offered by a faculty active in their own research endeavors.

Finally, the boundary between the way graduate students are taught and the way undergraduate students are taught increasingly is permeable. Many colleges and universities encourage and support students who are engaged in undergraduate research. To do this successfully, the teacher-scholars who guide these undergraduate researchers, just like the faculty who guide graduate researchers, have to be working at the frontiers of their fields. We will analyze the importance of undergraduate research in more detail when we return to the college bundle in chapter 9.

The scope and intensity of the research mission vary considerably across the diverse spectrum of colleges and universities described in the previous chapter. This variability in the resource intensity of the research mission often is unrecognized by arguments that lump research indiscriminately into the category of wasteful practices that will disappear in the cloud-based iCollege of the future.

Teaching, research, and mentorship require institutional support, so a related set of university activities also can be categorized as primary. The resources of a modern library (physical and digital) directly support the primary mission of knowledge creation. This requires both a physical space and a professional staff, and the role of both has changed substantially over the past forty years as digital technology has changed how people use library resources. Advising is another essential service that helps students navigate institutional complexities, understand the demands of the general education requirements, and master the details of departmental or program specializations. The faculty does some of this work, especially concentration advising. But advising increasingly has been professionalized over time. Other professional departments of the modern university are shared among many users. The information technology (IT) department, for instance, helps keep the academic enterprise running. Students and faculty alike depend on the IT staff to maintain classroom software and hardware, and to ensure that the university Internet, data, and communications systems run smoothly. Some of what this growing professional staff does is indispensable to the primary components of the academic bundle (teaching and research). But a lot of its value is shared with all of the administrative units that are needed to run a sizable institution, whether it's a college or a manufacturing firm.

There are many secondary services that are rolled into the bundle that American colleges and universities provide. The term "secondary" is not a judgment about importance. Secondary parts of the bundle are separable from the primary mission of teaching and research, and many of them are not the norm in higher education in other parts of the world. Some of these services reflect the historical evolution of the American education experience, and their persistence in American colleges and universities reflects both path dependence and a social choice for how to work with young people in the normal age range of first-time college students. The fact that American institutions put services in the bundle that other nations' universities leave out tells us nothing about the efficiency or inefficiency of American higher education. International comparisons that begin and end with cost per student are highly misleading.

Room and board makes up the largest aspect of campus life that we classify as secondary services within the bundle. Housing and dining in a campus space substantially define "residential education," and residence is a component part of many peer effects that help shape and channel the personal and educational growth that students experience inside a traditional four-year academic institution. At some colleges residence is required, sometimes only for incoming first-year students, but at times for all students. In most cases though, living on campus is an optional component of higher education. Living off campus and commuting for classes is quite common. Yet the fact that many students choose to live on campus tells us that this option has value. The 2010 census estimates that the primary residence of just over two million people was a college dormitory. Beyond housing and dining, the set of secondary services that most American colleges and universities offer includes a range of programs and offices that support students academically and socially. The set includes psychological counseling, health and wellness centers, career services, support for student clubs and organizations, and intramural athletic programs.

The last category in the bundle we'll call tertiary, and this means more than just being third. These are things that enhance campus life but that are even less directly connected to the primary mission of educating, retaining, and ultimately graduating students. Despite its expense, and its large footprint at many institutions, we would include intercollegiate athletics as a tertiary component of the bundle. Although universities elsewhere do sponsor athletic teams that compete, the United States is unique in having athletic competition as a significant financial enterprise run by the institution. We will say more about the fiscal footprint of athletics in chapter 9. Campus recreational centers, which are perhaps the canonical symbols of waste with their rock climbing walls, lazy rivers, and swimming pools, are another example of tertiary services that students use individually or in groups.[3] Lastly, college support for purely social events (everything from rock concerts to receptions for visiting parents) rounds out this group. All of these tertiary services enhance campus life, and most are peculiar to American institutions.

The College as a "Firm" and the Economics of Bundling

A traditional American college is a collection of academic and nonacademic components that work together to produce many different "outputs." These outputs generally are offered as a single package with minor variations, like which board plan you want to buy. Suppose a student could buy the services offered by a university separately on the market. This might seem preferable for a number of reasons. Few college students take advantage of all that a college offers. Some never use the counseling service, for instance, while others never choose to work closely with a professor on independent research. Moreover, a school with a fabulous English department may have a less stellar economics program. Why should a student be stuck with only the courses and programs offered by one (often small) institution if they could choose the best educational options one by one on a broader academic market?

We noted earlier that many students already forego some of the secondary items in the bundle. Commuter students pay their own living expenses if they choose to live off campus at universities that offer a residential option. These two services are the ones most often removed from the bundle, and that choice hasn't eroded the dominance of the modern multioutput university. The other components, like English classes, career services, athletic teams, libraries, genetics laboratories, student health services, and recreational facilities, are all bundled together and offered for a single price called "tuition and fees." Couldn't this bundle be picked apart? Instruction and skill acquisition could be purchased from many providers, with payment by course or by badge for skills learned. Career planning could be a separate enterprise offered competitively by services like LinkedIn or a growing array of copycats. A student could handle any personal psychological issues by hiring a counselor or psychiatrist in the private market. Even social activities do not need to be coordinated or funded by a centralized campus agency. Think of all those bars and clubs that inhabit the fringes of any college campus.

Economists have thought about this set of issues, and two strands of that thinking are important for explaining the persistence of bundling in higher education. The first idea stems from early work by Ronald Coase on why business firms exist at all, and a college is a firm in every sense that matters.[4] Once we understand the rationale for firms, the next relevant question is: why do some firms make more than one thing? Universities are a prime example of "firms" that "produce" multiple "outputs."[5] The existence of multiproduct firms depends on the idea of economies of scope, which was explored by John Panzar and Robert Willig.[6] Neither argument gets much attention in the public conversation about the American higher education system. This is a mistake. The long history of bundling higher education services within a corporate structure is not an accident that persisted due to random luck.

Typically economic models portray the economy as a collection of abstract interlinked markets. On these markets, competition through the price mechanism allocates goods and services to their highest-value use. If a disease decimates the pig supply, the market price of bacon goes up. People who value bacon less than the new price buy less expensive substitutes, or they enjoy bacon less frequently. Welcome to the world of supply and demand taught in every Econ 101 class. This model of how the economy works is very useful, which is why we teach it. But it's obviously a simplification because there is no role for complex organizations called firms.

Why do we need structured and hierarchical firms at all? Why isn't everything contracted in a market on demand, person to person, or by individuals coming together spontaneously to fashion complex items? Many transactions do take place directly in a market. I hire someone to put a new roof on my house. And the roofer buys shingles from one of the firms that make them. But these firms, both the roofer and the shingle supplier, make countless internal "transactions" daily, all without any market mechanism or prices to guide the resources that flow between different parts of the firm. In Coase's words, "If a workman moves from department Y to department X, he does not go because of a change in relative prices, but because he is ordered to do so."[7]

Outside of the firm, prices are the prime incentive for people to adjust their production and consumption choices as they make transactions on the market. Inside a firm these price-driven transactions are replaced by internal rules and procedures. Within the firm the entrepreneur-coordinator makes the decisions. These two ways of organizing production exist side by side. As Coase said, "The main reason why it is profitable to establish a firm would seem to be that there is a cost of using the price mechanism."[8] There are substantial transaction costs of buying every item and every labor service separately on the market and of negotiating individual contracts for everything needed to produce a product. To produce most goods of any complexity, costs are lower when an entrepreneur contracts with individuals to cooperate in making a final product.

Coase and the Foundations of the Modern Academy

The development of the medieval university shows Coase's idea at work. From their start, universities in Bologna, in Paris, and later at Oxford were organizations that we would recognize today. They hired faculty, established curricula, required examinations, held commencements, and awarded degrees.[9] An emphasis on research came later from German universities in the 1800s.

Higher learning certainly existed prior to the founding of colleges and universities, but it followed a master–apprentice approach without a formal organizational structure, a set curriculum, or degrees. Nathan Schachner describes the teaching of law in Italy in the twelfth century as conducted by "a few scattered, independent teachers who were willing to impart their legal knowledge."[10] This type of higher education "system" utilized a market exchange model. The student sought out a master or a master sought out students, and they agreed on the price of the exchange. Colleges or universities as organizations did not exist in Europe.

The shift to an organized institution of higher education happened in the twelfth and thirteenth centuries in Bologna and Paris, respectively. In Bologna, students came together to found the institution. They engaged instructors to teach them law and medicine. The origin of the student-run university traces to a group of foreign students who had collected in Bologna because a large group of well-known master teachers happened to be located there. As foreigners, these students did not have the rights that citizens of Bologna enjoyed, and they banded together to protect themselves from exploitation by the townsfolk.[11] This led to an increasingly organized university in which the students assumed, in Schachner's words, "more and more authority over the academic Studium, over lectures, over courses of study, hours, and methods—all the matters normally within the sole jurisdiction of a Faculty."[12] The model of individual arrangements between students and their teachers gave way as a new kind of educational firm grew, one in which allocation decisions "over lectures, over courses of study, hours, and methods" were controlled within the university. The fact that this occurred in Bologna and that it took the form of a student-led initiative against potential exploitation was largely accidental. But the economic advantages of this arrangement led to its continuation and to its spread to other circumstances that were very different.

At roughly the same time a very different process occurred in Paris.[13] Yet the outcome was roughly the same. A university-firm emerged and replaced individual exchanges. In Paris the impetus for the founding of the university came from the teachers instead of the students. Cathedral schools had previously employed teachers, but in many cases entrepreneurial "professors" took on private students in an open market. Teachers were not credentialed in a way that signaled quality to potential students, and poor information about this market meant that "propaganda and advertisement" likely harmed students and good teachers alike.[14] In response, the teachers came together to form a guild.

This guild played the role performed by the faculty and administration in a modern university. The guild continued to clash with the local church, which controlled who could be licensed to teach, and with local authorities who occasionally dealt with student miscreants violently. Anyone who thinks student problems with alcohol are a new phenomenon or that student uprisings began at Berkeley during the 1960s should study the Paris student riots of 1229 and the two-year strike that crippled the economy of Paris. After considerable commotion, in 1231 Pope Gregory IX—who was an alumnus of the University of Paris—issued a papal bull known as *Parens Scientiarum* (The Mother of Sciences), which granted the university the right

> to make regulations as to the manner and hours of lectures, the style of dress, the burial of their dead, the taxation of hospices (meaning the right of the University to fix what is deemed reasonable rents for the lodgings of its students in the houses of private citizens of Paris). . . . and most important of all, . . . the unqualified right of an aggrieved University to cease and suspend lectures, and go on strike until its demands are met.[15]

In Paris, just as in Bologna, the corporate university replaced the model of the student and teacher coming to individual agreements.

The university in Bologna initially was student organized (bottom up), while the university in Paris was run by a faculty guild (top down). Yet both foundation processes birthed institutions with very similar form and function, and in both cases neither founding group did it because they consciously wanted to reduce transaction costs. Nonetheless, the gains from reducing transaction costs were probably large, and spreading those gains made winners of students and faculty alike. Students now could find a place with recognized teachers much more easily than they could before. Similarly, teachers could collect students much more easily than they could before. The degrees and certificates earned by students who completed courses of studies at these schools came to be recognized as reliable markers of higher education. The effectiveness of this organizational structure led to its replication across Europe soon after its first flowering in Italy and France.

The University as a Multiproduct Firm

Coase's insights help explain why the reduction of transaction costs is a powerful organizing principle. The university provides value to students and teachers alike by reducing transaction costs. We have also described these universities as multiproduct firms. The set of services offered by colleges differs across countries, and it has evolved over time. In some countries, graduate programs and undergraduate education are kept separate. Some fields, such as art, music, and theology, are often (but not always) taught in separate schools. Some colleges and universities provide housing and meal plans, and others do not. Yet most higher education institutions in the United States offer many of the primary, secondary, and even tertiary components of the educational bundle.

Economies of scope lead to multiproduct firms, so it's important to be very clear about what this term means. There are economies of scope if the cost of producing two or more goods under one firm's organizational umbrella is less than the sum of the costs of having each good produced separately by independent firms. With economies of scope, a multiproduct firm in a competitive market would be able to outcompete a group of firms each producing a single product.

John Panzar and Robert Willig show how economies of scope arise when inputs that go into the goods or services that people buy are sharable within the firm. A sharable input, "once procured for the production of one output, would be also available (wholly or in part) to aid the production of other outputs."[16] Sharable input works like a public good within the firm. A public good, like the canonical lighthouse example beloved of generations of microeconomics students, isn't used up when one person uses it. The lighthouse's warning light, for instance, can be shared among many ships with equal effectiveness. Panzar and Willig offer a lot of examples of sharable inputs, like

> elements of productive capacity (such as electric power generators or transmission facilities) useable at different times for different outputs, indivisible equipment (or just a factory building) usable for more than one manufacturing process, heat sources only partially depleted by their primary uses, human capital applicable to the production of more than one output, or inputs (such as sheep) which inevitably offer by-products (such as mutton) from their primary production (such as wool).[17]

Panzar and Willig weren't thinking about universities, but shared inputs abound in higher education. A modern library is a prime example. As much as technological optimists would like to sell the idea that Google searching is a perfect substitute for a university's library resources, the differences are vast. Many important information resources remain behind a pay wall, but they are "free" to college users. My use of those resources doesn't generally reduce your ability to use them. Likewise, a library staff is a window into information management and data that is freely available to students and faculty. Although one can imagine congestion if twenty students ask for the same help simultaneously, in general the library's human resources are a public good to university users, much like the lighthouse is to ships at sea.

Much of the human resource base of a university also acts as a shared input for the variety of services that a school produces. This is true of the faculty, the administrative staff, and the professional staff. An academic administrator's time is limited, but most people who do administrative tasks can flexibly adjust between working on curricular issues, the budget process, the renovation of a building, or fundraising as the need arises. The faculty can flexibly adjust between teaching and preparation, mentorship, governance, or pure research. Some of these tasks are part of very different services "produced" by the institution. A professional IT staff member can move flexibly between supporting the teaching mission of the institution and crafting the web platform of the psychological counseling center or the office of career planning.

Let's return to two primary activities in the bundle, namely, teaching and research. A college education is more than a collection of randomly assembled classes. If there really is something to the way the classes fit together, there are likely to be shared inputs across departments and programs. If a university educates graduate students and undergraduates while also supporting faculty research, there are clear shared inputs. In the sciences the same expensive equipment that the faculty and graduate students use for professional scholarship and graduate dissertations is also available for teaching undergraduates and for undergraduate research. Physical spaces, lecture halls, and seminar rooms can be used for English classes, economics classes, and presentations from outside speakers brought in to enrich the university's intellectual life. College athletics departments use undergraduates and sometimes graduate students as players, though separate payment for athletic services may be around the corner. Public service projects often involve professors, staff, graduate students, and undergraduates. Shared inputs pervade higher education.

Economists have tried to measure the magnitude of economies of scope. Overall, the literature finds some support for the idea that scope economies exist, but it's not a unanimous position.[18] The problem with testing for economies of scope is that researchers are limited to examining things that can be measured fairly easily. Many of the studies have focused on big conglomerates of cost categories like "undergraduate education," "graduate education," and "externally funded research," because those are actual cost categories that exist. Defined broadly like this, the effect of having a graduate program on the cost of the undergraduate program would seem ambiguous. Having cheap graduate student labor available might lower undergraduate costs at an institution that teaches both undergraduates and graduate students (multiproduct). On the other hand, some of the faculty needed to teach graduate students might prove ill suited to teaching undergraduates.

In a sense, the literature on economies of scope suffers from the lamppost problem. We're looking for our car keys under the light, which is the existing highly aggregated data, when we know that we dropped them in the dark alley of unavailable data categories. Using overly aggregated cost data, you can easily miss or dismiss the bulk of the sharable input that makes the multiproduct university sensible. The impact on cost of all of the potentially sharable inputs that we talked about earlier goes unnoticed and unappreciated. The library's contribution as a shared input, for instance, is not measurable at all. Nor is the contribution of research activity to undergraduate education. Both of these examples of shared inputs tell us as much about the quality of programming as it does about the dollar cost, and quality is inherently difficult to measure with any precision. Lewis and Dundar highlight this kind of measurement problem as a caution in interpreting all existing studies of scope. "The quality of an educational environment for students that requires teachers, facilities, equipment, programs, services, and the mixture of these educational resources clearly affects the quality of its teaching output"[19] And differences in the quality of inputs or outputs can bias any measures of cost in higher education. The theory of economies of scope tells us to look at shared inputs to understand the benefits of the multioutput college, and shared inputs seem to abound in higher education even if we cannot precisely measure them at present.

Economies of scope are very different from economies of scale. Scale is about size. Many manufacturing processes get cheaper as the volume of output is ramped up. In higher education, there are indeed scale economies, and we alluded to them in the first chapter. If a school can grow from 1,200 to 2,400 without doubling the size of its faculty, its classroom space, and its library, then cost per student would go down as the school adds students. This is not what economies of scope are about. A small liberal arts college like Kenyon can experience economies of scope just like Ohio State, and these scope economies will lead the two schools to offer much the same bundle of services. Kenyon won't have a shot at the Division I football title, but it will have a decent chance of winning the Division III swimming title.

Colleges and universities share a similar organizational structure, and they offer a strikingly uniform bundle of services that defines American higher education. Institutions may be large or small. They may be dependent on tuition for the bulk of their revenues or they may depend instead on state appropriations. But they perform the same basic functions and house the same set of activities. Like any historical process, unpredictable events have helped to shape the development of the modern university. But we think there is great value in seeing the economic logic behind the formation and evolution of the modern university. Forming a university solved an economic coordination problem in ways that benefited students, professors, and the economy at large. The common set of activities within the bundle offered by most universities grew and developed within the framework of shared inputs that were already there in the first institutions focused solely on teaching and self-governance. The parts of the bundle with staying power are probably the ones that offer the greatest value to students given the alternatives available in the larger economy. In other words, they're the most economical.

In a hypothetical new world of unbundled education, a highly nimble and competitive market of knowledge providers will offer educational materials, and other entities will evolve to certify individuals who have accumulated groups of courses or measurable skills. The traditional university sector will shrink into a niche market as finishing schools for the wealthy. But in a world with significant scope economies, these new entities may remain hypothetical because they are outcompeted by an older institution—a traditional college— that can still do both of those functions together more cheaply. This is an issue we turn to more directly in chapter 9.

The Descent into Isomorphism?

The main message of this chapter is that despite the wide variety of institution types we identified in chapter 2, there are core activities that all colleges and universities share. We have argued that the organizations that produce higher education gradually assumed their current form in part because that form solved a basic economic problem of finding the least-cost way of producing a set of related services. There are other narratives that explain the similarities that American colleges and universities share. In *The End of College*, Kevin Carey builds a portrait of an inefficient "hybrid university." This is an institution that uncomfortably mixes practical training, liberal education, and high-level research. The hybrid university is inefficient to its core because it is an accretion of changes, almost all of which have increased cost while undermining educational coherence. As Carey notes, "instead of choosing, American universities decided to do all three things at once, with consequences that last to this day."[20] The hybrid university is supposedly in thrall to Harvard and all of its innovations, and the root of the dysfunction goes back at least to Harvard president Charles W. Eliot's "elective system." This system diminished the "classical core" of nineteenth-century liberal education by giving students choice. But it also supposedly encouraged scholars to teach their specialties to tiny audiences, pushing up cost and pushing most undergraduates to the useless fringe of the higher education enterprise. This same Harvard-centric view of American higher education's prestige-driven descent into disruption suffuses the narrative in *The Innovative University*, by Clayton Christensen and Henry Eyring, and in many other recent works about the supposed existential crisis in American higher education.[21]

In this reading of the historical record, Harvard's early twentieth-century search for faculty with the highest scholarly credentials led directly to a needless and costly overcredentialing of today's professoriate nationwide. Every member of the faculty at a hybrid college or university now is expected to hold that most rarified degree, the PhD. This credentialing competition then supposedly allowed narrow self-defined faculty research interests to displace a common educational mission. As a result, quality teaching is now de-emphasized and demeaned as an unworthy activity.[22] In this telling, even the idea of academic freedom becomes a way for the faculty to avoid accountability and teach what they please. Faculty entrepreneurial independence comes at the expense of the average undergraduate's education and at a huge cost to their family's bank balance.

The scientific and practical pursuits of the hybrid university then positioned American higher education to tap deeply into the well of federal support as the size of the federal fiscal footprint grew in the middle of the twentieth century. This financial wellspring includes the GI Bill, the Higher Education Act (and its sources of financial aid), and research support from agencies like the National Science Foundation (NSF). To Carey and others, the hybrid model is a socially irrational accretion of activities designed to be bad at undergraduate education. The only reason the model has endured for this long is because of this series of historical accidents that temporarily masked its inherent unsustainability.

In these narratives, the malevolent force maintaining the inefficiency of colleges and universities is "institutional isomorphism." This is the tendency for organizations in a similar field to evolve similar features over time. In many higher education narratives, this tendency is malignant at almost every stage of the process. Things like faculty tenure, institutional accreditation, the terminal PhD, and the role of research all push schools toward the same expensive model that devalues undergraduate instruction. Outside constraints then reinforce the negative forces of isomorphism. An excellent current example is the rankings game. The annual *US News & World Report* college rankings are based on well-known criteria, so we should not be surprised to see schools doing many of the same things to maintain or improve their position on the ladder. Isomorphism also supposedly breeds complacence. Industry leaders can't even contemplate other models, so the field becomes ripe for that new buzzword, disruption.[23]

We don't disagree with the proposition that higher education institutions are inefficient. We're not convinced, however, that any large organizations would pass an efficiency test. The Harvard-centric retelling of the story of American higher education based on pernicious isomorphism is hardly a closed case. For one, it's based on a caricature of the complex set of institutions that make up the system. As we showed in chapter 2, any discussion of US higher education that begins from statements about a typical university (hybrid or otherwise) is likely to be misleading, since schools vary widely in a huge set of dimensions. Diversity is what is typical.

If you look at what schools actually do, you will discover that their missions do have a substantial overlap. Schools as diverse as Kenyon College, with its undergraduate-only population of roughly 1,600, and Ohio State, with nearly 60,000 students on its Columbus campus, both offer a liberal education. At Kenyon, however, the third head of the hybrid monster—the option of practical career training—is very limited. If you read the mission statement at prestigious institutions and less selective schools alike you will see much in common. Faculty members overwhelmingly do have PhD degrees, and most are engaged in some form of professional scholarship. We would note that the same tendency to hire a faculty with terminal PhDs is true in most of the world's universities, and the institutions in places as different as France, Japan, and Saudi Arabia have evolved in response to very different historical circumstances. You'll also discover that most American universities have a counseling center, a career center, and a set of clubs and other services that all look basically similar. Much the same stuff goes on at most of these institutions, though it is tailored to the circumstances of each school.

Is this similarity due to the dead hand of Charles W. Eliot, and does it reflect an accumulation of inefficient practices at institutions driven by prestige competition to be more like Harvard?[24] If you observe that a certain model of LED television sells at roughly the same price at different stores in your city, you might infer that the firms selling TVs are all in cahoots, engaged in nefarious price fixing. The simpler answer is that this is how competitive markets work. In the higher education marketplace, we observe Harvard, Kenyon, and Northern Illinois University all offering a bundle of services that share many features, but that tells us nothing about efficiency. Isomorphism is not destructive by definition.

We think this commonality in structure and in practice at most colleges and universities results from a number of forces. Some do have long historical roots, and others are economic. For one, it reflects the similar mission of all of these nonprofit institutions. That mission arose in part from common values of the times. But university isomorphism also reflects a common understanding of best practices in education, and these practices have evolved over long stretches of time and through lots of experimentation. These practices will continue to evolve under the pressures we will outline more fully in the chapters ahead. In other words, there is no such thing as the final shape of the modern university. And lastly, the isomorphism that we observe also can be seen as a rational response to a set of economic problems that colleges and universities face together. The theory of the multiproduct firm offers a framework for understanding the evolution of the current structure of American colleges and why the system that we see remains durable even in the face of significant economic stress and technological change.

The idea that a substantial portion of America's colleges will simply disappear has high barriers to overcome. A new model of the sort that Kevin Carey calls "The University of Everywhere" would have to be so efficient that it overcomes the considerable transaction costs involved in collecting the set of related courses, badges, or qualifications required to complete a degree or some other new certification of knowledge. We already see students who take courses at lots of colleges and have institutions accept a large number of transfer credits. This way a student can collect courses and then become certified, though rules about how many transfer credits an institution will accept vary considerably. This is one way the current system is evolving to meet the needs of a generation of mostly older students, and it does not suggest that the current university bundle targeted at late teens is in any danger of imminent demise.

PART TWO

Threats

4

Internal Threat I

THE RISING COSTS OF HIGHER EDUCATION

EVERY YEAR NEWSPAPERS run front-page stories about the schools with the highest total costs of attendance, and we hear about the number of institutions that have surpassed the most recent milestone: $40,000, $50,000, and now $60,000.[1] In chapter 2 (Figure 2.2) we showed that only a small fraction of students face these astronomical list-price tuitions. For the 2014–15 academic year almost 52% of full-time undergraduates attended institutions whose list-price tuition and fees were below $12,000 per year. Fewer than 20% attended schools charging a list price above $30,000. And most students at these schools don't pay that list price.

Headline stories shape public opinion despite the fact that they are based on extremes, while more complex facts tend to get buried in technical reports. Perceptions, however, are very important. People who believe that a college education is out of reach are less likely to examine their options thoroughly, and there is indeed good evidence that Americans seriously overestimate what they will have to pay for a college education. In an early study of this, Ikenberry and Hartle showed that people overestimated the cost of attendance at a public four-year university by a factor of two.[2] This perception problem disproportionately affects lower-income and middle-income families who have less experience navigating the college application process. Perceptions also can influence which issues receive serious policy attention. Combatting high list-price tuition is an excellent example of a current cause célèbre, yet stabilizing or reducing list-price tuition will do little to raise college completion rates of at-risk students or improve social mobility.

The perception that college tuition is out of control is not just based on anecdotes. The Bureau of Labor Statistics (BLS) collects prices for hundreds of goods and services that Americans buy and uses this data to produce the

Consumer Price Index (CPI). According to the BLS, college tuition is indeed going up much faster than prices of other goods and services, including health care. These data often are featured in stories about the rapid rise in college tuition. We could have collected a great number of examples, but two make our point. In a 2013 story in the *Wall Street Journal* Douglas Belkin wrote, "In the past decade, college tuition has risen three times as fast as the consumer price index and twice as fast as medical care."[3] From the other side of the political spectrum, Katie Rose Quandt, writing in *Mother Jones* in 2014, said, "While the indexed price of college tuition and fees skyrocketed by more than 1,122 percentage points since 1978, the cost of medical care rose less than 600 percent."[4]

Health care costs are outrageous, so something must be seriously wrong with colleges and universities. Yet these statistics are just as misleading as the anecdotes that animate much of the reporting on college costs. The processes driving college cost and college pricing are complex, yet much of what is written about them is based on flawed and oversimplified statistics and unrepresentative stories. This chapter is intended as an antidote, and the story we tell here will motivate much of our later analysis of the turbulence buffeting the American higher education system.

Perceptions matter, but reality is important as well. Some families *do* pay high list prices, and this can steer the political process toward the interests of higher-income families that see these high list prices. Many others pay much lower list prices that have been increasing rapidly in recent years, especially at public institutions that have seen their state subsidies reduced. Rising tuition is indeed a potent internal threat. A Pew Research Center poll in 2011 found that 75% of the respondents believed that college was too expensive for most Americans to afford.[5] If true, colleges and universities cannot continue to exist in their current form even if new technologies don't disrupt them into extinction. If students stop coming, the business model of the modern college or university is clearly unsustainable. Our first job in assessing this internal threat is to dig into the realities of college cost *and price* so we can see how rising tuition may play out in the diverse US higher education system. Then we will turn to the value proposition, which is the other half of the problem.

If continually rising costs are part of doing business as usual, we need to understand the causes. Many believe the fundamental sources of rising cost are found in the history and the practices of colleges and universities themselves. The core problems of higher education today, in this view, stem from dysfunctional institutions abetted by public subsidy and by fortuitous changes in the economy over the past sixty years that have pushed up the demand for college credentialing. In brief, growing inefficiency inside the Ivory Tower is the primary driver of college cost in the dysfunction narrative. Colleges and universities from the most elite to the least selective (but trying harder) are engaged in an endless pursuit of prestige. The panoply of annual college rankings provides the steroids that drive a positional arms race fueled by profligate spending. In this no-win competition to be like Harvard, the by-product is needless tuition increases that punish students who just want the ticket to jobs and prosperity in the modern economy. This irrational and costly race persists because colleges and universities maintain a monopoly on accredited degrees, which are the credentials that matter in today's labor market.

Our task in this chapter is to evaluate the drivers of college cost and to assess the seriousness of this internal threat to the existing model of higher education delivery. First, we review the relationship between college cost and the price that is charged. Much of what is written in the press about tuition is confused because it assumes that higher education operates just like any private business. Second, we need to explain the important cost drivers in higher education and separate wheat arguments from the chaff. In our view, broad economic forces that are buffeting and transforming the global economy are the primary drivers of college cost. These economic forces are primarily technological. Lastly, we will evaluate the dysfunction narrative that shines a spotlight on poor incentives and bad decision making inside universities.

Costs and Prices

Higher education is a minefield of jargon. Terms like net tuition, cost per full-time-equivalent (FTE) student, and tuition discount rate permeate any serious conversation about the state of America's colleges and universities. Misunderstandings of this terminology color the way people use and interpret statistics about rising college tuition. Before we dig into the drivers of college costs and college pricing, we have to clean up this terminological swamp. We also need to describe the business model at work in nonprofit higher education.

We'll start with the crucial difference between price and cost. Most people have a working understanding of these terms from observing the way a typical for-profit business operates. A firm pays for labor, capital, rent, and raw materials, as well as for wholly or partially finished items it buys from other firms. That's its cost of production. Price is what the firm charges people who want to buy what the firm makes. To stay in business, a for-profit enterprise needs a price that covers the per-unit cost of the inputs used in making its product. Anything extra is a profit margin. If the firms in an industry see their per-unit costs go up, their profit margin takes an immediate hit. Losses force weaker firms out until a normal margin is restored. High margins draw new firms in, bringing the margin back to just what is needed to keep firms doing what they're doing. While profit margins are by no means constant, the competitive forces we have just described do limit them. If you have seen a new microbrewery set up in your town, you are watching this process at work. In this framework, if the price of something is rising for years without any fundamental change in the nature of the product or its quality, it's a good bet that the costs of producing that good or service have been increasing.

Prices and costs are a bit more complex in higher education. Not-for-profit firms dominate the traditional four-year sector in higher education, so profit margins are not part of the story. A not-for-profit college isn't single-mindedly motivated to maximize shareholder value. But it does have a bottom line, and it must break even over the long run to survive. The complexity comes from the fact that a college's revenue per unit sold is not the same thing as its price (or tuition). Colleges and universities receive revenue from many sources. First, they charge tuition, which is usually called "tuition and fees" because colleges often itemize certain parts of the bill separately. For most purposes the distinction is not important, and it certainly doesn't matter for the person writing the checks. Second, public colleges receive direct appropriations from state and local governments. Third, most not-for-profit colleges have endowments that produce an annual return, and they also receive spendable gifts from private individuals and foundations. Lastly, research carried out by the faculty often is sponsored by outside entities like the National Science Foundation. Universities that host this research use grant funding to cover some of their costs. Nonprofit colleges aren't the only institutions with such a diverse revenue stream. The same is true of other subsidized institutions like symphony orchestras, public mass transit systems, and libraries.

We can lump together state appropriations, endowment earnings and gifts, and sponsored research funds into a single pot called institutional subsidies. These revenue sources permit universities to charge a price (tuition) that does not cover cost, while still breaking even. As we showed in chapter 2 (Figure 2.7), over 90% of public universities get half or more of their revenue from these institutional subsidies.[6] Without institutional subsidies, students would have to pay a tuition that covered the full per-unit cost of their education, and the school likely would have to pare away many of the things it currently does. These institutional subsidies complicate the relationship between cost and price. We can no longer assume that rising prices must mean rising cost. Changes in subsidies can drive prices at nonprofits. This is a critical point. Much of the public discussion of rising college prices presumes that rising cost must be the reason for rising tuition. This inference is a step too fast unless institutional subsidies have been stable.

There is yet another layer of complexity in higher education pricing. The typical business cares only about its potential customers' willingness to pay, not their quality or other personal attributes. Colleges and universities are different. Student ability, diligence, and experience are important inputs into the educational production process. Students are not homogeneous flash drives that passively receive knowledge uploaded from professors. They are active participants in their own education in at least two ways. First, to succeed, they must have the intellectual capacity to learn complex and often abstract things. They must also have important character traits and noncognitive skills that allow them to persevere through lengthy tasks and to navigate a complex three- to six-year pathway to a credential. So most nonprofit colleges care about their students' characteristics, not just the size of the family wallet. Second, peer interaction is another significant part of the educational process. Students learn from each other in many ways and in many situations outside of the classroom or the professor's office. Any institution that is even minimally selective is very concerned about the "quality" of its customers and about the variety of attributes that will enrich an incoming class. At the most crass level—rankings and general publicity—colleges are motivated to find students who have a good chance to succeed in their school's particular environment. More seriously, nonprofit colleges and universities are mission driven, and crafting each incoming class is an important part of meeting that mission.

This is a critical difference between most colleges and universities and the larger private sector, and it affects how universities set tuition. Most important, from Harvard to Hiram, a college does not simply set the highest price that it thinks will lead to a full class. The owners of a Burger King franchise are trying to maximize profit. They do not use a winnowing process to exclude a willing customer who wants a hamburger. By contrast, a college or university must balance its needs for revenue against its desire to offer spaces to the students who can most benefit from (and contribute to) its program, and against its mission-driven aspirations to serve a social purpose. These goals are partly compatible and partly in tension.

Schools are under no obligation to charge every student the same price. Family income strongly influences willingness and capacity to pay, and students differ in their capacity to add to the institution's mission. In the search for the pricing strategy that accomplishes its goals, almost all schools use a range of need-based and merit-based discounts. Schools set list-price tuition and then offer "scholarships" that are often given impressive names to increase their marketing potential. In chapter 2 (Figure 2.3)we showed the magnitude and prevalence of tuition discounts. For schools that are adept at this process, they can extract enough tuition revenue to meet their needs while using discounts as a chisel to finely sculpt the group of entering students. We will present a simple model explaining the process of tuition discounts in chapter 6.

Given the multiple objectives that guide tuition setting, colleges and universities do not collect all the revenue they possibly could. This is very different from the behavior of most businesses. For example, among highly selective programs, the most elite do not extract the most revenue per student. The most selective schools face the highest demand for places, and they could use that high demand to charge a higher price. Yet they do not. Figure 4.1 plots the net tuition (list-price tuition minus all internal discounts) per student for thirty-one of the top fifty national universities in the 2014 *US News* ranking of the top national universities.[7] If higher demand, measured as applicants per student admitted, led schools to extract more revenue per student, we would expect a positive correlation. Instead, there is no significant relationship at all.

The average net price at elite institutions like Harvard and Stanford is very close to the national average net price for all private four-year institutions. This really shouldn't surprise anyone. For starters, the most highly

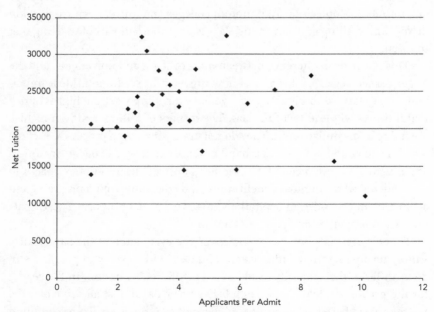

FIGURE 4.1 A scatter plot of net tuition and applicants per admit.

selective programs tend to be well endowed. This means they have more subsidy money they can use to hold down the price their average student pays. Less elite programs are often said to gear their behavior to imitate their more elite brethren. In price setting, however, Pace University isn't aping Princeton. Instead, keeping net price in line with less elite programs is a tool that allows places like Princeton to be as selective as they are. Leaving large amounts of revenue uncollected is a perfectly rational strategy for the elite to stay elite.

For many students, tuition discounting puts considerable distance between college prices and college costs. Universities don't like being accused of jacking up list prices just so they can put some of their seats on sale, but in fact this is what happens. And over the last twenty years, average discount rates have tended to rise at both public and private institutions.[8] Almost all colleges and universities could reduce their list-price tuition if they stopped the practice of giving tuition discounts.[9] For elite schools, they do not need the revenue they would receive if every student paid the list-price tuition, but a flat rate tuition paid by everyone would change the composition of the incoming class, reducing diversity and class "quality" in the eyes of the admissions office. And for many of the nation's less well-heeled programs, a one-price-fits-all approach would cost them significant amounts of revenue. *Not* discounting would be a survival risk.

The final part of the pricing story involves donors and government sources that award grants or scholarships directly to students to help make a college education more affordable. The federal government funds Pell Grants and Supplemental Educational Opportunity Grants (SEOG) for students from low-income families and offers tuition tax credits that help families with incomes high enough to take advantage. State governments also fund grants for needy students or students that show particular academic merit, and various private organizations award scholarships to student to help defray college expenses. We will dig much deeper into direct student grants in chapter 7 when we explore the state and federal commitment to higher education.

The prevalence of tuition discounts, grants, and scholarships makes college pricing very complex. Here are the three distinct tuition concepts to keep in mind:

1. List-price tuition—This is the tuition posted in the catalog. Some students do pay the full list price, but many students pay less because they receive a discount from the institution or they get a grant or scholarship from some entity other than the school.

2. Average net tuition to the institution—This is the average amount of tuition revenue the school receives per student after paring away internal tuition discounts. Total tuition revenue is just this number times the full-time student population.

3. Average net price to the students—This is the average tuition actually paid by students. It is the list price minus the tuition discount offered by the institution and grants, scholarships, and tuition tax credits provided by entities other than the institution. Average net price to the student is less than average net price to the institution.

List Price, Net Price, and Cost

When someone makes a statement or quotes some statistic about college tuition, look to see if the author has a clear tuition concept in mind. As we'll now show, these three tuition measures move very differently over time. And college cost follows its own path. Anyone who wants to get past sound bites needs to dig into why.

Figure 4.2 shows the evidence about college tuition and the price of medical care that birthed the quotes at the beginning of the chapter. These are

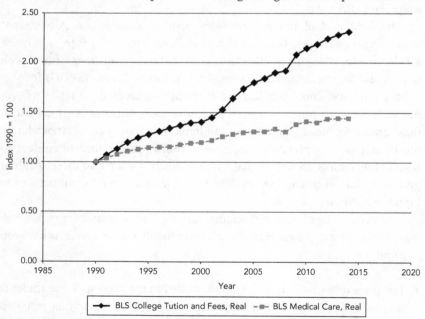

FIGURE 4.2 Real college tuition and real cost of medical care, 1990–2014.

"real" price indexes using data the BLS collects to compute the CPI. A real price index increases over time if the price of the product or service in question rises more rapidly than the overall price index. Both price indexes have risen over time, which tells us that college tuition and the price of medical care have gone up more rapidly than the overall CPI. And real college tuition has indeed increased faster than the real price index for medical care. Does this mean that college costs are soaring out of control? That is the conventional wisdom, and it is quite wrong.

The BLS uses list-price tuition in its price indexes. This is unusual, because whenever possible the BLS collects prices actually paid for the goods and services included in the CPI.[10] For medical care, the BLS most assuredly does not use the "charge" you see on your doctor's bill. If you have medical insurance, the "price" used by the BLS is your copay plus the amount the insurance company pays the doctor. If you have ever looked at a bill (the EOB, or explanation of benefits), you will see that the insurance provider has negotiated a steep discount on the doctor's charge. Almost no one pays the list price, so to produce an accurate CPI the BLS is keen to get the real "transaction price." Yet the BLS does not do this for college tuition.

In Figure 4.3, we see why the difference between list prices and transaction prices matters a great deal for college tuition. The steeply rising BLS list-price tuition index is repeated from Figure 4.2. The other two series are indexes for the average real *net price to students* at public and private four-year schools.[11] Two clear stories emerge. First, the average transaction price of a year in college does not behave at all like the average list price. Over a considerable time period we see that the average transaction price has gone up much more slowly than the average list price. The BLS data that scream from the headlines substantially overstate the increase in prices that the average student actually pays. Second, the average transaction price at public universities is much more volatile than the net price at private nonprofit schools. This volatility comes largely from substantial swings in state support that mostly get passed through to tuition. State government finances went into reverse in the early 2000s during the dot-com bust and again later in the decade following the financial meltdown.

In Figure 4.4, we move from net price paid by students to what public universities actually spend to provide the service. Now we see that the list price index wildly overstates the growth in cost at public institutions. Cost per full-time student at public universities has risen less rapidly than real income per capita in the United States over the same time period. The reason that college has not become more affordable for the middle class has more to do with changes in the income distribution than with profligate spending sprees

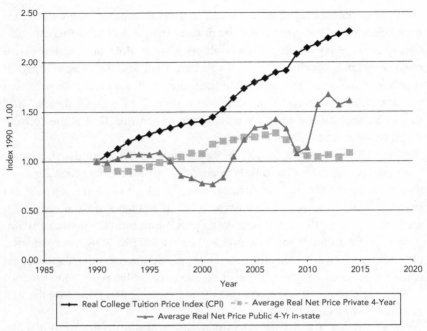

FIGURE 4.3 Real college tuition and real net price of college, private nonprofit and public four-year institution, 1990–2014.

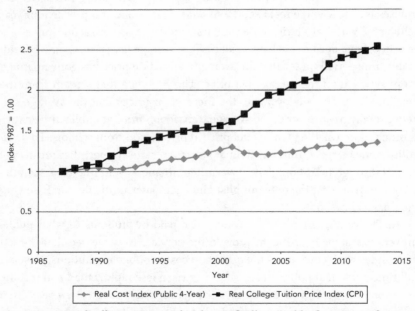

FIGURE 4.4 Real college tuition and real cost of college, public four-year, 1987–2013.

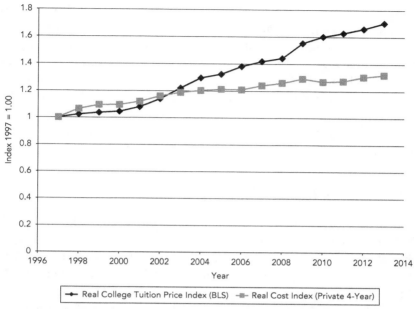

FIGURE 4.5   Real college tuition and real cost of college, private four-year, 1997–2013.

at prestige-driven schools. We will explore how national trends in household income affect higher education in chapter 6.

Figure 4.5 gives the same comparison for private four-year institutions. Because of changes in the way the cost data are calculated, we can only present this comparison from 1997 to 2013. Even over this shorter time period, we see the same pattern. The CPI based on list prices overstates the increase in the cost of producing a year of schooling at private colleges.

Much of the hyperventilated talk about the ills of modern colleges and universities is based on looking at list prices and concluding that *costs* are growing out of control. Like grist for the mill, stories of lazy rivers and sushi in the food court provide the emotional raw material ready to be processed into an indictment of universities' faulty cost controls. The analysis then continues by describing ways that colleges can cut costs, presumably without reducing the quality of the education offered. Without passing judgment on the specifics of any college or university's spending, the national facts of rising cost don't fit the apocalyptic story. Equating list-price movement with changes in cost is not sensible in higher education.

Although we have made some important points about the exaggerated language of crisis, we can't close the book right here. First, we must heed the message of chapter 2 about diversity. Our price/cost comparisons are averages, and there is a considerable dispersion around those averages. Schools that are far from the average may face a very different future, and we need to identify the likely suspects. Second, some students do pay the list-price tuition, and they (and their parents) have faced dramatically increasing prices. They are a significant part of the politics of higher education. Third, even if the average real cost isn't rising nearly as rapidly as the list price, it's still rising. This means that the costs of providing a college education are growing more rapidly than the inflation rate. This could still create problems for many colleges and universities.

What Drives College Costs?

College costs have gone up faster than the overall inflation rate for so long that it has become part of the landscape of higher education. Figure 4.6 lays out the national data on real cost per full-time student from 1948 to 2013.[12] This is an average for all types of colleges and universities, public and private. We see three distinct periods. From 1948 to the mid-1960s, higher education costs rose more rapidly than the inflation rate, so the real index is rising. Then from the mid-1960s to the early 1980s, the rise in higher education costs moderated and average costs actually rose more slowly than overall inflation. In this

FIGURE 4.6 Index of real higher education costs, 1948–2013.

period the real index is flat or falling. Finally, after the early 1980s, higher education costs again began to accelerate faster than the overall inflation rate, so the real index bends upward again. Despite the moderation of the 1970s, the overall trend is clear. In thirty-eight of the fifty-six yearly changes for which we had annual data, college cost increases exceeded the overall inflation rate.

This pattern of cost increase is not at all uncommon. There are other industries whose costs and prices exhibited this up, flat, and up pattern over the same span of years, and those industries share many features with the higher education industry. These "like" industries include dental care, medicine, legal services, life insurance, and bank service charges, to name a few. The historical pattern of rising cost in these industries over long stretches of time is so striking that it's not likely a simple coincidence. Instead, it's driven by three fundamental characteristics these industries all share.

First, all of them provide services instead of physical goods. Data from the National Income and Product Accounts show that the price index for services soared by more than a factor of twelve from 1947 to 2013, while the price index for goods rose only 4.5 times over the same time period. If you want a one-sentence explanation of why college costs have gone up more rapidly than the inflation rate, here it is: it's a service.

The reason for this is well known. Technological progress over the last century has dramatically raised labor productivity in the manufacture of things like automobiles (more cars produced per hour worked) or in the production of agricultural commodities like wheat (more bushels per labor hour). Raising labor productivity in the service sector is more difficult, and this is especially true in personal services where quality is strongly determined by human interaction. Few people want to go to the fastest barber in town, and aspiring students don't seek out the college that crams the most students into each class. Likewise, most people don't prefer the doctor who zips through ten patients per hour without reviewing their medical history. Yet service industries hire labor in the same national market as other industries. Productivity growth in goods-producing industries holds down cost compared to service industries, whose productivity is more stagnant. In addition, the usual measure of labor productivity (output produced per labor hour) does not effectively capture changes in service quality over time.

The tendency for costs to rise more rapidly in service industries than in goods industries is called "cost disease." The term comes from William Baumol and William Bowen's 1966 book about the economics of the performing arts.[13] Live performances are a good example of an industry with little potential for productivity growth. No sensible person would value the higher labor productivity of a three-person string quartet. Although technological innovation in the 20th century dramatically expanded our ability to hear recorded music, the market for live performances has not withered away. In chapter 8, we will evaluate the future potential of sophisticated artificial intelligence and automated online content to displace the "live performances" of face-to-face instruction. But whatever the future may hold, cost disease is a critical part of any serious explanation for rising college cost over the past century.[14]

The second similarity between industries like higher education and the services of dentists, physicians, and lawyers has to do with the education level of the service providers. Barbershops and colleges both produce services, and both have had fairly stagnant labor productivity, but the cost of a haircut has not risen as rapidly as college cost. The reason is that the labor force of the hair care industry and the labor forces of colleges and universities have very different average levels of educational attainment. The gap in earnings between someone with a college degree and someone whose education stopped with a high school degree has widened substantially since 1980. Labor market data show that the annual rate of return to a year of college, which had bounced around just under 10% from 1940 to 1980, climbed steadily after 1980 to over 15%. Over the same time period the wages of those with only a high school degree have stagnated. This changing wage gap will play a prominent role in later chapters, both as an environmental challenge and as an argument for the continuing value of the credential.

The third similarity these education-intensive personal services share is how they respond to changing technology. Most manufacturing firms choose to adopt new techniques, software, or machinery if this change allows them to cut costs while still meeting the quality demands of their customers. This is not generally how technology decisions are made in higher education. Colleges and universities have to meet an educational standard of care. In addition to their supposedly timeless and mission-driven commitments to liberal education, colleges have to prepare students for the demands and the standards of an evolving labor market. That market is saturated in new technology, so colleges and universities tend to be fast adopters of the newest equipment and subject matter even if the new is more expensive than the old.

Any university that held down costs by steadfastly maintaining the techniques and technology of the 1960s could be charged with educational malpractice. The story is easy to tell in the STEM fields (science, technology, engineering, and mathematics), where expensive lab equipment that did not exist a generation ago is now commonplace and new methods have permeated the curriculum of the average undergraduate. But the same process is at work in most academic fields. In economics, our students take classes in subjects like econometrics that were rudimentary in the 1970s, while political scientists and sociologists (and their students) have become adept at using Geographic Information Systems (GIS) modeling. These tools were given life by modern computing technologies, and our students now routinely do work that was unimaginable a generation ago. As a result, colleges and universities often have to invest in new technology and new professional staffing even if it drives up the cost of the education. A similar process has been at work in many other industries. Just think of how a doctor's office functioned thirty years ago, and of how surgical procedures have evolved over the same time frame. Our choice of the term "standard of care" is deliberate.

Counseling and student services offer another example of meeting a standard of care. The Higher Education Research Institute has surveyed incoming college students for many years.[15] One part of the survey asks students to rate their emotional health. In 1990, 57.1% of the respondents rated their "emotional health" in the "top 10%" or "above average." By 2014, that percentage had fallen to 50.7%. Also, in the 2014 survey, 9.5% of the respondents "frequently" felt depressed. Colleges and universities have responded to this pressure by putting more resources into counseling and other student services. This spending does boost student retention and graduation, but it also pushes up cost. We will have much more to say about student services when we tackle the hypothetical unbundling of higher education in chapter 9.

We have identified three factors that explain why college cost tends to rise more rapidly than the inflation rate: (1) higher education is a service, (2) compared with most other industries higher education relies on highly educated service providers, and (3) higher education has to meet a technological standard of care. Yet college cost rose more slowly than the inflation rate for over a decade between the late 1960s and the early 1980s. Why this exception to the rule? Any theory of the cost drivers in higher education has to explain this period of cost moderation, as well as the overall upward trend. If your explanation of rising college cost focuses on dysfunction in the academy—things like administrative bloat, prestige games, excessive spending on research, or the evils of academic tenure—you are left trying to explain why a dysfunctional system had a burst of functionality, or you need to tack on a special story just for this time period. Our "fundamentals" explanation has no such difficulty.

Two parts of our three-part story help us explain the period of flat to declining real cost. First, cost disease only pushes up the real cost of services when there is robust productivity growth in the overall economy. This makes real cost rise in the sectors of the economy (like personal services) that haven't experienced the productivity gains. The period of flat real costs for higher education coincides with a well-documented slowdown in overall productivity growth, which made cost disease less virulent. Figure 4.7 documents the falloff in productivity growth that characterizes the period from roughly 1967 through 1982.[16]

This moderation of cost disease was reinforced in the 1970s by changes in the college wage premium. In this decade, the gap in earnings between someone with a college degree and someone whose school completion tops out with a high school degree actually declined. In the 1970s, this earnings gap was at its smallest in the entire twentieth century. The college wage premium turned around and began a pronounced increase beginning in the early 1980s, just when the real cost of higher education started to rise again.

Our story of why higher education costs have gone up more rapidly than the inflation rate over most of the post–World War II period is inherently comparative in nature. In an inflationary time most prices and costs are rising, but some persistently rise more rapidly than others. Explaining why requires identifying the similarities that characterize the industries whose costs tend to increase either faster or more slowly than the overall inflation rate. We found a whole set of industries whose historical cost and price behavior closely resembled the path of higher education costs in Figure 4.6, including the slowdown

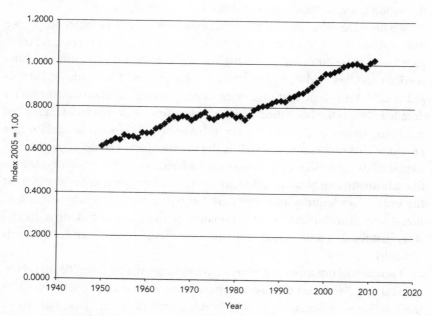

FIGURE 4.7 Index of total factor productivity, 1950–2011.

from the mid-1960s to the early 1980s. They are personal service industries whose employees are mostly highly educated, and they tend to be industries that adopt new technology to meet a standard of care rather than for pure cost reduction. Our explanation of the major forces driving college cost focuses on the broader economic environment in which colleges and universities (and other industries) operate. We do not think that industry-specific explanations offer a better story for rising college cost, and we don't think that the evidence of similarities across so many different personal services is just a coincidence. Occam's razor is on our side.

To this point, our argument is short on assigning blame. We have not supplied any juicy stories of university presidents frivolously trying to make their institutions the most expensive in America. This doesn't mean that people making choices aren't a part of the story. Human agency actually is very important. Universities must respond to their changing environment, and their reactions are choices made by administrators and boards as they grapple with pressures and opportunities. In response to cost disease, a college could try to keep pace with national productivity growth by expanding class size. When the cost of employing highly educated labor expands, a college could respond by hiring fewer PhDs into full-time positions (and many have indeed done this). When new technologies spread through the economy, a college could respond by delaying adoption of any cost-increasing new tools and focusing the curriculum and the support services on older, less expensive practices and approaches. Each of these responses would reduce the quality of the education it offered even as it ameliorated cost growth. The past history of college behavior tells us that most schools have made the quality-preserving choice in response to cost pressures, and where they have had to surrender quality they have tried to minimize the harm to their long-term mission. Going forward, however, we need to evaluate how these choices likely will be made in a future environment with different constraints and different opportunities.

The three cost pathways of the past may persist, but they are not inevitable. Advances in distance learning technology may indeed break the link between class size and the quality of instruction. New modes of artificial intelligence–assisted online information delivery may even break up the expensive bundled university. That would certainly lessen the impact of cost disease and potentially allow higher education to escape its clutches completely. The factors that have driven up wages for college-educated workers relative to high school graduates may begin to abate. Any decline in the college wage premium would reduce cost pressures in a wide range of education-intensive industries like higher education. And lastly, we may see a slowdown in the development of expensive new technologies, often embodied in equipment that colleges and universities have felt compelled to adopt as they work to maintain the educational standard of care. Just because broad economic forces can explain past increases in college cost does not mean that we are fated forever to have costs that rise more rapidly than the inflation rate. The future isn't predestined. Before we examine these possibilities, we need to evaluate an alternative view of rising college cost.

The Dysfunction Argument for Rising College Cost

Much of the contemporary criticism of American higher education takes a very different tack. Instead of broad economic forces, increasingly wasteful and inefficient behaviors inside the academy are the primary culprits behind rising costs. In some ways this is a more optimistic view. Inefficient behaviors might be changeable. Strong leadership from college presidents and their governing boards could possibly set things right. In addition, inefficient organizations should lose out in a competitive market. The higher education industry has many of the hallmarks of a competitive market—a lot of sellers and millions of buyers who increasingly have good information about their options. Indeed, we have ample evidence that the barriers that once insulated institutions and gave them local and regional market power have dissipated.[17] Perpetual inefficiency is a difficult idea to maintain in any market with a reasonable amount of competition. An organization that finds ways to curb inefficiencies should gain an edge over others that continue to waste resources. Eventually this competitive advantage should translate into gains of some sort, measured in growth, programming quality, or that coin of the academic realm, prestige.

In this section we review the claimed inefficiencies that figure so prominently in today's narrative of sky-high tuition. Before we begin, we'll put our cards on the table. Higher education is indeed an inefficient industry. But we are deeply skeptical that inefficiency stories go very far in explaining rising college cost. For starters, the data in Figure 4.6 suggest that inefficiency must have increased dramatically over the past seventy years, except, of course, between 1967 and 1982, when real higher education cost increases abated.

Many of the features of academic life and culture that create the supposed inefficiencies have been with us for quite some time. This includes academic tenure and the accompanying pressure to succeed in research. Tenure has been dying a slow death at most institutions. In the 1993–94 academic year

62.6% of colleges had tenure systems. Twenty years later in 2013–14 that number had fallen to 49.3%. For the institutions where tenure is available, it is almost always reserved for full-time faculty members, and full-time faculty members have decreased from 59% of the faculty in 1993–94 to 51% in 2013–14. If tenure is an inherently inefficient practice, the problem should have diminished.

Administrative Bloat

In recent years, professional staffing at colleges and universities has grown considerably. This growth often is tagged as "administrative bloat." The term naturally suggests waste and excess leading to needless increases in cost. Professors often are inclined to endorse this view. Ask any professor to identify an administrator who isn't necessary, and he or she may suggest three. But before we jump on this bandwagon, let's take a close look at the data to see just how much growth has occurred, and in what parts of the administration.

A 2010 report by the Goldwater Institute of Arizona State University gives some data, and those concerned with administrative bloat often cite this study. The punch line is straightforward: "Between 1993 and 2007, the number of full-time administrators per 100 students at America's leading universities grew by 39 percent, while the number of employees engaged in teaching, research, or service only grew by 18 percent."[18] This information suggests a growing problem. The useful employees form a declining share of the academic labor force, and the number of administrators per student is rising.

The data in the Goldwater report come from the Integrated Postsecondary Education Data System (IPEDS) of the Department of Education. IPEDS contains a wealth of detailed information about colleges and universities, including information about their employees. IPEDS puts college employees into seven categories: (1) faculty, (2) executive/administrative and managerial, (3) other professional, (4) technical and paraprofessional, (5) clerical and secretarial, (6) skilled craft, and (7) service and maintenance. The Goldwater report combined executive/administrative and managerial with other professional to gauge the size of the "administration." The administration is the administrator plus his or her entire staff. Measured this way, the administration has grown quite rapidly.

A 2014 report by the Delta Cost Project takes a slightly different approach. It keeps the two parts of the administration separate. The data in this report also come from IPEDS and are measured as the number of headcount employees per 1,000 FTE students. They present separate data for public and private research universities. For public research universities, the data show that executive/administrative and managerial employees fell from 14 per 1,000 students in 1990 to 11 in 2012, while other professionals grew from 53 to 73 over the same time period. All of the growth in "administration" came from growth in staff, not management. For private research universities, executive/administrative and managerial grew from 30 in 1990 to 41 in 2012, and other professional grew from 72 to 102. For private universities, the growth in staff was three times as big as the growth in management. What is termed "administrative bloat" is not driven by growth in deans and vice presidents as much as it is driven by growth in the staffs of deans and vice presidents.

Who are these professional staff people, and where do they work? We don't have good national data on this, but we can delve into the numbers at our own institution, the College of William and Mary. We may think our institution is special in many ways, but we don't believe that our administration and staffing numbers are all that unusual. The Office of Institutional Research at William and Mary has kept detailed records of staff backing up the reports they sent to IPEDS since 1994. These data include job title and department, so we could largely identify where these people worked and what they did.[19] We have good information for 1994–2005. This is shorter than the Goldwater time span but the trends should be apparent.

The William and Mary student body grew very little over this time span, from 6,926 FTE students in 1994 to 7,197 FTE students in 2005. This growth of 271 FTE students happened over a time span in which the number of headcount professional staff grew by 231. Headcount professional staff per 1,000 FTE students grew from 43.5 in 1994 to 73.9 in 2005.[20] The professional staff clearly has soared over this time period. But two questions remain. How much of this growth in professional staff are people whose salaries added to costs that are passed on to tuition payers, and can we reasonably apply the term "bloat" to those new staff positions?

We allocated the professional staff into nine units: (1) academics—staff that reported to an academic unit, (2) athletics—staff that reported to the athletic department, (3) business and human resources, (3) central administration—staff that reported to the president or provost, (4) development, (5) enrollment management (admission, financial aid, and registrar), (6) information technology, (7) libraries and museums, (8) student services, and (9) other. In two instances we shifted staff by function. Law librarians were assigned to libraries and museums instead of academics despite the fact that they report to the dean of the law school, and admissions officers in the schools of business, education and law were assigned to enrollment management, despite the fact that they reported to their deans.[21]

The overall staff headcount increased by 231. Academics contributed 97; information technology contributed 36; development contributed 30; athletics contributed 24; enrollment management contributed 16; student services contributed 14; and both business and human resources and libraries and museums contributed 2. There was no growth in central administration. Do these increases in staff add to cost, and is there any clear evidence of waste?

Let's start with the addition of thirty staff members in development. "Development" is a euphemism for fundraising. Extra development officers only add to costs that have to be covered by tuition or state subsidy if they're not doing their job successfully! A brand new development staff member is expected to bring in new donations at least as large as his or her salary, and an experienced officer is expected to bring in five to ten times his or her salary. Some of the donations aren't spendable. They add to the endowment. But at the usual draw-down rate from endowment, the discounted present value of the flow of spendable funds from a brand new development officer already exceeds salary if the new hire merely meets expectations.[22] According to a 2012 study conducted by the Council for Advancement and Support of Education, the median contributions raised per dollar of annual operating costs spent on fundraising is $6.38.[23] Of course we cannot attribute all of this to the efforts of the development office. Even if a college had no fundraising effort, or a very lean one, some gifts would come in anyway. But if the marginal contribution of an added development officer is only half of this median, then that officer pays back his or her employer with a flow of earnings whose net present value is a big multiple of the cost to the institution of bringing a new hire onto the payroll. The Commonwealth of Virginia has substantially reduced its appropriation to William and Mary. For us, the search for private support has driven over 12% of the increase in the College's administrative hiring. This is clearly not bloat.

Of the ninety-seven new staff members who reported to academic units, forty-nine had their salaries and benefits funded by grants and contracts. When a faculty member, for instance, is awarded an external grant from a foundation, some of the grant money often can be used to fund professional staff (and graduate students). These jobs are often termed "soft money" positions. The extra staff administers the project or directly aids in the research and outreach the granting agency intended to support. Since these positions come with their own funding, they do not add to costs that must be paid through tuition hikes or added state support. To the extent that any of these staff positions create spillover benefits to other campus programs (including students), the soft money is subsidizing the broader activity of the university.

So far in our brief accounting, at least 30% of the staff growth is covered by extra revenue and so does not contribute any pressure on costs that have to be covered by tuition. We could make a similar argument for other additions to the academic staff. For example, we have a new director of the master's of accounting program in the school of business. This program did not exist in 1994, so the position is a net new administrator. But the program itself is also new, along with its tuition-paying students. This kind of addition is like a development officer or a staff member on soft money. It adds to both revenue and cost, and therefore the position is partially or completely self-funded. We cannot make a definitive count of the number of positions like this. It's just an example to show why one should not simply label all staff increases as cost drivers.

Some of the growth in staff does not reflect an increase in college employees but rather an upgrading of positions. When Professor Archibald joined the faculty of the economics department in 1976, the department consisted of twelve faculty members and one department secretary who typed all tests and papers. Now we have twenty-eight full-time faculty members and one department *administrator* who doesn't type anyone's tests or papers. Department secretaries are classified as clerical employees by IPEDS and department administrators are classified as professional staff. The department is seemingly more productive, with twenty-eight professors and one support person compared with twelve faculty members and one support person, but because the secretary was reclassified into an administrator, we somehow became less efficient by using more professional staff per faculty. This position upgrading is a common phenomenon at the College, and it is common across the US labor market. Labeling it as bloat in higher education may be politically useful, but it is not really honest.

Some increases in staffing seem quite compatible with the standard-of-care component of our explanation of college cost drivers. The information technology staff grew by thirty. This is a response to growing needs of the institution (faculty and students alike) in a world that relies increasingly on computers and software. Similarly, the ten extra staff in student services is arguably a response to the steady pressure of rising demand in areas like counseling, career planning, and medical care. Finally, part of running a college or university involves dealing with an expanding set of requirements from governments and accrediting agencies. More (and more intrusive) regulation has led to some increase in professional staff. If this is bloat, it is a national problem and not something particular about higher education.

We do need to exercise real caution in invoking an evolving standard of care to justify increasingly large professional staffs on college campuses. In many cases the standard of care is self-defined, and this leaves the door wide open for ex post justifications of waste. A college's definition of the appropriate standard could indeed be too broad. Yet it's equally problematic to assume that any cost-increasing addition to the professional staff is unproductive bloat. One way of getting around this problem is to compare what is happening at colleges and universities with what is happening in the rest of the economy. This is the context that is missing from most of the public discussion.

Statistics for employment by occupation for the entire economy help us to put staffing changes observed in higher education into perspective. Unfortunately, the Occupational Employment Statistics collected by the Bureau of Labor Statistics changed the universe of industries covered in their classification scheme between 1994 and 2005. But we can compare the data for 2000 and 2015. Those years should reflect the continuation of trends that started during the time period covered by our William and Mary data. In 2000, there were 2,642,910 workers employed in "computer science and related jobs." This represented 2.04% of total employment. By 2015, the number of employees in these same occupations was 3,853,870, which was 2.79% of total employment.[24] Given this kind of increase in the overall economy, no one should be particularly surprised that the professional IT staff at an information-intensive institution like William and Mary grew from 25 in 1994 to 61 in 2005. A second example compares university employment of clerical workers with trends in the broader economy. In 2000, the occupational categories for "executive secretaries and administrative assistants" (occupational code 43-6011) and "secretaries, except legal and medical" (occupational code 43-6014) had 3,068,040 employees, or 2.36% of the workforce. In 2015, these same two occupational codes had declined to 2,947,610 employees, or 2.14% of the workforce.[25] In 1994, the College of William and Mary had 402 employees in the IPEDS category of clerical and secretarial. In 2005, that number had decreased to 383. William and Mary's hiring patterns mirrored changes in the overall economy.

The administrative workforce in higher education has increased, but that fact alone is not evidence of bloat or waste. Some new staff positions are funded by outside revenue streams. Others generate significant revenue flows to support and subsidize other university programs. What looks like new staff may also be the result of a reclassification of workers, and this may well be associated with an increase in productivity on campus. Lastly, some of the increase in staff is associated with running an up-to-date educational enterprise that meets the needs of current students and provides state and federal regulators with the reports they demand.

Amenity Competition

Luxurious dorms, fancy food courts, and athletic facilities with rock climbing walls and "lazy rivers" frequently feature in stories about the transformation of colleges from lean educational institutions to fat country clubs. Is there an arms race competition needlessly turning campuses into spas, and are these amenities a significant cause of rising cost? In the same way that administrative bloat is a pejorative and easily politicized term that becomes much more nuanced under close examination, Country Club U also merits scrutiny. We should not simply trust university presidents who are tempted to justify every expense as simply meeting a new and necessary standard. Likewise, we should be skeptical of nostalgic notions of the Spartan virtues of a reimagined halcyon past.

By far the most important nonacademic cost that students face if they attend a residential program is room and board. What "should" the quality of these offerings be like in an academic setting? There is no doubt that the quality is substantially higher today than when the authors of this account were undergraduates. Critics of contemporary food and living options on campus often use the standards of their own experience as a benchmark for what is acceptable and right. We think that this is an unreasonable standard. When we placed changes in university employment in some national context, we softened the hardest edges of the charged idea of "bloat." Likewise, finding some context for room and board may help us to think carefully about excess amenities on campus.

In January of 1960, real disposable personal income per capita in the United States was $11,894, measured in 2009 dollars. As of June 2015, it stood at $37,891. That's a more than threefold increase. Things have changed in the United States since most of the critics attended college. Restaurant meals are a much more important part of the eating habits of Americans than they used to be. The size of American houses and apartments has expanded and the size of American families has shrunk, so students are used to more personal space. Students are coming to college with different expectations than before. Most schools have not kept their 1960s-style living arrangements and told students to "Get used to it; this is college." Yet despite touting their improving lifestyle amenities, most schools recognize that their living arrangements don't quite match home for a substantial portion of their applicants. When we ask our own students about having a roommate, most report that they never had to share a room with a brother or sister.

Even if some improvements seem warranted, at this point many critics will use the analogy of a positional arms race to suggest that the rising standards are excessive. If just a few colleges or universities upgrade their dining and housing options, all the others will be compelled to follow or they will lose out to any school that leapfrogs over them in the amenity department. To hang on to your spot in the rankings, every school overspends on amenities. As intuitively appealing as the arms race argument may be, we do not think that the quality upgrading we have seen is good evidence of an arms race. In a positional arms race, college A's competitors are colleges B, C, D, and so on. But there is another competitor whose behavior could be the driving engine. Even if all the colleges could sign an arms control treaty that limited amenity upgrading (frivolous or otherwise), the arrangement would fail in the face of rising standards for off-campus dining and housing options. The private sector alternatives are continually reflecting public preferences, and if private sector alternatives are improving, then few colleges could afford to drop out of that competition. College dining and housing have all three of the most important real estate attributes—location, location, and location. But there are limits to the "get used to it; this is college" command.

The economic model of residential colleges and universities is based on filling dining halls and dorms. How well does the cost of college room and board track private sector alternatives? Perhaps surprisingly, our own evidence (Archibald and Feldman, 2011) is that they track quite closely. Between 1965 and 2005, the real price of board charges did rise slightly more rapidly (by less than .4% annually) than the price of "purchased meals" in the CPI. But the index of "purchased meals" prices is periodically adjusted for quality improvements. The price index of college meal plan charges is not. Given the real improvement in food quality and food choices on campus, there is no case for claiming that board plan charges are out of control compared to their private sector alternatives. And you can ask students if they think the quality of campus food plans is excessive.

There is one argument about overdone amenities that squares with the incentives universities face. We have already seen that schools use price discrimination extensively, some for class sculpting and others for revenue maximization. For most schools, holding on to full-paying students is important. One way to do this is by gearing enough of the lifestyle amenities to the preferences and income of the full-paying audience. This likely adds somewhat to cost growth, but it is not an explosive arms race. And an amenity-control treaty cannot solve the problem. Gearing the average level of amenities to the preferences of full-paying families is only a problem because of the egalitarian impulses of the academy. In the nineteenth century, when most students lived and dined off campus, well-heeled students lived and ate in palatial settings compared to their poorer brethren. One of the motives of moving to a residential model was to forge more community by bringing students together under more equal conditions. Today's universities would not tolerate first-class to steerage-class pricing differences for living arrangements. This is a defensible choice, though it may lead to an average quality of amenities that is higher, and thus more expensive, than if they offered no-frills options at a lower price for their poorer students.

The argument also applies to the climbing walls, lazy rivers, and other health club–like features now found at many college campuses. In the past, recreational athletic facilities were rudimentary. Nonathlete students had to share facilities with the athletics department, and team practices and games kicked the "normal" students off the courts and fields. Increasingly, student recreational facilities and athletics department facilities are separated. Many schools have built modern facilities that have exercise equipment, weight rooms, swimming pools, climbing walls, and, yes, the occasional lazy river. The quality of the health and fitness options available to students has indeed improved. When one of us (Feldman) was a student in the mid-1970s, Kenyon College's athletic facility was a renovated World War II airplane hangar. The current facility, built in 2006, is a substantial and long-overdue improvement.

These athletic and recreational facilities are not part of meeting a standard of care. If they did not exist, we would not be guilty of educational malpractice. Like dining and housing, poor or nonexistent recreational facilities might lead students to migrate off campus. And in the market for full-paying students there is a pressure to meet their preferences. Colleges and universities often don't charge students a market price for the use of the institutional recreation facilities, so the business model of a contemporary college would not face a mortal threat if recreational facilities were downgraded throughout the industry. Paring back could save some money. It would, however, diminish the sense of community on campus and it would likely diminish the overall fitness level of the college community. These might well be significant factors. The recreational gymnasium on our campus has a thriving social scene, one that keeps students together on campus. And it probably contributes more to the fitness level of students than would a private recreational facility charging private facility fees. A single lazy river embedded in a new recreation facility is a visible symbol of waste and a substantial public relations black eye for all colleges.[26] Yet the real value of meeting the health and wellness needs of contemporary students is hard to quantify and often goes unreported.

We have offered two contending viewpoints about the drivers of college cost, and we have made a judgment between them. The dysfunction stories form the dominant narrative in public discussion, but we think that it's a story with weak foundations. Yet we agree that the status quo likely costs more than it could or perhaps should. You might notice that we mounted no defense of lazy rivers. Still, the cost consequences of true excesses probably are small. The major drivers of college costs are as follows: (1) higher education is a service, and productivity growth in services lags productivity growth in goods; (2) higher education relies on highly educated service providers, and the income gap in favor of highly educated workers has grown; and (3) higher education institutions adopt technology to meet a standard of care, even if meeting that standard pushes up cost.

Any serious attempt to control cost must address one or more of these three factors. The future of higher education depends in large part on how the diversity of institution types in various corners of the higher education market react to the stresses and the opportunities they face. Will we find ways to increase productivity within the current model, or will change come by embracing more education delivered over the Internet? Will we be able to ratchet down the acceptable standard of care and produce a no-frills college experience at a much lower cost? Or will we find the resources to continue to fund the current higher education system? These are questions we will address in detail in the coming chapters.

5

Internal Threat II

WILL STUDENTS KEEP COMING?

IF COLLEGES AND universities continue to use roughly the same business model and strive to meet a rising standard of educational care, the cost of providing a college education is likely to rise more rapidly than the inflation rate. Someone has to pay these costs of a technology-saturated high-touch experience. State governments have ratcheted down their commitment. This is an issue we will take up in detail in chapter 7. Unless governments at all levels boost spending per student or we see an unexpected burst of private philanthropy, more of the costs will be borne by students and their families. This is a significant internal threat to traditional colleges and universities, and it will be compounded if students lose faith in the power of a traditional college education to improve their economic circumstances. Those who forecast doom for the traditional college or university say that the double whammy of increasing costs and declining payoff spells very tough times ahead for colleges and universities. This threat is fundamentally related to bigger social and economic forces that have affected wage growth in the US economy and that have changed how income and wealth are distributed. Yin and yang are hard to separate, but we will take up these environmental threats in chapter 6. Likewise, we will also save the technological disruption claims for later. For the moment, let's examine the possibility that rising cost and declining payoff will inject turmoil into the traditional model of higher education.

Before we discuss the private and social payoff to higher education, we need to take a look at demographic trends. The pool of college-age students in the United States is an important factor in higher education demand. If the pool is stable or growing, even if college costs are rising and the payoff to college is falling, traditional colleges and universities are going to have an easier time. On the other hand, if the number of college-age students in the

United States is falling, the threat from rising costs and falling payoffs will be magnified.

Demographic Trends

The number of high school graduates remains one of the most important indicators of the *potential* demand for places at American colleges and universities. Nontraditional students (those over age twenty-five) do make up a large percentage of overall enrollment in higher education, but that percentage has been fairly stable since the 1990s.[1] The four-year nonprofit sector is the heart of the traditional college experience. At public universities 88% of full-time undergraduates fall in the usual seventeen- to twenty-four-year-old age range. For private nonprofit schools the figure is 86%. For this sector of the higher education industry, demographic forecasts remain important.[2] The Western Interstate Commission for Higher Education (WICHE) has published forecasts of the number of high school graduates for thirty years. The latest edition starts with the high school graduating class of 2009–10 and goes through the high school class of 2027–28.[3]

Figure 5.1 gives the national forecasts along with the actual data for 1996–97 to 2008–09. The darker and thicker line represents the forecasts for 2009–10 to 2027–28. High school graduate cohorts grew fairly steadily from 1996–97 to 2009–10, but thereafter they bounce around in a fairly narrow range. The end of steady growth in the usual raw material of the college-going population is not good news for colleges and universities. Yet the forecasts aren't dire either, especially given historical enrollment patterns and forecasts of future enrollment behavior. The number of high school graduates falls just a little under 190,000 students from its peak in 2010–11 to the trough in 2013–14. This represents a 5.6% decline. In those same years, enrollment did not fall. A greater fraction of high school graduates progressed to some form of higher education. Likewise, forecasts of future enrollment numbers at four-year schools continue to rise despite the relatively stable demographic picture.[4]

The potential downside of demographic developments is not shared evenly. The most selective colleges are in the best position to weather slowing population growth without feeling great pressures to change. The applicant pools of the schools in this group have been expanding and deepening over time.[5] Less selective schools will be under greater pressure to find ways to enlarge and diversify their applicant pools. This will likely involve some combination of program development to appeal to a wider domestic audience (and this takes resources), foreign recruiting, and cost cutting.

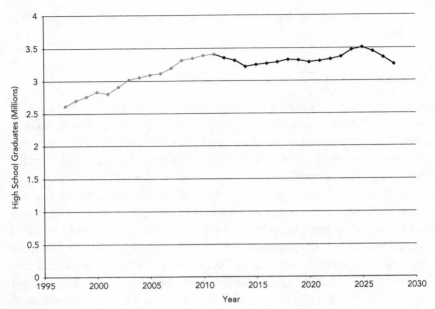

FIGURE 5.1 Actual and projected high school graduates, 1997–2028.

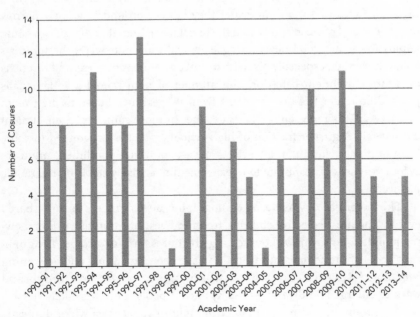

FIGURE 5.2 Four-year college closures, 1990–91 to 2013–14.

The schools under the greatest stress are likely to be small private colleges that depend on full classes to meet their payroll. These schools are well below efficient scale and some will need to enlarge to survive. Others may need to merge programs with similar institutions or become more specialized in professional pursuits that are in high demand. Still others will face insolvency, though the numbers that disappear likely will be far smaller than the catastrophists predict. The data on college closures do not show any effect of recent or past declines in the number of high school graduates. Figure 5.2 gives the number of four-year colleges that closed each year from 1990–91 to 2013–14. There is no trend, the overall numbers of closures are small, and closures are dwarfed by new nonprofit start-ups entering the field.

The other major decrease in the number of high school graduates in Figure 5.1 is at the very end of the forecast (2025 to 2028). This large (7.3%) decline reflects low birth rates during the most recent recession of 2008–09 and the slow recovery afterward. Births peaked in 2007 and then fell by 1.58% in 2008, by 2.76% in 2009, and by 3.1% in 2010. As the economy recovered, the fall in the number of births moderated. The number of births fell 0.02% in 2012 and 0.52% in 2013. This means that with more data from years of economic recovery, the drop in the number of high school graduates at the end of the data likely will ebb.

The regional variation in the forecast may be more important than the overall national trend. The WICHE study breaks the nation into four regions: the Northeast, the South, the Midwest, and the West.[6] Figure 5.3 shows the path of actual and forecasted high school graduates by region. Once again, the forecasted numbers are thicker and darker. The South is the only region with favorable demographic projections (an 8.5% rise in high school graduates). The West is in relatively good shape, with only a minor 1.3% decline. The Northeast may see a 10% falloff, while the Midwest is forecast to experience a 12.4% decline. The declines are not sudden in any region. The only reason the West shows any overall decrease is because of a relatively steep decline at the tail end of the forecast, and the later years have the greatest chance of forecast error. Regional forecasts have added uncertainty because regional migration is another source of forecast error.

Nonetheless, regional differences may be important because the application process that sorts students to schools is not fully national in scope. More students do attend schools in another state or region than in the past, but 57.1% of students still attend a school within a 100-mile radius of their home.[7] Schools whose recruiting is largely local or narrowly regional will have to work hard to broaden their appeal if they are located in an area of demographic decline. This will affect two types of institutions most strongly. The first are

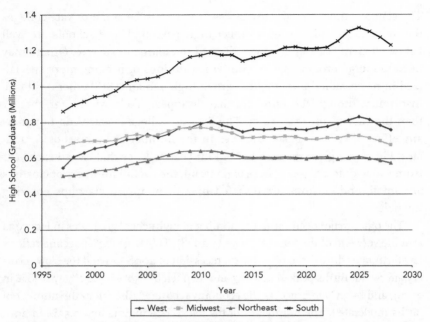

FIGURE 5.3 Actual and projected high school graduates by region, 1997–2028.

nonselective state institutions, especially schools whose students mostly commute to campus for classes. The second are the smaller private colleges that currently have little draw beyond their locality or state.

There are a limited number of options for dealing effectively with demographic decline. One is to eat your neighbor's lunch by attracting applicants away from other local or regional schools. This is a zero-sum game, but it can work for schools that have some existing advantages. Those advantages can lie in simple geography. Boston may be preferred to rural Pennsylvania, for instance. But the advantages could lie in carefully nurtured specialties like an excellent and well-designed liberal arts core, a robust study-abroad program, good engineering or other STEM (science, technology, engineering, and mathematics) offerings, or a successful preprofessional program in medical or information technology services. Surviving the demographic slowdown, however, need not be a zero-sum process. Regional schools can band together to utilize each other's programmatic strengths while economizing on the fixed costs that come with proliferating offerings. Two schools forty miles apart, for instance, might share an equipment-heavy physics or chemistry department. Reduced duplication means more resources for the programs that differentiate the institution, however slightly, from their competitors. Lastly, schools in regions of demographic decline can find ways to broaden their appeal to students in other regions, and internationally. This may take some up-front investment in recruiting and program development, both of which may make the institution's finances appear worse in the short run.[8] Nonprofit institutions tend to be inherently risk averse, but survival for some of the most at-risk schools may require a more entrepreneurial approach to investment and risk taking. Risk means the potential for failure, and some institutions may indeed fail.

The final portion of the WICHE forecasts shows how the racial and ethnic composition of high school graduates is likely to change over the next fifteen years. Table 5.1 gives the percentages of high school graduates by racial and ethnic category for the beginning year of the data (1996–97), the last year of the actual data (2008–09), and the final year of the forecasts (2027–28).

Non-Hispanic whites are expected to shrink as a percentage of high school graduates and Asian/Pacific Islanders and Hispanics are expected to replace them. The ethnic and racial make-up of student populations at colleges and universities will be very different by the end of the time period. Many of these students will be the first in their family to attend college, and many will come from households in which English is not the first language. As a statistical matter, a rising Hispanic share of the student population also will mean a rising share of lower-income students in the applicant pool. These are issues that schools have experienced for many years, and student support services have been built around the needs of first-generation, lower-income, and minority students. The problems may not be fully new, but the magnitude of the challenge will grow. Colleges and universities will have to adapt, and portions of the university budget that are currently in the cross-hairs as wasteful—like student services expenditures—may be crucial to weathering the coming changes.

Table 5.1 Racial and Ethnic Composition of High School Graduates, 1996–97, 2008–09, and 2027–28 (Projected)

Year	American Indian/ Alaska Native	Asian/ Pacific Islander	Black Non-Hispanic	Hispanic	White Non-Hispanic
1996–97	0.94%	4.45%	13.11%	9.91%	71.59%
2008–09	1.11%	5.47%	14.97%	15.95%	62.53%
2027–28	1.20%	8.60%	14.13%	24.28%	51.78%

The thirty-year arc of demographic change will move the US higher education system into a world of new demands from students and new constraints on university decisions. Selective institutions, even selective institutions in demographically declining regions, will be able to recruit nationally and internationally. These schools will have an easier time adjusting to national and regional demographic shifts. Less selective institutions, on the other hand, will have more difficulty maintaining their current size without becoming even less selective. They will face increasing pressures to recruit nationally and internationally and to cut costs in ways that preserve and expand distinctive and/or revenue-producing programs. Declines in state funding have pushed state-supported institutions to try to attract more out-of-state students. State-supported schools in declining regions are likely to ramp up this activity. This strategy may work for some flagship schools, but it's a difficult model for less selective schools, particularly during a time in which the overall number of high school graduates is stagnating. Recruiting out-of-state students, after all, is a zero-sum game nationally.

Finally, the changing racial and ethnic make-up of high school graduates creates challenges and opportunities. Colleges and universities that can find ways to appeal to Hispanic students, to integrate them successfully into their institution, and then to graduate them will have a much better chance of thriving in the future than colleges and universities whose behavior and programming remains rooted in today's ethnic and demographic reality. This book isn't a "how to" manual for colleges that want to survive, but we can mention some simple and fairly obvious strategies. Recruiting minority faculty has been an ethical imperative at most schools for at least the past generation. It's not an easy task given the small pool of potential minority faculty and the draw of nonacademic careers for them. But for schools facing a demographic squeeze, the desire to recruit minority, and especially Latino, faculty becomes a practical imperative as well.

The Payoff to a College Education

College attendance rates depend on more than the projections for the number of high school graduates. College going is also influenced by changes in family income, the social stigma (positive or negative) of being only a high school graduate, the ease and availability of credit for financing the cost of college attendance, and the economic payoff to going to college. Given the facts of rising tuition and some recent evidence of weaker starting salaries for some graduates, many commentators have suggested that a college education is not a sound economic proposition. In this view, too many young Americans are expensively overcredentialed. This view is almost always buttressed by references to studies showing how little learning takes place on campuses today.

Before we embark on our discussion of the economic and social payoff to earning a college degree, it's worth noting that college leaders seem relatively unconcerned that doubts about the value of higher education will threaten their cherished status at the pinnacle of the educational pyramid. In November and December of 2014, the *Chronicle of Higher Education* asked college leaders to rate "the most important outcomes for college graduates."[9] First on the list was "having an appreciation for the value of lifelong learning." This was rated a most important outcome by 66% of public four-year institution leaders and 63% of private four-year institution leaders. Much further down the list was "having a job requiring a college degree," which was rated a most important outcome by only 18% of public four-year institution leaders and 15% of the private four-year institution leaders. This apparent lack of focus on training students for specific jobs annoys many parents. A May 2011 study by the Pew Research Center finds that the public has a very different sense of the purpose of going to college.[10] For 47% of those surveyed, the main purpose of a college education is to teach work-related skills. Only 39% thought that the main purpose of college was to help a student grow personally and intellectually.

The attitude gap between parents and administrators may be more apparent than real. We have already noted that a student who becomes a lifelong learner may pick up some very valuable work-related skills. Lifelong learning requires a broad knowledge base and an ability to analyze and deconstruct arguments from various viewpoints, including via careful use of the scientific method. It also helps to be a good communicator, orally and through effective writing. All of these traits of the lifelong learner should add real value to a person's work-related skill set. Specific skills, which can indeed be learned in a college setting, point people toward particular initial jobs. The more general skills of the lifelong learner are what help people move smoothly between career paths. This too is a job skill.

The economic question isn't whether a college degree prepares students to do a particular job, but whether the process of earning a traditional degree enables students to be productive people in whatever career path or paths they eventually follow. To get a handle on this rather large question we must tackle a series of smaller and more specific questions. First, we need to ask if there is a positive economic payoff to college on average. There is a vast amount of evidence on this point and the simple answer is an overwhelming yes. Second, this is only the beginning of the story because there is a variance or spread of the economic returns to college. We need to examine that spread of the return to see if it's rising. Perhaps there is a growing fraction of the undergraduate population for whom the investment in a college education is a financial loser. Third, we need to recognize that by its very nature, measuring the returns to education is a retrospective test. It can only tell us about the benefits for people who earned their degrees in the past. The future may follow a different course. In particular, the payoff may change if more (or fewer) people go to college. This question has no definitive answer, but we can sketch out potential scenarios.

The thorniest question is last. If intelligent, talented, and driven people succeed in college, and intelligent, talented, and driven people succeed in the labor force, perhaps college training isn't really "causing" higher incomes. This is the problem of selection bias. How do you evaluate the independent contribution of education on people's earnings? Are those lifelong learning skills really making people better employees? In principle, this is an easy matter to settle. Run a controlled experiment that randomly assigns high school graduates to the workforce or to college. Then, after controlling for differences in ability, we could see if the college group outperformed the noncollege group using some clear measure of performance, like earnings. If we find no significant difference, college education would be unmasked as an economic fraud. We would have shown that colleges are doing nothing more than picking out high-ability people to accept, and those are precisely the people who would have made good employees anyway. Of course, an experiment like that is completely unethical. But we have other ways to make the data talk.

Average Economic Payoff

It's easy to identify with the parents of a recent graduate who has no job and who is back at home living in the same room with the same stuffed toys on the shelf and the same punk or metal band posters adorning the walls. This kind of anecdote can be very powerful. It leads easily to pronouncements that "college is no longer a guarantee of economic success." The evidence about that guarantee is quite clear. College never has been, and never will be, a guarantee of economic success. On average, however, college is a very good economic investment.

In 2014, Jaison Abel and Richard Deitz of the New York Federal Reserve Bank presented a very thorough analysis of the costs and benefits of graduating from college. They collected data from the Census Bureau, the Department of Education, and the College Board to estimate the rate of return to earning a four-year college degree. Their data spanned the forty-three years between 1970 and 2013. At first glance their data suggest that the payoff to college is declining. The wages earned by college graduates have been flat or falling in real terms over the last decade, and at the same time college students have faced rising tuition. These facts are often peeled off from context to suggest that the rate of return to college is declining, or worse, that college no longer pays.

But to determine the rate of return to college, or to anything else, the costs and benefits have to be compared to an alternative. Abel and Deitz compare the average college graduate who finished a BA to the average high school graduate whose schooling stopped with just a high school degree. A person who invests in an education builds a stock of human capital. The costs of this human capital investment are the tuition payments plus the foregone income the person could have earned by working instead of continuing in school. The benefits are the wage gains from working with a college degree compared to the wages (plus four years of extra experience) of the jobs available to high school degree holders. As with most investments, the costs appear first and the benefits follow. Abel and Dietz compute the rate of return on this investment just the way a firm would compute the rate of return on an investment in physical capital such as a machine or a building.

The results are unambiguous. They conclude, "After climbing impressively between 1980 and 2000 the return to a college degree has held steady for more than a decade at around 15 percent, easily surpassing the threshold for a sound investment."[11] This result is perhaps surprising given that the starting wages of many college graduates have declined in real terms since 2000, while tuition has increased. Two things are important. First, the wages of the typical person who stopped with a high school degree have declined even more than the wages of college graduates. This decreases the opportunity cost of spending time in college. Second, because of increases in financial aid, the real net tuition faced by students has not gone up nearly as fast as list-price tuition. This is what we examined in chapter 4.

This 15% rate of return to earning a degree likely understates the true return to college because it is based on earnings of people who stopped their education after a four-year degree. One of the benefits of a four-year degree is that it makes further education possible. None of the individuals in Abel and Dietz's data went on to become lawyers, doctors, dentists, or college professors or to earn MBAs. Graduate education comes with both costs and benefits, so the impact on the rate of return is not a simple calculation. Studies of the return to graduate and professional degrees suggest further significant increases in income, which is why the return on investment calculated by Abel and Dietz is an underestimate.[12]

Marginal Returns

There are several reasonable ways to critique these average calculations. The marginal return may be quite a bit lower than the average. Very talented and very well-prepared students have always gone to college, and they have also done very well in the after-college job market. These individuals bring up the average, so the average is not necessarily a reliable predictor for the student just on the margin of going to college or not going to college. A significant body of empirical research finds that this is not a concern. The returns to students on the margin are at least as high as the returns to students at the average of the group.[13] This is more than a bit curious. As economists we're used to thinking about diminishing returns. If we assume that colleges and students match up on the basis of student talent, we would expect the last student accepted (the marginal student) to be less talented than the average student. And so we would expect the marginal student to do less well in college and in the labor market after college. Why does this sensible argument not do a very good job of predicting outcomes for students over long stretches of time?

The answer lies in the haphazard mechanism that matches students to universities. A lot of good students who could succeed in college fall through the cracks. For starters, seventeen-year-olds are heavily involved in the process. As anyone with a passing familiarity with the age group knows, not all of them behave sensibly about long-term decisions. But family financial constraints and university selection mechanisms also play an important role. Some very talented students do not move into higher education at all. Some do a poor job of choosing between two-year and four-year programs. Applying to college is complex, and financial aid processes often trip up good students who have no family experience to guide them. Although the sorting hat remains far from efficient, Archibald, Feldman, and McHenry show how it has gotten better over the last forty years.[14] This is the reason we do not observe diminishing returns as the pool of students in college has gotten larger.

Figure 5.4 illustrates how the sorting process has improved over time using one of the most important predictors of college success. We break the national high school grade point average (GPA) distribution into ten equal groups, or deciles. The first decile is the bottom 10% of the high school GPA distribution, and we move progressively up to the tenth decile, which is the highest-performing 10% of graduates. The height of the bars gives the fraction of students from that decile who attended a four-year college, using two big longitudinal data sets separated by over thirty years.[15]

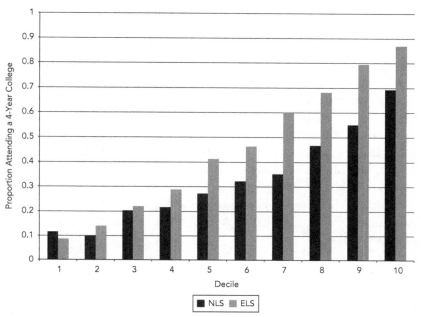

FIGURE 5.4 College attendance by high school grade point average decile, NLS-72 and ELS:2002.

GPA is one of the best predictors of college success, so it's a good indicator of the quality of matching. And since we are using deciles of the distribution instead of numerical GPAs, this measure isn't affected by grade inflation. In addition to capturing information about a student's cognitive ability, GPA rank also tells us about important noncognitive traits, like stick-to-itiveness, that correlate quite closely with success in college. Not surprisingly, the percentage of students who go to college steadily increases as we move up the deciles into the higher part of the national GPA distribution. This was true for the high school class of 1972 (the dark gray bars), and it's also true of more recent high school graduates (light gray bars). But it's also something of a shock to see how many highly ranked students don't go to a four-year program and how many low-ranked students do.

The college-going rate has soared over time. In the 1972 sample, from the National Longitudinal Study of the High School Class of 1972 (NLS-72), one third of the pool of high school seniors attended a four-year program within the first three semesters of their graduation. For the high school seniors of 2004, from the Educational Longitudinal Study of 2002 (ELS:2002), the figure had risen to 47%. How is it possible to avoid diminishing student quality of college attenders if you're sucking an increasing fraction of the high school graduating class into four-year schools? The answer is that you do a much better job of getting students from the top half of the GPA distribution to go, and this is exactly what the United States has managed to do.[16] The group of students in college today has roughly the same GPA percentile profile as their predecessors a generation ago, and the story is the same if we replace the GPA distribution with the distribution of test scores. Additional attenders today are no worse than the average attender a generation ago. Despite a drumbeat of commentary about the failings of the American K-12 system, Altonji, Bharadwaj, and Lange offer good evidence that the characteristics of youths that correlate with positive adult outcomes are improving instead of worsening.[17] This is another reason diminishing returns haven't led to worse outcomes for college graduates. We are nowhere near having an overeducated population.

The college-matching machine remains far from perfect. Things like family income or parental education continue to steer students into, or away from, the higher education pathway independent of the student's own characteristics. There is still a lot of room to raise attendance rates before we must of necessity begin to experience diminishing returns. For instance, if we achieved a 90% four-year attendance rate among the top four GPA deciles, we could raise the attendance rate at four-year colleges from 47% to over 52% while improving the average quality of students in college.

There is yet another reason not to presume that the return on investment of a college education must fall as more students choose to attend. A somewhat less talented or motivated student is indeed less likely to graduate and more likely to have a lower-earning career path than a more talented or driven colleague. The marginal student of lower "quality" may indeed not get as large an economic bounce out of trying college. But his or her chances in the market without a degree are probably lower as well. As a result, the gain to that student from improving his or her skills in college relative to what that student could earn with only a high school degree—that is, the delta over not going—may be large enough that the ROI is the same *or better* for him or her than it is for his or her more talented roommate. Jennie Brand and Yue Xie offer very good evidence that this is indeed true.[18]

Distribution of Returns

If no one with a college degree ever failed in the labor market, we would not need to think very deeply about the economic payoff of going to college. We know that the averages of the two earnings distributions are far apart, which is why earning a degree makes excellent economic sense if you think you are anywhere near typical. But some people with a college degree do earn less than some people who only have a high school education. In other words, the earnings distributions of high school–educated and college-educated people overlap. There are indeed well-educated Uber drivers and sociology majors waiting tables. On the other end of the distribution, there are also college dropouts and college avoiders inventing apps for Apple and creating vast software empires. These are juicy anecdotes indeed. Much of the rhetoric about the "end of college" is based on the idea that the pool of underemployed college graduates languishing in economic mediocrity is large and growing.

If the variance of wages for the college educated is rising over time, that would make the distribution of earnings spread out. We would see the fraction of the college graduate population that fares poorly in the labor market rising over time. This is something we can test by asking a simple question: what's the likelihood that a person with a college degree winds up earning more than the median income of the group that holds only a high school degree? The answer comes from the census's American Community Survey, which gathers data from 2.9 million households per year. Figure 5.5 shows the fraction of college graduates in the twenty-five- to thirty-five-year-old age range who earn more than the median high school graduate.[19] The diagram is quite boring since it shows no trend whatsoever.[20] There are two takeaways from Figure 5.5. First, the average economic return to a college degree is high and has been fairly constant. Second, there has been no increase in the dispersion of college returns that would suggest that a greater fraction of college graduates are economically unsuccessful.

The fraction of the college educated who earn less than the high school median is roughly 22%. This number needs to be interpreted with caution. It's not a measure of the fraction of college degree holders who are economic failures. The data capture the earnings of working adults between the ages of twenty-five and thirty-five. This includes recent college graduates who are still in the process of finding their way, or who are off building connections in low-paid internships, and it includes settled thirty-four-year-old high school graduates who have experience and seniority in a good job. It excludes the unemployed, who are more likely to have stopped with a high school degree. Yet earning a college degree is not a guarantee of economic success, and it never has been. For some people who were graduated with a meaningful degree, if at age seventeen they could have accurately glimpsed their economic future they might not have chosen to spend their time and money on further education.

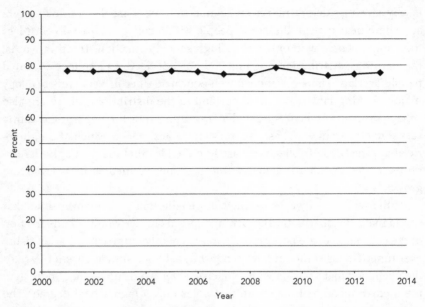

FIGURE 5.5 Percentage of college graduates who make more than the median high school graduate, 2001–13.

Although the likelihood of economic failure for a college graduate is low, it's not inconsequential. There are a number of reasons for the existing earnings dispersion among college graduates. A 2015 study by the Georgetown University Center on Education and the Workforce uses US census data to show the considerable dispersion both across graduates with different college majors and among college graduates with the same college major. For example, the median annual wages of college-educated workers aged twenty-five to fifty-nine who majored in petroleum engineering was $136,000. The similar median for workers who majored in early childhood education was $39,000. Petroleum engineering is the college major with the highest median wages and early childhood education is the college major with the lowest median wages. Table 5.2 gives the twenty-fifth, fiftieth and seventy-fifth percentiles of wage earnings for all bachelor's degree holders and for bachelor's degree holders in the most popular major in fourteen different major categories.[21]

This study received a lot of publicity because the difference in the means was so stark. Should students and families make decisions about which majors to pursue based on rankings of mean salaries? This might make some sense if a student is equally capable of performing well in all or most majors, but people have heterogeneous abilities and widely divergent preferences.

Table 5.2 Wages by Major for Largest Major in Each Major Category

Major Category	25th Percentile of Wages	50th Percentile of Wages	75th Percentile of Wages
Agriculture and natural resources	$37,000	$53,000	$81,000
Architecture and engineering	$66,000	$93,000	$123,000
Arts	$33,000	$49,000	$74,000
Biology and life sciences	$39,000	$56,000	$84,000
Business	$43,000	$62,000	$92,000
Communications and journalism	$38,000	$54,000	$84,000
Computers, statistics, and math	$56,000	$83,000	$114,000
Education	$35,000	$46,000	$60,000
Health	$52,000	$66,000	$85,000
Humanities and liberal arts	$37,000	$53,000	$81,000
Industrial arts, consumer services, and recreation	$35,000	$49,000	$67,000
Law and public policy	$39,000	$54,000	$79,000
Physical sciences	$41,000	$61,000	$89,000
Psychology and social work	$35,000	$49,000	$73,000
Social science	$48,000	$76,000	$114,000

The data on the dispersion *within* any given major reveal a lot of information, and this information often is ignored. For example, English is the most popular major in the humanities and liberal arts. An English major at the seventy-fifth percentile of the English major wage distribution will do better than all but one of the other fields at the fiftieth percentile of their various distributions. In addition, Anthony Carnevale and Stephen Rose show that within occupations, even in low-paying ones that don't "require" a degree, bachelor's degree holders significantly outearn those with only a high school degree.[22] If businesses are rational, they must be paying those higher wages for a reason.

The other important lesson, however, is that there are a large number of college graduates whose wages after college are not high. The wages at the twenty-fifth percentile for several of the majors are quite low. We cannot tell what an individual arts major at the twenty-fifth percentile would have been able to earn with just a high school degree, but the wage bump is small enough that his or her investment in a college education had a low, or possibly even negative, rate of return. As we mentioned previously, some people seem alarmed when they realize that college is not a guarantee of economic success. We'll shout it from the rooftops. No one should go into college thinking that economic success is guaranteed! And no one should think that any and all borrowing is justified by the payoff. Table 5.2 does offer a cautionary tale about student loans. If your talents or preferences steer you toward a low-income major, do not overuse debt to finance your education. This may mean selecting a school whose net price is lower for your income level or searching for a program that offers more grant aid relative to loans.

Does College Education Cause Economic Success?

The average college graduate may be a clear winner in the labor market, but two questions remain. First, if colleges simply attract talented people who would have succeeded in the labor market anyway, is the significant economic return we are attributing to college a mirage? The return we see may have little to do with college education. Students with greater ability also are more likely to succeed in college. The demands of schoolwork are easier for them, so going to college is less "costly" than for high school students whose academic potential is weaker. The group in college is not a random sample of the population. As a result, there may not be any causal link between education and prosperity. The high average return to education may just reflect sample selection bias.

The second question is about what earning a college degree actually means. Perhaps the only value of earning a degree is the signal it sends to employers that the graduate is likely to be a good employee. What goes on during those four to six years does not matter. Completing a degree reveals that the student can learn, can show up on time, and can follow rules set by professors, departments, and registrars. College may be just an elaborate device to help employers screen prospective workers for desirable traits.

Uncovering causality is one thing science is potentially good at revealing. But in the social sciences many of the big questions can't be studied experimentally. As we mentioned earlier, every university's "human subjects committee" would take a rather dim view of a proposed randomized trial to study whether the "treatment group" of college attenders enjoys better lifetime economic outcomes than a "control group" made up of people randomly kept out of college. But social scientists have dealt with the problem of selection bias very creatively.

The research strategy is to find a "natural experiment" where part of a population is randomly treated by some natural event or policy change. This can very closely approximate a controlled experiment. One approach is to use data on identical (monozygotic) twins. The variance of ability in identical twins is very low, so differences in economic outcomes for identical twins are most likely "caused" by measurable differences in education. In an early twins study, Orley Ashenfelter and Alan Krueger found that an additional year of schooling increased wages by 12% to 16%.[23] The average number of years of schooling in their sample of twins was over fourteen (which is between two and three years of college), so they are catching the effects of higher education in their estimate. Other studies using twins, as well as studies using siblings, have found broadly similar results.

Another natural experiment comes from the military draft lottery system instituted during the Vietnam War. Starting in December of 1969, conscription into the army was determined by a random lottery based on date of birth. As a result, Vietnam veteran status is highly correlated with draft eligibility. This means that a particular group of young men qualified for GI Bill benefits while others didn't, and the selection was random with regard to abilities that could affect their earnings later in life.[24] Veterans who were randomly drafted eventually achieved more years of schooling, and each additional year increased their earnings by about 9%.

There are other strategies researchers have used to estimate the returns to schooling that avoid contamination by these selection effects, and there are more recent studies that don't rely on the value of a college degree earned in the 1970s. People who grow up near a college, for instance, are more likely to go to college than are people with similar characteristics (abilities) who live farther away. Using this selection method, David Card found that the earnings gain for an additional year of schooling ranged between 10% and 14%.[25] A more recent study of college graduates in the 2000s looked at Florida high school graduates whose high school grades left them right at the borderline of the state university system's grade cutoff for admission to a state university.[26] Students who barely exceed the standard are essentially identical to those who barely missed it, so the assignment of students to college is random. The average threshold-crossing student who was induced to enter a college program stayed 3.8 years. And within 8 to 14 years after finishing high school they earned 22% more than students who were just below the cutoff for admission.

In any empirical literature about something as big and complex as how schooling translates into earnings, you will find schools of thought that fight over the details of whose approach is best. Some researchers build complex models of the labor market, and others use simpler statistical models. Some authors have found lower rates of return, and others have found higher rates of return. The estimates may vary, and Oreopoulos and Petronijevic offer a good review, but the case is clear.[27] This is a settled question. Going to college causes economic success.

These gains can flow from two very different sources. The knowledge and skills students acquire in college can raise their productivity in the labor market. On the other hand, getting a diploma can be a screening device. Completing a degree sends a signal that these graduates have unobservable traits that make them desirable employees. If signaling is important, we would expect someone with a degree to have higher earnings than someone with the same number of years of schooling but who for some reason didn't earn a diploma. This earnings bump is what is called a "sheepskin effect."[28] If you spend any time reading popular accounts of higher education's failings, you will hear that what goes on in class is increasingly useless and that the only value of college is from its screening role. The sheepskin effect is taken as sufficient proof.

There is now a long research record that has established the existence of this degree bump. But the presence of a sheepskin effect does not confirm that college is just a simple screening device to help firms infer things about a person's hidden traits. Seeing a sheepskin effect is necessary for screening to play a role, but not sufficient. That's because the sheepskin bump may also be caused by real productivity differences between workers, not just unseen traits that are innate. As Hungerford and Solon note, graduates may be "disproportionately comprised of efficient learners who complete their diploma programs because their productivity is enhanced by education."[29] Moreover, some people earn a degree after three years. Most take four. But some complete their degrees in five or even six years. Part of the sheepskin effect comes from people who have been working while in school. Much of their degree bump may come from job experience, not from any college screening value. As a result, the sheepskin effect may not be telling quite the story that many commentators want it to tell.

Acquiring a college degree does have a larger payoff than acquiring 120 disjointed college credits. Likewise, the sheepskin effect does tell us that screening/signaling may play a role in the value of a degree. But the fact that there is an earnings bump from getting a degree is not evidence that time spent in a traditional college curriculum is otherwise worthless. Whatever the failings of contemporary classroom instruction, higher productivity seems to emerge at the end of the process. There is a role for knowledge gains and skills acquisition, as well as signaling. The wide dispersion of wages by undergraduate major suggests that specific pathways through the undergraduate experience confer different skills and knowledge, and that those learned things affect productivity. The wage data in the Georgetown study come from college graduates, so they all had the sheepskin effect. Employers understand that most college graduates come with certain general background skills. And as dense as a transcript may be, it's not hard to glean basic information about more quantitative versus more writing-intensive pathways through a college curriculum. But a petroleum engineering major, an accounting major, and a nursing major have also picked up very different job-related skills during their college careers, and those skills have a large effect on their average productivity in the labor market.

If earning a college degree is simply a signal, it's an incredibly inefficient and wasteful one. If all college does is provide employers with an indication that graduates will be good employees, then there are $100 bills lying on the floor and no one has seen fit to pick any of them up. Some for-profit corporation could replace a bachelor's degree with a rigorous application process that mimics colleges' own and offer a one-year internship that would uncover the valuable hidden traits that employers covet. Alternatively, large employers could internalize this whole process by doing the task in house. Offer college-bound students immediate internships with a promise of good wages afterward. Students would save four years of time and thousands of dollars. Firms could find talented employees willing to work for slightly less than the going wage for a college graduate. This type of arrangement always seems just around the corner. The fact that it stays in the future implies that the current education system, for all its faults, offers students and society more than an expensive screening device.

Finally, recognizing the importance to parents and students alike of the labor market payoff, that payoff is not the only private and social benefit that flows from traditional higher education. There is increasingly rich evidence that education bestows benefits beyond the monetary "investment" gains that dominate public discussion. When comparing college graduates and high school graduates with the same income level, college graduates self-report greater happiness than do people with less education. This could flow from the different kinds of jobs they tend to do. College graduates report greater job satisfaction and they work more often in fields with greater prestige. They are also unemployed less frequently, which reduces financial stress. College graduates also are healthier and substantially less likely to have ever experienced a divorce. This is true after adjusting for the difference in incomes between the groups. College graduates tend to be less today oriented. They don't discount the future as heavily as people who stopped with a high school degree. As a result, they are much more likely to hold off on child bearing until they are more financially secure. College graduates even tend to smoke less (tobacco) than high school graduates.[30]

6

Environmental Threat I

THE NOTION THAT soaring cost is undermining the whole college enterprise is mostly overblown rhetoric. Hyperventilated talk about students priced out of the American dream of college attendance is based in large part on list prices that do not reflect what the vast majority of students actually pay. Claims of rising institutional inefficiency don't seem well founded in evidence either. The major drivers of college cost are larger economic processes that are mostly beyond the control of institutions. Schools must respond, of course, and their choices largely reflect their different capacities to maintain the quality of what they offer. Improvements in amenities, which supply great anecdotal fodder of waste and misplaced priorities, are at worst a second-order cost problem. And these investments in facilities often have a willing audience to pay for them. In the near-term future there will still be lots of college-age students, though the growth of the college-age population will not be as robust as in the past. The economic returns to college are impressive and have been fairly stable. This is true for the average student, and for students in most majors. To this point there is little in our narrative to suggest serious turbulence shaking the American higher education system. This is about to change.

This chapter is the first of two focused on threats from the broader environment. The first threat comes from changes in the income distribution. Income in the United States has become much more concentrated at the top. The problem is actually global in scope, since the forces for rising wage and wealth inequality are mostly technological and not specific to the US economy. The United States does not have the same redistributive policy mechanisms as in many other developed nations, so the impact of rising inequality plays out differently in a US context. Rising inequality is not a new phenomenon. The United States was at its most "middle class" in the decades immediately following World War II. But the gap in earnings between the top and the bottom began to grow in the late 1970s, and that process has continued to this day. The cumulative effects of rising inequality have played a significant role in college pricing decisions over the last forty years. It has affected how students choose among education options, and it has affected the way many families finance educational investments.

The economic pie has grown quite a bit since the 1960s. As we noted earlier, real disposable income per capita in the United States was 3.2 times higher in 2015 than in 1960.[1] If today's income distribution looked more like the middle-class society of 1960, we would be having a very different conversation about access to higher education. College cost, as high as it is, would not be categorized so readily as a crushing burden based on stories of eye-popping list prices at elite colleges that serve a small fraction of the college-going population. As the economic pie has expanded, however, most of the benefits are flowing to families at the very top of the income distribution. Figure 6.1 shows the evolution of family income in the United States since 1947. The figure gives the upper limit of income for each fifth of the income distribution. For example, the bottom line is the upper limit of what a family in the bottom fifth

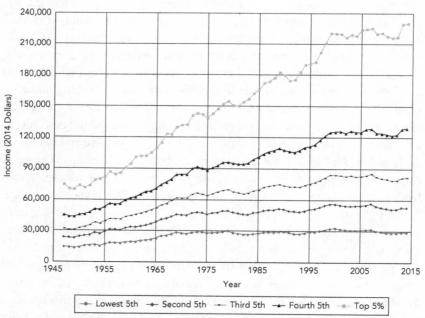

FIGURE 6.1 Real family income by fifths of the income distribution and the top 5%, 1947–2015.

(lowest twentieth percentile) of the income distribution earns. Twenty percent of families earn less than this amount. We have also included the lower limit of the top 5% of family incomes. Only 5% of families earn more than this amount. These measures of family income are in 2014 dollars so they are corrected for inflation.[2]

Three patterns are clear. First, until roughly 1980, real incomes at all levels were growing; everyone was getting better off. After 1980, growth stopped for the bottom two fifths of the income distribution. Second, over this long stretch of time the income distribution has widened considerably. Incomes were more bunched together in 1960 than they were in 2015. In 1960, a family at the ninety-fifth percentile earned 4.9 times what a family at the twentieth percentile earned. By 2015, that gap had widened to 7.9. This is not just the rich getting richer faster while everyone else gets richer more slowly. The bottom fifth and the second fifth have experienced very little real income growth over a full fifty-year time span. There is some real income growth at the sixtieth percentile, and considerable growth at the eightieth percentile. Between 1960 and 2015, a family at the sixtieth percentile saw real income growth of over 91%, while a family at the eightieth percentile enjoyed a 114% rise. But the largest gains accrued to people farther up the distribution. In 2014 dollars, a family at the ninety-fifth percentile of the income distribution *gained* $141,657 of real income over this time period. That *gain* is 4.7 times as much as a family at the twentieth percentile actually earns in 2015.

The third important fact is that family income stopped rising at the turn of the twenty-first century for all but the wealthiest families. Between 2001 and 2014, the average family at the sixtieth percentile lost almost 2% of its income ($1,542 in 2014 dollars), while the family at the twentieth percentile lost roughly 9.5% of its meager income ($2,992). The only families still experiencing real income gains are those in the top 5%, and the biggest gains are found in families in the top 1% and above. This sixty-seven-year evolution of family income in the United States has affected how colleges set tuition and how families finance paying for it.

Tuition Discounting

We turn first to tuition setting, and in particular to the discounting process we introduced in chapters 2 and 4.[3] Tuition discounting is part of what is called the "high-high" strategy. Colleges and universities following this strategy set high tuition and offer high financial aid packages. The alternative to the high-high strategy is the "low-low" strategy, where colleges set low tuition and offer low levels of financial aid. Both strategies can ensure that college will be affordable for the kind of students the school seeks to recruit. In the 1950s and 1960s, most state-supported colleges and universities followed the low-low strategy, and private colleges and universities mostly followed the high-high strategy.

State-supported institutions recognized that the low-low strategy, made possible by generous state appropriations, was wasteful in the sense that it provided the benefit of low in-state price to lots of high-income families willing and able to pay much higher tuition. Milton Friedman's pithy take on this was, "why should families in Watts pay taxes to subsidize families in Beverly Hills who send their children to UCLA? "[4] The low-low choice can be justified in two ways. As a political matter, generous state appropriations garner more support when the benefits of low tuition are spread widely and not concentrated on the poor as in a welfare program. Pursuing a low-low strategy also has an effect on incentives. Low in-state tuition is a simple program for people to understand. Its simplicity means that fewer families will conclude, erroneously, that college is simply out of reach based on list prices that often do not apply to them. The low-low strategy lost effectiveness in many states during the tax revolt of the 1970s, and it has continued to erode as pressures on state budgets have shifted spending toward health care, K-12, prisons, and other priorities that can't pay for themselves through user charges like tuition.[5] State-supported institutions are now well down the path of shifting to a higher tuition model, and the more selective and better endowed among them are also following through with increased levels of institutional aid. As a result, tuition discount rates are rising at public institutions, though they remain much lower than discount rates at private institutions.

To understand the impact on tuition of changes in the income distribution, we have to look within the tuition-setting processes of a college or university. Figure 6.2 lays out the framework we'll use to understand discounting. In the short run we will take the size of the institution as fixed. Its buildings, faculty, and staff determine that size. The institution knows how many students it would like to enroll (E^*) and how much revenue it needs to maintain its desired quality. Some of that revenue may come from government appropriations or from private giving and the returns on the school's endowment. The school also knows how much of that revenue it needs to extract in the form of average tuition from each student (AT^*). The area of the box ($AT^* \times E^*$) gives the tuition revenue dollars the school needs to collect to make ends meet in the short run.

The college wants to enroll the highest-quality group of students compatible with collecting the required amount of tuition revenue. We will assume

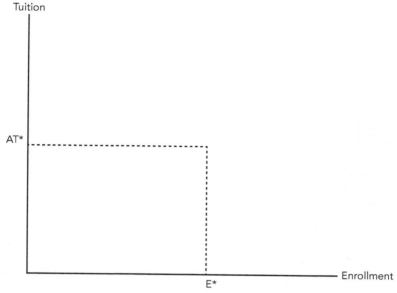

FIGURE 6.2 The tuition requirement of the institution.

that the institution is "selective," so it has a group of applicants greater than E*. All selective programs must have a mechanism to rank students. For example, they might employ a ten-point scale. Students rated ten are the highest-quality students from the institution's perspective. These students will have the best test scores and high school grades, and they may offer something special. They may be accomplished athletes or musicians, or they may offer a compelling personal story. They may also provide geographic, economic, or ethnic diversity. The school would love to fill the incoming class with tens, but it may not be able to come even remotely close to hitting its revenue needs or its enrollment goals from that group alone.

The first step in the process is to see how much revenue the school can obtain from students with an admission rating of ten. To do this, the institution has to estimate how much these students and their families are willing to pay. Most schools have a lot of information they can use to assess this. Students may have had siblings or other relatives who earned a degree there. Some applicants may have applied through an early decision program or actively pursued the institution in some way. They may have filled out financial aid forms, which reveal a lot of information about their parents' income and assets. On the other hand, schools also know that their tens are very attractive to other schools. Competing schools may offer large scholarships, and this will affect what these families are willing to pay.

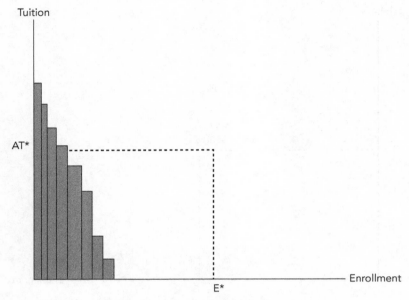

FIGURE 6.3 The willingness to pay of top-rated students.

Figure 6.3 gives an example of how much revenue our hypothetical school might be able to get from the tens it reasonably expects to say yes to an offer of admission. The height of the bars represents the family's willingness to pay. The diagram is constructed by placing students from left to right in declining order of willingness to pay. We'll assume for the moment that this school can design its aid packages to capture the full willingness to pay from this group of students. Even so, in this example the institution cannot meet either its revenue requirement or its enrollment goal from the students with the highest admission rating. The area on the willingness-to-pay bars above AT* is not as large as the part of the required revenue box not covered by a willingness-to-pay bar, and the group of tens who would accept a place at this school is smaller than E*.

To meet its revenue and enrollment goals the school has to consider students with lower admission ratings. Repeating this exercise for students with successively lower admission ratings eventually leads to the group of students with the highest-possible average admission rating that satisfies the school's tuition revenue and enrollment requirements. Figure 6.4 illustrates this outcome. In the figure, the area covered by the willingness-to-pay bars above AT* is exactly equal to the area below AT* not covered by a bar. If each student is charged his or her willingness to pay, the average tuition will be AT*, and the school will successfully sell all of its seats. Institutions accomplish this by setting the list-price tuition (LT) based on the preferences of the families with the highest willingness to pay and giving the remaining students tuition discounts. The discounts are usually given nice scholarship names. That is a costless form of advertising for schools since families prefer saying that Jane or Johnny got a scholarship rather than a discount.

Most schools are "need aware" in their admission decisions. To take in AT* in net tuition on average, a selective college may need to enroll some eights who are willing to pay full price instead of some nines who are not. Some schools in the hyperelite can be "need blind" in their admissions process. A need-blind approach recruits the best-possible class regardless of the families' capacity to pay. With a few tweaks, we can still use Figure 6.4 to think about need-blind admissions. For a school in the hyperelite like Stanford, many families whose young people are indeed tens in Stanford's talent distribution would be willing to pay a multiple of the current list price. The willingness-to-pay bars at the very left of the figure are much higher than the list price set by the school. By not extracting the full measure of willingness to pay, these schools leave revenue on the table uncollected. This means there is some play in where to set the list price to generate AT* in revenue per student while also taking in the best-possible incoming class. In this way, a school like

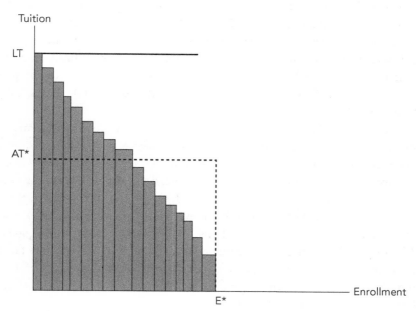

FIGURE 6.4 Pricing and enrollments goals met

Princeton only goes down the list to applicants ranked lower than ten because of competition for those tens from Yale, not because a seven's or eight's family is willing to pay more for the spot in the class.

This framework is clearly a simplification. The real tuition-setting process is more haphazard and uncertain. Schools do not truly know each student's willingness to pay. Nor do they know exactly how many students in each ranked group will accept offers from the school. Schools make guesses about willingness to pay using rules of thumb or with some type of forecasting model, and they make offers of admission based on long experience with the "yield" on those offers. Their forecasts can deviate from reality rather unexpectedly from year to year, with unfortunate results for enrollment or revenue. Nonetheless, our simple model captures the essence of the enrollment management process that selective institutions use to meet their multiple goals.

This process does not fit every school. In some states, the legislature or a state board sets tuition at public universities. For schools that have no control over tuition there are fewer levers the school can pull to craft the incoming first-year class. Yet some public institutions are selective and they do use discounting to manipulate the characteristics of the incoming class. This applies to many public flagships. Also, this enrollment management model is not a good description of how for-profit schools operate. For-profit schools depend very heavily on access to federal Title IV funding, like Pell Grants and Stafford Loans, so they do have an interest in having enough of their students exceed a bare-minimum-quality standard. But they do not offer scholarships to attract particularly talented or diverse students to benefit their peers in the residential mix. If you examine the online "net-price calculators" at most for-profit schools, you will see that most students pay a set price with little or no internal discount. The financial aid students receive at these institutions is mostly federal grants and loans.[6]

Now that we have laid out the framework for how enrollment management works, we're equipped to evaluate the consequences for tuition setting of changes in the American income distribution over the last fifty years. Our argument in chapter 4 gives reasons that college cost will drift upward somewhat faster than the overall inflation rate. Unless a school can match these extra costs with increases in nontuition revenue sources such as gifts, endowment earnings, or state appropriations, it will face an unavoidable choice. Take in more net tuition per student or cut spending. If there isn't pure fat in the budget, schools that cut spending per student will see the quality of their programming decline both absolutely and in comparison to schools that have found a way to increase net revenue.

From the late 1960s through the end of the last century the top third of American families experienced rapidly rising real income. In this period tuition discounting enabled many schools to cover their rising costs without pricing out lower-income students. As the wealthy got wealthier, tuition discounting facilitated a set of college goals that differed by school type—class sculpting for the elite schools, improving revenue flows for both the elite and the highly selective programs whose applicant pools were growing, and simply "making the class" for less selective schools whose finances were driven by filling seats. On top of helping schools to meet institutional goals, in a national environment of rising income and wealth inequality tuition discounting increasingly acted as a form of private income redistribution. This is not a bad thing. Between the mid-1970s and the late 1990s, the real value of the maximum federal Pell Grant lost almost half its purchasing power. As the federal government backed away from supporting low-income students, schools themselves were picking up more of the task and more of the tab.

We can use Figure 6.4 to show how different schools might respond to changes in the income distribution in the late twentieth century. If the cost of providing a quality education is going up, then we would see AT* rising over time. Selective colleges and elite institutions alike were experiencing a sustained rise in the number of academically strong applicants, many from families with soaring incomes. Using Figure 6.4, the willingness-to-pay bars toward the left of the diagram were rising rapidly for many of the tens, nines, and eights the school winds up enrolling. Selective schools could increasingly raise the list price and fill the freshman class with full-pay students without losing many quality points. But they might prefer to trade off a portion of the potential revenue gain from increasing the list price by filling some of their spots with very desirable students from families with less capacity to pay. At the margin, a selective school in this situation might happily allow some low-income tens to displace some full-paying sevens or eights. More schools, in other words, could adopt or move toward the need-blind admissions policies of the true elite.

For elite universities like Harvard or Stanford, the competition for the limited number of spots in the freshman class has become even more intense. These schools in the academic firmament have indeed used their increased selectivity to hit a rich and rising revenue target while simultaneously raising the quality of the incoming class. For schools further down the pecking order and schools whose applicant pool includes few students from wealthy families, the income gains of the top half offered less scope for revenue gains. Yet even for less selective institutions, an increase in the willingness to pay from any portion of their applicant pool allowed them to hit their enrollment and quality goals more easily by pushing the envelope on discounting.

The economic landscape changed in the early twenty-first century. Enrollment management problems look very different when family real incomes are flat or falling for all but the top few percentiles of the income distribution. Many of the students who make up an "optimal" class now come from households whose willingness to pay is declining. This falling willingness to pay now even afflicts families at the eightieth percentile of the income distribution. Once again using Figure 6.4, most of the willingness-to-pay bars now are shrinking. Many students who the institution could only attract with tuition discounts will need larger discounts. This requires more revenue from full-pay students. Yet many upper-income students are unwilling to pay full list price anymore. They too will need discounts. To secure the revenue the school will have to raise list-price tuition on top-income families whose incomes are still rising and on families that have saved diligently for their children's college expenses.

As a result, the fall in income for families from the median all the way to the eightieth percentile is itself a force for rising list-price tuition at selective institutions that consciously use discounting as a tool of enrollment management. Many institutions also have expanded their recruitment of foreign students in part to cope with the need for more full-pay students. Again, this is not a bad thing. It allows schools to hit a revenue target built around maintaining quality programming while discounting for capable students who otherwise would not be able to attend or who would have to go deeper into debt to do so.

The other consequence of flat family incomes is that some colleges have had to alter their admission practices. Ideally, need-blind admission is the best practice for the school and for society if the revenue target can still be met. This will not work if the highest-quality set of students does not include enough students with a high willingness to pay. This is the need-aware situation in which schools face a tradeoff between student quality and revenue. With need-aware admission, the institution admits the highest-quality students it can until it can no longer afford to give tuition discounts and then admits the remainder of the class from students who are very likely to attend without a discount, or with only very small discounts. Over the last twenty years we have seen more schools moving away from need-blind practices toward need-aware admissions.[7]

The problem of dealing with rising cost (AT*) is an additional headache. Schools that are seeing flat to declining net revenues per student from the incoming class will find that they cannot hit their revenue target and fill their seats without lowering their student quality goals (being even more need aware). This can create a vicious cycle if it induces fewer high-quality students to apply in subsequent years. Likewise, failing to hit a revenue target can be equally damaging if it forces an institution to cut the quality of its programs. This is not a problem faced by highly selective schools whose applicant pools are still rising in quantity, quality, and overall family resources. But it is a real fear at smaller and less selective schools that have no particular distinction to offer. Their problems are compounded if they currently recruit from a narrow regional base that is less wealthy, and if they are in areas in demographic decline. This is the perfect storm that may cause some schools to close their doors if they cannot find ways to manage the turbulent waters of the next thirty years.

Figure 6.5 shows the results of the most recent tuition discounting survey by the National Association of College and University Business Officers (NACUBO). The NACUBO survey covers 411 private colleges.[8] There are no state-supported institutions in the group. In the NACUBO data the tuition discount rate is institutional grant dollars as a percentage of gross tuition and fee revenue. To calculate this percentage the institution figures what its tuition revenue would be if all students paid 100% of the list-price tuition and fees and calculates the fraction of that tuition revenue the institution does not

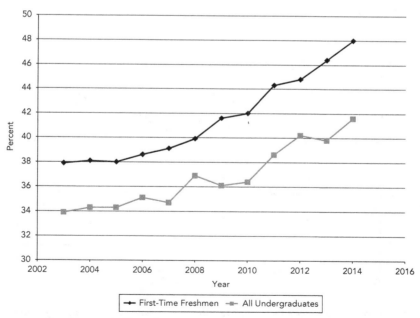

FIGURE 6.5 Average tuition discount rates, 2003–14.

receive because it has given students a discount. As the income distribution has spread out, this has led to more tuition discounting, both for first-time full-time freshmen and for all undergraduates. The discount rate for freshmen is larger than the school's overall discount rate in part because the discount is often given as a fixed dollar amount. At the University of Miami, for instance, a student may receive a flat $20,000 Dickinson Scholarship for each of his or her four years. But that scholarship makes up a smaller fraction of the bill over time as the list price continues to rise.

Figure 6.6 gives the percentage of first-time, full-time freshmen receiving institutional grants in the NACUBO data from 2003 to 2014. Institutional grants have always been common at these private institutions, but in recent years the fraction of students receiving a discount has been rising. The proposition "I'm a special student; I got a scholarship" is losing its power, and this is giving many institutions a serious headache. In the past, scholarships were a special mark of distinction even if they were need based. When the majority of students get one, the lack of a scholarship is likely to be seen as a black mark. Also, when scholarship support cannot keep up with cost growth, many students wind up receiving very small amounts of institutional aid. These schools may not be able to meet as much of their students' demonstrated need

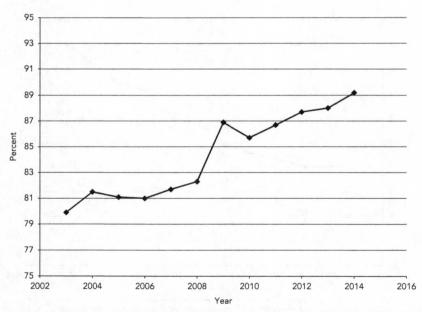

FIGURE 6.6 Percentage of first-time full-time freshmen receiving institutional grants, 2003–14.

as they met in the past. Affected students end up being asked to pay far more in net tuition. These students face the prospect of incurring larger debt or trading down to programs that may not be the best fit for them.

There is a second reason behind this upward trend in the discount rate. In addition to income distribution pressures, more and more schools are using merit-based financial aid, and this reduces the willingness-to-pay bars of students who are very attractive to multiple institutions. This puts pressure on any institution that is trying to meet enrollment and revenue targets while still maintaining the desired quality of its student body. For schools that were not leaving any revenue uncollected, at least one of those goals will have to give.[9]

Competition for students using merit-based tuition discounting is inherently a zero-sum game. A great number of small and minimally selective private colleges recognize this. They understand that if their rivals begin to discount more aggressively for the better students, they will have to respond with deeper discounts to attempt to meet targets for students, quality, and revenue. The last two figures showed that institutions in the NACUBO data are giving back close to 50% of gross tuition for their first-year students by giving close to 90% of them institutional grants. This has the look of a very mature arms race. To the extent that the discounting is merit based instead of need based, it creates no access to higher education.

The solution to the merit-based arms race is an arms control treaty. A good agreement is one that is easy for the parties to monitor. This makes cheating difficult to conceal, so schools are less likely to try. Higher education has some experience in trying to control the worst aspects of the merit aid arms race. In the 1950s, MIT and a group of eight Ivy League schools agreed to admit students based solely on merit and distribute aid based solely on need. The "Overlap Group" agreed to common standards of need, and the financial aid officers of the group met each spring to ensure that students accepted to multiple institutions within the group (an admissions overlap) had their financial situation evaluated in common. The meetings were well known to the government, and the purpose of the effort was to ensure that private aid and public money created maximal access for needy students. The Department of Justice, however, thought this was price fixing, which is a violation of the antitrust laws. As soon as the suit was filed, the Ivy League defendants signed a consent decree ending their collaboration. MIT resisted, claiming that the Sherman Anti-Trust Act should not be interpreted as applying to charitable gifts. After a ten-day trial in a Philadelphia court, the government prevailed and the Overlap Group was history.[10] Absent congressional action to exempt higher education from this interpretation of price fixing, the most viable method for curbing the merit aid arms race is gone. This is a possible policy remedy to some of the turbulence in higher education's waters.

Quite a few small private colleges are in financial straits in an environment of increasingly aggressive tuition discounting. They are the institutions with the weakest capacity to secure revenues in the face of broad declines in willingness to pay from families with above-median incomes. To cope, they need to make their programming distinctive enough so that some families in the applicant pool are willing to pay more. Institutions judged "ordinary" are at greater risk of failure in a world of flat family income and increasing price sensitivity from higher-income families. In addition, schools at risk have to find a way to be distinctive without dramatically increasing the cost of what they offer. If distinctiveness comes with a big price tag, that would push up the school's revenue needs. In this way the competition to offer amenities or special programs to students could be a financial trap every bit as large as the discounting competition problem it is designed to fix.

The data on tuition discounting by admission selectivity shows how the changing income distribution puts pressure on less selective colleges and universities. In Table 6.1, we see that the average tuition discount rate for first-year students is not related to selectivity.[11] The discount rates are all bunched in the same fairly narrow range. By contrast, the percentage of students receiving institutional grants is clearly related to selectivity. Highly selective schools enroll many more full-pay students. This means that the size of the average discount at the most selective schools has to be higher than the size of the average discount at the less selective schools. In other words, Stanford's first-year class includes a higher percentage of full-pay students than lower-tier schools can attract, but the Stanford students who do get grants get really big ones on average. Highly selective schools have made themselves distinctive in a variety of ways, and they are using this advantage to appeal to talented

Table 6.1 Tuition Discounting and Selectivity

Acceptance Rate	Average Tuition Discount Rate (Freshmen)	Percent Receiving Institutional Grants (Freshmen)
<25%	47.2%	67.3%
25% to 49%	42.2%	72.8%
50% to 74%	47.5%	93.7%
≥75%	46.8%	93.3%

students from low-income families. These students from less wealthy circumstances get discounts that are very large on average. By contrast, less selective schools need to offer tuition discounts to almost everyone, so their average discount is much smaller. Less selective institutions use tuition discounts to fill the class. More selective institutions use discounts to sculpt the class.

When we think about turbulent waters ahead in higher education, among the schools at greatest risk are the less selective small private institutions that are dependent on tuition for a large share of their revenues. The presence or absence of a few students is very important for small schools. Larger schools can shrug off a freshman class that is ten or twenty students short of ideal. Smaller schools cannot. In these cases dorm rooms go unrented, meal plans go unsold, and tuition coffers are closer to empty. At smaller schools the margin for error is much tighter. If real income for the majority of households in the nation continues to stagnate and the cost of providing a high-quality education continues to creep up, these schools will have a difficult time surviving. They have been using tuition discounts to lure students, but as the average tuition discount rate creeps up, some of these institutions may not be able to earn enough revenue from tuition to keep their doors open.

Student Debt

For most families earning median incomes and below, financing a college education has required a combination of institutional aid and borrowing. In recent years, stagnant family incomes for all but the very top-earning families has made financing college expenses out of current income much more difficult even for families at the sixtieth and eightieth percentiles of the earnings distribution. These families do not qualify for much (if any) need-based grant aid. The result is more debt financing of the college bill for families up and down the income scale. This rise in student loan debt has changed the national conversation about education. Problems that once were confined largely to struggling working class families have worked their way up the income distribution, with large effects on the politics of higher education.

To most observers, the rising list price of a year in college together with rising levels of student debt is sufficient evidence that college has become less affordable. Before we dig into the data on debt, we should explain the weasel words "to most observers." How could anyone argue that college hasn't become less affordable? We're sticklers for precision, so we want to be very clear about what the term "affordable" actually means.

Many people think about affordability as though buying an education was just like purchasing something nondurable like clothing or restaurant meals. Nondurables are usually purchased out of a family's current income. Buying an education, however, is an investment, and it's an investment that does not depreciate over time. The decisions involved are closer to the process of buying a car or a house, or when a firm thinks about the long-run costs and benefits of adding plant and equipment. We have already shown that the economic return to college is high, and the lifetime value of earning a degree has grown considerably over time. As a long-run investment there is no obvious reason to think that acquiring a degree has become less affordable, even though one may have to borrow more to acquire it.

That said, let's start by thinking of a year in college as just like buying a nondurable good or a service. One common measure of affordability is the share of the family budget spent on something. If the share is rising, many people say the product or service is less affordable. This really isn't a logically defensible definition. Here is a simple numerical example to explain why.

Suppose a family's income is $50,000 this year. With that income the family buys a bundle of goods and services, and maybe saves some of its income. That bundle is the family's material standard of living. As part of that bundle, the family spends $10,000 to send its daughter to college. In this year the family spends 20% of its income on higher education. In the following year the family's real income rises to $54,000. Once again, the term "real" means that we have deflated the family's money income by whatever inflation occurred as measured by an overall price index.[12] Suppose the real cost of the daughter's college education rises to $12,000. Now the family has to spend 22.2% of its real income on higher education. What a family can afford is measured by the real value of the bundle of goods and services it can buy with its income. In the first year the family spent $40,000 on goods and services other than college. In the second year the family could spend $42,000 on goods and services other than college. This family's income allows it to buy a larger bundle of goods and services in year two than it did in year one, even though some components of the bundle are more expensive. In other words, this family isn't forced to consume less of anything. The family's purchasing power after paying for college has gone up by $2,000, even though the cost of a year in college has risen by 20%. In this example higher education has not become less affordable.

Crafting an example like this isn't an academic exercise. As we have noted, real per-capita income has tripled since 1960 because overall labor productivity has tripled. We have demonstrated why service prices have gone up much more rapidly than the overall price level, while goods prices have risen more slowly. Productivity growth is slower in artisan-like services than in factories, fields, and mines. One result is that the share of income spent on services has risen. In the late 1940s, the average family spent 72.9% of its income on goods and 27.1% on services. By 2012, the percentages had flipped. Services took up a whopping 60.3% of the budget, while goods only took up 39.7%. Despite the fact that services "eat up" ever more of the budget, the average family consumes more of them in real terms, and more goods in real terms as well.[13] In a world of rising overall labor productivity, an increase in the relative price of a portion of the bundle that people buy does not mean that anything has become less affordable.[14]

Any good or service whose price rises more rapidly than the inflation rate does indeed become *relatively* more expensive compared to other goods and services. When that happens, people often choose to substitute less expensive alternatives even if they have the real purchasing power to buy just what they were purchasing before. Sandy Baum and Alice Ma highlight this difference between what they call "actual" and "perceived" affordability.[15] People's perceptions do matter. Many lower-income families see the rising list-price tuition and conclude that a college education is unattainable, even if that list price is not what they would pay after the dust settles on the financial aid process. This sense that college is unattainable affects decisions about what subjects or curriculum their children pursue as early as the middle school years. These decisions can then become a self-fulfilling prophecy that keeps many students from pursuing an education that could very well have been within reach. Wealthier families also can misperceive incentives. Tuition tax credits are a policy designed to make college more affordable for middle- and upper-middle-income families. The tax credits reduce the net price of attendance. But because the credits come in the form of a tax refund in April, people often think of it as an income boost unrelated to the cost of a year in school. The complexity of college pricing makes constructing good incentives difficult.

Rising income inequality over the last half-century also has changed the college affordability equation because a much smaller fraction of the population looks like the average. Until the last few years of the twentieth century, the incomes of families in the sixtieth percentile of the income distribution and above were growing, and the growth was quite strong for those in the eightieth percentile or above. Strong income gains for this group meant that college tuition increases did not reduce affordability. Families could send their children to college and still see their standard of living improve.

But after 1999 that was no longer true except at the top of the income distribution. For a family whose real income is stagnant, any big-ticket item whose price rises faster than the inflation rate becomes less affordable out of current income. To buy the same quality year in college, they will have less income left over after paying the tuition bill. Families toward the top of the income distribution do not receive need-based grants, so they feel the full effect of increases in list prices. For families at the bottom whose income has fallen, affordability also worsens if increases in state, federal, and institutional aid do not fully offset rising tuition. If we think of paying for college like paying for a restaurant meal or a new piece of furniture, college affordability went in reverse for a substantial majority of the population starting in the late 1990s.

Decreasing affordability out of current income also means that to maintain a family's standard of living while its children are in college requires a change in how the family finances the college bill. With a constant real family income and a rising college price, families must tap savings or borrow. The expansion of borrowing for college expenses is a direct consequence of the flat family incomes illustrated in Figure 6.1. Student loans for college expenses come from several sources. Federally subsidized student loans are available for students from low-income families, and unsubsidized loans are available to all students. Private loans are available for students who have exhausted their eligibility for federal loans, but they often have higher interest rates and sometimes require a cosigner. Parent PLUS loans are available if parents are willing to borrow for their child's education.

Before we discuss the expansion of college lending and its effect on the economy, we want to reiterate that much of the public discussion about affordability is rooted in the idea that college is a type of consumption good. If paying for education is viewed as an investment, much of the current apocalyptic rhetoric about college debt seems overblown. Framing the question is important. As we saw in chapter 5, the rate of return to an investment in college is roughly 15% and it has been constant. The increase in loan financing for college is the result of a number of related forces. The first is declining affordability in a consumption sense. The second is the general recognition that investment in education still has a substantial long-run payoff.

Figures 6.7 and 6.8 show the average student debt of bachelor's degree recipients at public and private nonprofit institutions. There are two bars for each year. The solid bar is the average debt for students who had loans, and the cross-hatched bar is the average debt for all students. The cross-hatched bar is considerably smaller than the solid bar because it includes a large number of zeros for students who did not take out loans. Even if we restrict the discussion to students who borrowed, the 2012–13 average debt levels of $25,600 at

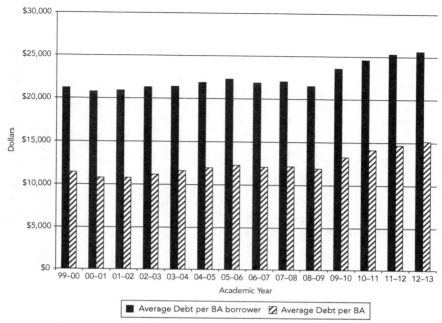

FIGURE 6.7 Average debt for bachelor's degree recipient, public institutions, 1999–2000 to 2012–13.

public institutions and $31,200 at private nonprofit institutions are not astonishingly high. The average debt is close to the cost of attendance (tuition, fees, room and board) for a year of study at these two types of institutions.[16] This is not an unmanageable debt burden for most people.

What would a person who borrows the average amount have to repay? The answer depends on the interest rate on their loans and which repayment option they choose. Table 6.2 shows the options facing someone who is single, who borrowed $32,000 at a 6.8% interest rate. This was the rate on federally subsidized loans until 2007, when it declined. We have assumed the borrower lives in Virginia and earns a modest $35,000 per year right now, though this number tends to rise rapidly for college graduates as they gain work experience. This information is not difficult to acquire. Anyone can go to the Department of Education's student aid website (studentaid.ed.gov) and determine their repayment situation and options before ever borrowing a single dollar. A person whose current salary is low might choose extended repayment or an income-contingent plan. For a graduate whose starting job pays well, the fixed repayment option would make more sense (and dollars). Overall, for an investment with a

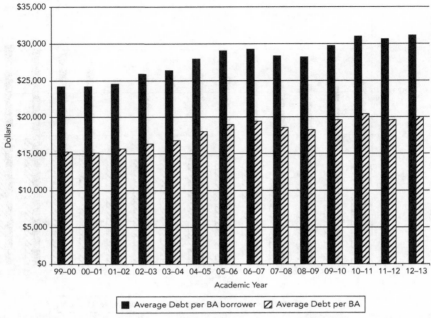

FIGURE 6.8 Average debt for bachelor's degree recipient, private nonprofit institutions, 1999–2000 to 2012–13.

lifetime value for most people of between $250,000 and $1,000,000, these carrying costs remain modest.

If we view college as an investment with a lifetime payoff, borrowing sums that are anywhere near the average amount is a very sensible proposition. For that average student, the economic payoff to earning a degree more than justifies borrowing the full average cost. Christopher Avery and Sarah Turner examined this question in their provocatively titled article, "Student Loans: Do College Students Borrow Too Much—Or Not Enough?" On balance their answer supports the "not enough" thesis.[17] Students who do not seek out an education or who drop out for fear that they will not be able to repay the loans are often making a bad economic decision.

Newspaper and magazine stories that lead with anecdotes about an undergraduate who has borrowed over $100,000 have latched on to extreme cases. Generalizing based on outliers is dishonest, though it may sell copy. We recognize that averages themselves may mislead, so we should also look at the dispersion around the averages. If the number of students with very large levels of debt is soaring, the problems with student debt may be disguised by looking at the averages. The best data for this purpose comes from the National

Table 6.2 **Sample Repayment Options for Federal Student Loans**

Repayment Plan	Repayment Period	Monthly Payment	Total Interest Paid	Total Amount Paid
Standard	120 months	$368	$12,191	$44,191
Graduated	120 months	$212 to $637	$15,552	$47,552
Extended fixed	300 months	$222	$34,631	$66,631
Extended graduated	300 months	$181 to $317	$40,173	$72,173
Income-based repayment (IBR)	161 months	$217 to $368	$19,039	$51,039
IBR for New Borrowers	236 months	$145 to $368	$32,611	$64,611
Pay as you earn	236 months	$145 to $368	$32,611	$64,611
Income-contingent repayment	181 months	$265 to $314	$19,909	$51,909

Postsecondary Student Aid Survey (NPSAS). Table 6.3 is taken from *Trends in Student Aid* and it gives the cumulative debt of bachelor's degree recipients from the last three NPSAS surveys in 2003–04, 2007–08, and 2011–12.[18] The number of students with a cumulative debt greater than $40,000 is indeed increasing. In the 2011–12 NPSAS survey, 12% of graduates of public institutions had debts this high. The 2011–12 figure for graduates of private nonprofit institutions was 20%. At for-profit schools, 48% of graduates had loan debts exceeding $40,000. Since there are many more graduates of public institutions than of the two types of private institutions, the percentage for all graduates is only 18%.

Table 6.3 clearly shows that students are taking on increasing amounts of debt. Perhaps surprisingly, it also shows that a significant percentage of students leave college debt free. By no means are all students saddled with debt. Even at private nonprofit institutions, which are the schools with exceedingly high list-price tuitions, a significant number of students have sufficient family help or are willing to take on a serious job while they are in college that they end their college careers with no debt. The table also shows that students at for-profit schools finance their tuition bill very differently. Debt is much more common in the for-profit sector. This may well reflect the fact that students going to for-profit institutions tend to be much older.

Table 6.3 Cumulative Debt of Bachelor's Degree Recipients in 2012 Dollars by Sector, 2003–04, 2007–08, and 2011–12

	Year	No Debt	<$10,000	$10,000 to $19,999	$20,000 to $29,999	$30,000 to $39,999	>$40,000
Total	2011–12	30%	10%	13%	18%	12%	18%
	2007–08	33%	15%	21%	16%	8%	8%
	2003–04	35%	24%	26%	10%	4%	2%
Public	2011–12	34%	12%	14%	18%	10%	12%
	2007–08	36%	17%	21%	14%	6%	5%
	2003–04	38%	26%	23%	9%	3%	1%
Private Nonprofit	2011–12	26%	8%	12%	20%	14%	20%
	2007–08	26%	11%	22%	17%	11%	13%
	2003–04	28%	19%	32%	12%	5%	4%
Private For-profit	2011–12	12%	4%	7%	14%	16%	48%
	2007–08	11%	6%	15%	27%	23%	18%
	2003–04	15%	15%	32%	21%	13%	4%

Debts incurred for a bachelor's degree are only part of the story. Table 6.4 gives the total debt accumulated for undergraduate and graduate study by the type of graduate degree students received.[19] This table shows that the debt incurred by students who complete graduate degrees can be very large. The category "doctoral professional," which includes chiropractic, dentistry, law, medicine, optometry, pharmacy, podiatry, and veterinary medicine, is particularly striking. More than half (54%) of these degree recipients leave school with more than $120,000 in debt. These degree programs tend to take longer than master's programs and have fewer fellowships and assistantships than the degrees in the doctoral research category. The result is that students in these professional programs take on much more debt. At the same time, these programs prepare graduates for careers in fields that are very lucrative on average, and the variance in earnings in many of these career paths is well known. As a financial matter, taking on a sizeable debt to earn a professional degree whose payoff is reasonably clear makes better sense than taking on a similar amount of debt for an undergraduate degree.

Rising college debt is a part of the turbulence buffeting higher education. The roots of this issue are reasonably clear and lie in family income trends, college pricing behavior, and the increasing cost of providing a high-quality and

Table 6.4 Cumulative Debt in 2012 Dollars for Undergraduate and Graduate Studies, 2003–04, 2007–08, and 2011–12

	Year	No Debt	<$40,000	$40,000 to $79,999	$80,000 to $119,999	>120,000
Total	2011–12	27%	26%	24%	12%	11%
	2007–08	26%	40%	23%	7%	4%
	2003–04	27%	52%	15%	5%	2%
Doctoral	2011–12	33%	28%	14%	10%	16%
Research	2007–08	33%	30%	14%	8%	8%
	2003–04	31%	38%	21%	8%	2%
Doctoral	2011–12	11%	7%	12%	16%	48%
Professional	2007–08	10%	17%	26%	20%	28%
	2003–04	11%	22%	31%	25%	11%
Master's	2011–12	26%	29%	27%	12%	0%
	2007–08	27%	43%	24%	5%	1%
	2003–04	28%	58%	12%	2%	5%

up-to-date service for students. The recent debt data also reflects the toxic legacy of the financial crisis and recession that began in December of 2007. How large is this problem, and could it be the next financial bubble to burst in the US economy? The precarious financial health of America's law schools often is seen as a harbinger of things to come in the entire higher education sector as students become ever more dependent on debt to finance their education.

Law Schools as a Case Study

Juris Doctorates (JDs) represent a significant share of the doctoral degree professional practice category in Table 6.3, and we expect that a considerable fraction of the graduates with over $120,000 in cumulative debt are JDs. Recent *US News & World Report* information on law programs includes a ranking of the debt burden of law students who borrow. At current top-ranked Yale Law School, the average graduate who borrows leaves Yale with a debt of $117,000. The debt burden of students at many low-ranked or unranked schools is much higher. The average borrower leaves Florida Coastal needing to repay over $162,000. At most law schools 75% to 95% of students need to borrow to finance their legal training. Since many graduate students are financially independent from their parents, taking on debt often is their only option.

In the past, going to law school was widely understood to be a ticket to a prosperous future for students willing to invest the three years of tuition and hard work required to get a law degree. This is no longer the case.[20] The fraction of law school graduates whose job actually requires passing the bar exam has decreased. Starting salaries for those lucky enough to land a job in the field have stopped rising. Some new lawyers do move quickly into the top 1% of the income distribution, but many barely reach the top 5%, which is territory that many talented BA holders can reach without a law degree. And we have already seen that the real income of the top 5% group has not grown much in quite some time. Yet tuition at law schools has been driven up by the same factors that drive up college tuition. As a result the value proposition offered by law school, which includes the heavy debt burden that many law students carry, has become less and less appealing. Figure 6.9 shows the number of applicants at American Bar Association–accredited law schools from the fall of 2000 to the fall of 2014. The number of law school applicants has fallen by more than 40% from its peak in 2004.

With shrinking numbers of applicants, law schools have faced unpleasant choices. Some have seen incoming classes shrink, which reduces revenue flows. Others have had to reach further down into their applicant pool to admit students they might not have considered several years ago. Some law schools may be forced to close their doors. With full cohorts of full-paying students,

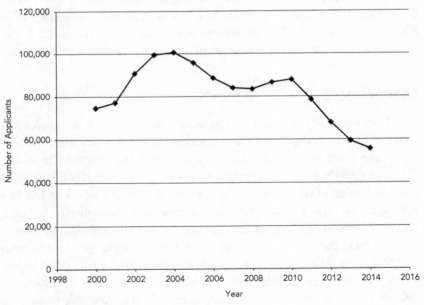

FIGURE 6.9 Law school applicants, 2000–14.

law schools once were cash cows for their universities. Unlike humanities seminars for undergraduates, the average law course was fairly large, so the cost of an expensive law professor was spread over a lot of students. And unlike many STEM (science, technology, engineering, and mathematics) fields, law professors do not require expensive equipment to do their research or teaching. The cash-cow days are gone at many institutions. Many law programs are seeing smaller incoming classes, and some programs have begun to discount tuition aggressively in search of the good students in a shrinking pool. At some institutions, the law school now needs to be subsidized by the larger university, and for stand-alone law schools the crisis is existential.

In our view the notion that law schools are the canary in the coalmine is very weak. A legal education is a riskier investment than it was in the past. Does this tell us anything about undergraduate education? We think not. Students who decide not to go the law school route have other attractive options. They can seek out other professional programs with better or more secure payoffs, or they can go directly into the job market. On the other hand, students who decide not to go to college at all have very few attractive options in a world that has seen the wages of high school graduates stagnant to declining over the last half century.

The law school example does not tell us a story that easily generalizes to the American higher education system as a whole. Nonetheless, the speed with which law school applications declined is indeed sobering. There are roughly 200 law schools in the nation. Their problems are a small hiccup to higher education in general. If the same tsunami swept away a similar fraction of the incoming classes at all of America's colleges and universities, many colleges and universities would indeed fail. On the other hand, the evidence about family income and college debt, as problematic as it is, does not easily translate into an existential crisis for a substantial portion of America's colleges and universities. The evidence about long-term changes in the American income distribution reinforces what we have seen in the demographic data. Smaller and less selective schools are in for the roughest ride. This effect many be compounded by changes in public investment in higher education, and that is the issue to which we now turn.

Environmental Threat II

PUBLIC DISINVESTMENT

WE TURN NOW to one of the most politicized parts of our story—public investment in higher education. Government financial support for higher education is a complex mix of programs financed by states and by the federal government. It can be usefully divided into three types. The first is funding that flows directly to institutions. This comes primarily from state government appropriations to cover operating expenses of public colleges and universities, and from state appropriations and bond issues for capital projects. The second category is financial support that goes directly to students, and this funding comes from separate federal and state programs. Most state governments offer some combination of need-based or merit-based grants and scholarships for state residents attending state-supported schools. Many states also allow resident students to use state-funded scholarships to attend a private college or university located in the state. The federal government is a large contributor to direct student support through the Pell Grant and Supplemental Educational Opportunity Grant (SEOG) programs for low-income families, and via subsidized loans and tuition tax credits affecting a broader slice of the population. Lastly, the federal government and some state governments award grants for research undertaken at public and private institutions.

Like so much of the contemporary American political discourse about policy, much of the national conversation about public funding of higher education takes place inside increasingly partisan echo chambers of the like-minded. You can see these parallel intellectual universes on display in any congressional hearing, or on the op-ed pages of newspapers and activist blogs. Simple ideological sureties often replace nuance and complexity. This leaves little room for a shared framework for thinking about incentives and about how complex organizations operate. When evidence is used, it is picked selectively to confirm biases or support interests more than to inform rational decision making about the costs and benefits of public policies.

Our complex stew of national and state higher education funding policies affects students and institutions in ambiguous ways, and this ambiguity often doesn't align well with firm ideological frameworks. Nonetheless, on one side of the ideological tussle we hear impassioned claims that the magic of unfettered and unsubsidized markets can solve the college cost problem. In this view, public subsidies do positive harm by driving up college tuition. Inappropriate analogies with the medical market's insurance-driven inefficiencies abound. On the other side we have those who believe that legislatures have needlessly or callously abandoned higher education despite evidence that some forms of government assistance have not receded. This side often argues that free is the right price for everything of social value. And from both sides we are regularly treated to finger wagging about wasteful university priorities and practices of the sort we discussed in chapter 4. We will not claim complete dispassion in what follows. Others will decide how well we have read the evidence and evaluated the incentives. We will, however, inject some of the nuance and complexity that is so often missing in contemporary accounts of the evolving state and federal financial commitment to the American higher education system.

Changes in public funding of higher education have indeed affected cost, price, and access to higher education, often in ways not fully appreciated by the public. We will show that colleges and universities do have the ability to siphon off some of the subsidy that their students receive from state and federal sources, repurposing it for other university goals. But the evidence suggests that most of that financial support actually gets to students in the form of a lower net price of college attendance. In plain language, student subsidies create access. Our understanding of the process of tuition setting convinces us that federal subsidy is not an important driver of college tuition at nonprofit colleges and universities. But federal student subsidies may be a significant driver of tuition in the for-profit sector that has expanded so rapidly over the past quarter century. On the other hand, cuts in state appropriations for public university operating expenses have put significant upward pressure on tuition at public institutions, and this may be the most important factor affecting access and outcomes in higher education. If this continues, we risk cementing in place a haves and have-nots higher education system in which the schools that serve the most vulnerable (and growing) segment of the American population are the most underresourced.

Institutional Support

In many ways, state-supported institutions are like a private nonprofit university that has one very large donor whose generous gift comes with many strings attached. As the president of any college will tell you, finding a large new donor can transform an institution. On the other hand, in the case of public institutions, some of the strings attached by their big donor can make efficient operation of the institution quite difficult. In most states, public institutions are feeling the effects of two changes in the fiscal behavior of their big donor. The first is the long-term decline in the real value of state appropriations per student. The second issue is that state revenues, which have always been volatile, have become even more volatile in recent years. Volatile revenue flows make planning more difficult, and when state revenues nosedive, public universities are sometimes forced to make midyear budget cuts of substantial magnitude. This problem is almost unknown at private nonprofit schools.

Large donors also want to exert control over university programming, and state legislatures are not exempt from this attitude. The level of political micromanagement varies across states. In Virginia where we teach there is no state-mandated programming, and compared to many states the Virginia system gives its component institutions a lot of autonomy. By contrast, the state of Texas mandates a forty-two- to forty-eight-credit distribution requirement with very specific line items. All students, for instance, must take twelve credit hours of US history and government, although they are permitted to use subjects such as Texas history and government as a substitute. This mandate alone is 10% of the credits required to graduate, and the full Texas core constitutes 35% to 40% of the necessary credits. Universities that have their own ideas about educational best practices then must layer additional requirements on top of state-mandated ones. Many students from wealthy districts often can place out of a significant fraction of a state's mandated core requirement using advanced placement courses and dual enrollment credits earned at local community colleges. This makes completing a degree on time much easier for them. On the other hand, students from a more disadvantaged background find that extensive state mandates may tack on an additional semester or year to their stay in college.

You can often hear a snarky quip about public financing at some highly selective public universities. It goes sort of like this: "once we were state supported, then we became state assisted, but now we're simply state located." In our own state, the University of Virginia receives only 10% of its operating revenue from the state. That percentage is down from 35% in the late 1980s. But few of the nation's public institutions are this financially independent.[1]

As we mentioned in chapter 2, 82% of students at public universities attend institutions that get 20% to 50% of their operating revenues from state coffers.[2] Despite substantial decreases in real appropriations per student, these schools remain very much state supported.

One of the most difficult parts of running any business is forecasting revenues. And most businesses have to make commitments before they are sure of those revenues. Colleges and universities have to maintain buildings, hire faculty and staff, and equip classrooms. They do this without knowing precisely how many tuition-paying students will show up in the fall. Every school has experienced summer melt. These are students who commit to the institution in the spring, but who for one reason or another do not show up in the fall. Some students even leave during freshman orientation. This tuition revenue uncertainty is a bigger worry for smaller schools. Another source of uncertainty is variability in annual giving from alumni. For schools with a sizable endowment, there is also the market uncertainty that can play havoc with endowment earnings. Typically institutions insulate themselves from this uncertainty by spending last year's gifts, not a guess of this year's gifts. They also spend from endowment based on the portfolio's performance averaged over several years.

State-supported institutions face the added burden of state budget uncertainty, and with it the political uncertainty of how the legislature will choose to act in response to economic shocks. States typically live with balanced budget mandates, so when the state is in trouble, public colleges and universities are asked to do their part. "Their part" is often disproportionate because higher education spending tends to be more discretionary than many other lines in the budget, and because unlike most other state agencies state institutions have an independent source of income from students. State governments have revealed over many years that as much as they don't like to see rising tuition at public universities, they like raising taxes even less.

Figure 7.1 shows how short-term state budget uncertainty has become even more virulent over the past fifteen years.[3] As one would expect, state tax revenues follow the overall economy. When the economy is growing (solid line), state revenues grow as well (dashed line). Tax revenues have been consistently more volatile than gross domestic product, especially on the upswing. Improvements in economic growth have led to larger improvements in revenue. In the two most recent economic slowdowns, however, we have seen extreme contractions in state tax revenues. In the past, state tax revenues seemed protected on the down side of the business cycle. This is no longer the case.

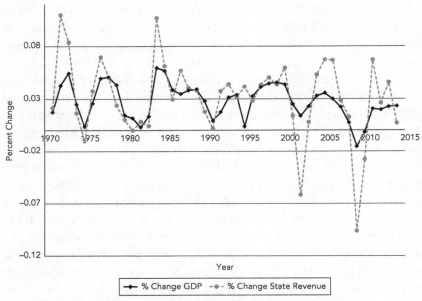

FIGURE 7.1 Percent change in real gross domestic product and real state tax revenue, 1971–2014.

These contractions in state revenue sometimes force midyear budget cuts, which are a big problem for any institution whose costs are mostly fixed. For universities, faculty and staff are under contract, the utility bills have to be paid, and the students expect services, some of which are difficult to cut. In these situations schools suspend all faculty and staff searches, and they may cancel classes taught by contract teachers who aren't permanent employees. These reactions have an immediate effect on students' ability to get needed classes, and the result is often a form of class rationing that means extra costs for students who cannot get what they need and who may be required to extend their stay in college. To add some scale, if the state prunes $6 million from the budget of a midsized state university, that's the equivalent of a private institution losing over $120 million of endowment.

Midyear cuts are unusual. Normally state-supported institutions can count on the legislature following through on appropriations decisions made for any particular year. But the politics of the appropriation process means that any long-run budget forecast must be hedged. Some states do have biennial budgets, but the second year of funding is subject to re-evaluation based on the evolution of state tax revenues. If state tax revenues lag behind forecasts, the second-year appropriation will be cut. Many states also control tuition levels, so longer-run revenue forecasts are clouded with uncertainty. This puts state-supported institutions at a permanent disadvantage in planning capital improvements and program changes, since they involve extra staffing and maintenance costs that aren't easily adjusted. Private colleges and universities have a much surer understanding of their longer-run revenues.

In most cases state universities also cannot move state appropriations from one year to the next. Unlike tuition or donations to a private institution, state money is "use it or lose it." This means that state institutions cannot save, even if transferring revenues across fiscal years would be prudent and might facilitate good long-run planning. State governments are likely to swoop in and grab any "surplus" in a university's budget to help cover some other state agency facing a shortfall. Knowing that you cannot count on carrying funds forward from one year to the next often leads to end-of-budget-year spending sprees.

These planning issues are an important impediment to building more efficient public institutions, but the most important and transformative feature of the economic landscape is the long retreat of real per-student state appropriations for higher education. For the United States as a whole, the real value of state appropriations per full-time student is lower today than in the 1980s. The top line in Figure 7.2 shows the evolution of real state appropriations per full-time-equivalent student from 2000 to 2014. In economic expansions real appropriations rise, but the retreats during economic downtrends dominate. The experience for most states is very similar. Over the span from 2000 to 2014 only four states, Alaska, North Dakota, Illinois, and Wyoming, increased state appropriations per full-time-equivalent student. The new reality is that state university tuition must rise more rapidly than the inflation rate merely to make up for state cutbacks, and rise even more to maintain quality in the face of cost disease and technological change.

We can offer two explanations for this sea change in public university finances. The first is structural, and rooted in constitutional mechanisms at work in some states. The other reflects long-term shifts in state priorities, many of which seem common to most states. As we explained in our 2006 paper, the growth of tax revenues has been curtailed in many states because of tax and expenditure limitations (TELs) imposed as part of what is commonly called the tax revolt. Starting in 1978 with California's Proposition 13, which limited property taxes, a number of states have imposed limitations on the amount of revenue the state can raise and/or spend. In some states, even tuition collected by state universities is considered state revenue subject to aggregate caps. In those states a tuition increase crowds something else out of the budget, so the legislature is loath to allow tuition increases even

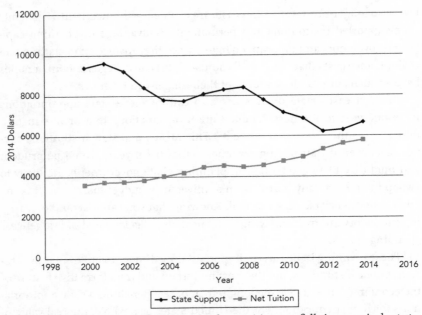

FIGURE 7.2 Real state appropriations and net tuition per full-time-equivalent student, 2000–14.

if they are warranted. Some states also have supermajority requirements for tax increases, and this is also associated with reductions in state support for higher education.

Second, even in states whose revenues have continued to grow, other priorities have squeezed higher education spending. The Medicaid program has been responsible for some of the squeeze. In 1990, higher education accounted for 14.6% of state general fund expenditures, and Medicaid accounted for 9.5%. By 2014, higher education's share had fallen to 9.4% and Medicaid's share had increased to 19.1%. Expenditures on elementary and secondary education and corrections also have grown more rapidly than expenditures on higher education. Between 1986 and 2013, state higher education expenditures grew 5.6% while expenditures on elementary and secondary education grew by 69% and expenditures on corrections grew by 141%.[4] Colleges and universities are getting a smaller slice of the pie, and in many states the pie of public spending itself is shrinking as a portion of the state economy.

The bottom line in Figure 7.2 shows real net tuition revenue per student, which has risen over time. Often with a lag of a year or two, state-supported institutions have replaced lost state appropriations with tuition revenues collected from students and their parents. The funding of state institutions is being slowly and somewhat erratically privatized. The increase in tuition revenue has proceeded at a different pace at different institutions. This is a wrenching transition. State-supported institutions have traditionally embraced a low tuition model. Many state residents and legislators alike are wary of completely erasing a tradition that gave citizens access to higher education at minimal cost to the family. But legislative choices in many states over many years are producing that outcome in slow motion.

The increase in net tuition revenue displayed in Figure 7.2 comes from two sources. First, state institutions have been forced to increase the tuition paid by state resident students. This group constitutes the bulk of most schools' potential revenue. In the 1974–75 academic year the average list-price in-state tuition at four-year state-supported institutions was $2,469 in 2014 dollars.[5] By the 1999–2000 academic year real list-price in-state tuition had risen 94.6% to $4,805. In the first fifteen years of the new century real list-price in-state tuition rose another 90.2%, from $4,805 to $9,139. By comparison, the last fifteen years have witnessed a smaller 40.8% rise in real list-price tuition at private nonprofit colleges and universities.

Tuition increases at state institutions are politically unpopular, and state legislatures often prevent or limit the increases that state universities propose in response to appropriations cuts. Schools are told to absorb the cuts and "do no harm" to their students. But the plausible ways schools can absorb budget cuts all harm students in one way or another. Class size grows. The number of classes shrinks. Student support services that improve retention and graduation rates are weakened. These are all costs on the students in time, money, and life chances. These unintended consequences ultimately create pressure on the legislature, so limits on tuition growth tend not to last very long. Political memory tends to be short, so the cycle repeats in each economic downturn.

Although they draw the bulk of their students from within the state, most state-supported institutions enroll some students from other states and from other countries. This is a second source of extra net tuition for increasingly cash-strapped public universities. Some institutions have made concerted efforts to increase the number of out-of-state and overseas students who enroll, since the tuition premium from these students is often quite large. Highly selective state institutions also have pushed the envelope on tuition increases for these nonresident students. State legislators' constituents are all state residents, so they are not generally concerned with out-of-state tuition as long as the average nonresident student's tuition bill isn't being directly subsidized by state appropriations. In the 2014–15 academic year, the list-price tuition for out-of-state students averaged $22,958, which is more than two and a half times the $9,139 list-price tuition for in-state students.[6] Most state institutions are not under political pressure to keep the list price for nonresident students "affordable" or to meet the financial need of nonresidents.

Although nonresident students are an increasingly attractive source of revenue, there are political and economic constraints on how state schools market themselves to nonresidents. At highly selective flagships, for instance, legislators are under pressure from constituents to make more room for state citizens. Increases in the population of nonresident students can become a political football since they seemingly displace state residents who could have taken those spots at premier flagship schools. Legislators often are impervious to the counterargument that nonresident students relieve some of the budgetary stress the state and its colleges and universities jointly face. Some states deal with this political issue by mandating that their public institutions enroll no more than a certain percentage of nonresident students. To take more nonresident students requires growing the entire institution. Many schools are loath to do this since growth doesn't solve cost problems for larger universities, and for smaller and midsized ones it can change the character of the entire institution. For selective flagships that could easily double the percentage of nonresident students if they had the freedom to do so, these constraints strongly affect their admissions processes. Maximum percentages often aren't met at less selective public universities. These institutions have a harder time attracting high-paying out-of-state students who could attend similar-quality programs in their own states at much lower in-state prices. To tap this market shows us again why universities that want to preserve or improve their quality must build some distinguishing features or programs that are not replicated at hundreds of competitors. It's also an argument for state schools to pursue overseas full-paying students who have fewer options at home and who positively value the US experience, even at a less selective state school.

Students like Pradhi Gupta in chapter 1, who attended our mythical North Central State, do help pay the bills. There is good evidence that state funding cuts and foreign enrollment are indeed related. Bound, Braga, Khanna, and Turner have recently examined this relationship. They find that a 10% cutback in state appropriation is associated with a 6% rise in foreign enrollment at US public universities.[7] Given the strong economic growth over the past few decades in large economies like India and China, the pool of qualified students from families with the wherewithal to pay list price for a US education has grown rapidly. The extra revenues produced by foreign enrollment create real benefits for US students well beyond the opportunity to interact with students with different backgrounds.

Private fundraising is another option institutions can use to increase revenues. In recent years, state-supported schools have become much more aggressive at tapping alumni donors. In the middle of the last century, colleges and universities in many states had forged a tacit agreement about fundraising. State-supported institutions lobbied the legislature, while private nonprofit institutions went after private donors. Many state universities had dabbled in private fundraising, so endowments did exist at public institutions. For historical reasons a few public institutions, like the University of Texas system and the Texas A&M system, had large endowments.[8] But public university efforts to promote private philanthropy were dwarfed by the networks developed by their private counterparts. As state support has ebbed, that tacit agreement has eroded with it. State institutions have become very aggressive at seeking gifts and bequests to create the same kind of endowment support long utilized by their private counterparts.

President Taylor Reveley of the College of William and Mary puts it rather colorfully. "Philanthropy is the absolute life's blood of the schools that are going to succeed in this century, public or private. We're after it tooth and claw." William and Mary recently initiated a $1 billion capital campaign, and Reveley quipped that "six hundred million doesn't get the blood flowing. A billion, on the other hand, is a round number with some body and flavor."[9] Public universities must go a long way to catch up with their private counterparts. Of the institutions whose total endowment already exceeds $1 billion, the University of Virginia is the leading public institution in endowment dollars per student (at $400,000 in 2014). Within the billion-dollar club, however, Virginia only ranks twenty-eighth in endowment per student, nestled just behind Middlebury College and looking longingly at schools like Wellesley and Rice whose endowments per student are twice as high. The University of Texas system with its seemingly massive endowment of over $25 billion spreads the return on that fund over 216,000 students. As a result, its endowment per student is 30% smaller than Union College's.

Succeeding in this fundraising game is a difficult tactical and cultural problem for public institutions. The natural givers are the alumni. But the alumni with a large capacity to give attended a very different institution that was well funded by the state. When they were students in the 1950s through the 1980s the campus buildings were named after state senators, past college presidents, or beloved old professors, not big donors. And when they were students, the freshman orientation did not lay the groundwork for a lifetime of giving back to the institution. As public universities ramp up their "development" efforts, these older generations of alumni need to be educated about the new financial realities at their alma mater. This isn't easy, and the percentage of alumni who donate remains much smaller at public universities than at private colleges and universities that have long stressed a lifelong financial connection between the school and its graduates. Inculcating a giving ethic in the current generation of public university students is a long-term investment that may see significant returns in the 2040s and beyond, but not so much today.

Public universities may indeed be able to convince alumni that current needs are substantial, but there is an additional problem in getting alumni to be the solution. If a million-dollar gift to the university is matched by a decrease of $50,000 in the state's annual appropriation, the state has effectively taxed away the gift. To convince donors to support the operating budget under these circumstances, you must also convince them that state support will continue to decline no matter what they do. Otherwise, donors are likely to give for new initiatives (like centers for this and that) that cannot easily be taxed rather than to areas of greatest need within the university's general operating budget.

While state-supported colleges and universities have labored hard to replace lost state appropriations, the evidence on spending per student tells a very clear story. Educational and general (E&G) spending covers instruction, student support, and the other operating expenses of the institution. In 1987, public institutions spent 88 cents on average for every dollar spent at private nonprofit colleges and universities on wages and salaries in E&G categories.[10] By 1999, the ratio had fallen to 81 cents. And by 2010, it had fallen further to 73 cents on the dollar. Unless public institutions are increasingly more efficient than their private counterparts, this long-term trend must have consequences for the quality of public university offerings. One piece of evidence for this shows up in college rankings.

University administrators genuinely detest ranking systems like the one published annually by *US News & World Report*. Rankings are all about rungs on a ladder, not the quality of the programming. To preserve their position, schools have an incentive to care too much about the specific measures used by the ranking scheme. But changes over time within a single ranking system do show us how public institutions are falling behind their private competitors in measures of quality. Within the *US News* rankings, state-supported institutions have moved down over time because their resource base is eroding. The 1990 rankings included five state-supported institutions in the top twenty-five of the "national universities" category. The University of California at Berkeley was the top-ranked public institution, holding down the thirteenth spot. UCLA took the seventeenth position, followed at number eighteen by the University of Virginia. The University of North Carolina was twentieth, and the University of Michigan came in at twenty-first.[11] In the 2015 rankings only two state-supported schools remained in the top twenty-five. The University of California at Berkeley was number twenty and UCLA was twenty-third. The other schools had been pushed entirely out of the top group by private institutions that moved up.

Many view this erosion of state support with great alarm. In the past, all students with college potential could count on the option of attending a state-supported institution at low or negligible tuition. This is the low-low world we described in chapter 6. Many people can trace the start of their successful career to a low-cost public university education. In an opinion in the *New York Times* in 2015, Tom Hanks says of Chabot College, a community college in Hayward California, "That place made me what I am today."[12] People who went to college in a prior world of generous state support can see the slow privatization of their alma mater, and to many the change is unwelcome. Others recognize that the state university has been a major economic driver in their state. As but one example, the research and the extension work done by the local state university can be critical for farmers and industries in the state. Falling state support can curtail some of these activities. Many a state's leading newspapers frequently chastise the legislature for shortchanging higher education, but these calls produce little change. Taxpayers have little appetite for tax increases, and state budgets have other compelling needs.

Forecasting the future of America's state-supported universities is complicated, and sweeping generalizations are unwarranted. For some institutions, the future is indeed fraught with financial stresses and difficult, risky choices. Nonselective public institutions in many states face the full weight of changing state priorities and have few ways to respond. Cost cutting will further compromise the quality of their academic offerings and the capacity of their vital support services to deal with the academic adjustment problems of their more vulnerable students. And as their net tuition approaches or surpasses the levels at lower-tier private colleges, they will find that they have moved out of their market niche into a world filled with much greater competition. Many of these public institutions already reflect the diverse demographics of the future, and many serve a substantial population of low-income families. These are also the schools that will face the greatest pressure, and the greatest temptation, to replace a substantial portion of their traditional face-to-face coursework with the lowest-cost online alternatives. This will be sold as farsighted stewardship of public resources. We will explore the promise and the risks of an online educational future in the next chapter.

We already know that there are social consequences of starving America's less selective public institutions. Over the last half century the proportion of a high school cohort that moves directly into four-year college programs went up substantially. In the early 1970s roughly a third of high school seniors moved into a four-year program within the first year and a half following high school graduation. By the early 2000s this had risen to 47%. Yet in the latter years of the century, the completion rate began a sustained decline. College attendance is a means to an end. Finishing is the goal. Many things could cause declining completion. Entering students could be worse than in the past, or the characteristics of the schools they attend could be changing. Bound, Lovenheim, and Turner used survey data from the high school classes of 1972 and 1992 to evaluate the causes of declining college completion rates.[13] At four-year programs, they found a marked decrease in institutional resources per student at less selective public institutions where the declining completion rates are concentrated.

Highly selective public universities face the same environment of declining real appropriations per student along with the budget uncertainty that comes from the politics of the state business cycle. Yet the future of the highly selective institutions is not as grim. The most selective public institutions have the greatest capacity to emulate the financial behavior of their private brethren. These are the institutions most likely to succeed in ramping up private giving. Their selectivity also gives them more flexibility in tuition setting, given the right alignment of political forces in their state. The data are quite striking. In 1987, the average state flagship university spent 1.42 times the amount spent on "wages and salaries in E&G" categories at other state-supported four-year institutions per full-time-equivalent student. This multiple has increased steadily, to 1.66 in 1999 and to 1.75 in 2010.

This is important because for most public universities the transition from low-low to high-high has not fully happened. The model of low tuition and low aid is dead or dying, but they are stuck in a purgatory of mid-mid. List-price tuition is creeping up, which erodes their competitive position while burdening many of their lower- and middle-income "customers" with a higher net price. Yet most public flagships are not extracting as much tuition revenue as they could from families that have a significant capacity to pay. Without that revenue they cannot discount like private colleges while also maintaining the quality of their programming. Instead, they find themselves recruiting in a world where families with an income of $150,000 or below see that the cost of a year at Stanford often is lower than the cost of a year at the state flagship.

In the absence of a sustained turnaround in state higher education funding, achieving a stable revenue trajectory that reduces the net cost for middle-income families requires a different pricing model for public institutions. The College of William and Mary has implemented a plan, called the William and Mary Promise, that is an experiment in how to fund a public institution differently. The College "promised" certain things to students and to the state of Virginia in the new plan. One is tuition stability for families. For students who matriculate in a particular academic year, the list price is guaranteed for four years. The next promised benefit is for middle-income families who earn less than four times the federal poverty level (families making roughly $100,000 per year or less). This encompasses over 70% of Virginia families. These families are promised a lower net price under the new plan compared to the old pricing system. This is accomplished by replacing some loans with tuition grants. For families making $40,000 or less, the College maintains no-loan, all-grant aid packages. The College also promised the state an increase in the number of in-state admissions slots. In return, the College increased the list-price tuition for in-state students by 69% over the following four years, broken into yearly steps. This substantial rise in list-price tuition from $9,264 in 2012–13 to $15,674 in 2016–17 generated a predictable increase in college revenue.

This is an option for any highly selective public university that can compete for students with good private institutions. At these schools in-state tuition would remain subsidized, but the size of the subsidy is reduced for high-income families. At present, highly selective public institutions are leaving a lot of potential tuition revenue uncollected, and collecting even a portion of it can give them a better planning horizon and a chance to close the funding gap with their private peers, all without harming lower- and middle-income families. On the other hand, by mimicking the high-high pricing behavior of private colleges and universities, they also introduce all the pricing complexity of private institutions.

Support for Students

Direct student support comes in three forms. First, state governments and the federal government provide grants to students. These grants are gifts that do not have to be repaid. Second, the federal government provides loans to students. This relaxes financing constraints and permits some students to invest in some form of postsecondary education instead of moving directly into the workforce. It permits others to seek out higher-cost institutions that might be a good match for them but that they cannot afford out of current income. Loans have to be repaid, so they do not directly reduce the net price. They may indirectly cut the cost a small amount by offering submarket interest rates. Third, the federal government provides tuition tax credits to students and families to help cover a portion of college expenses. Unlike institutional aid from state appropriations, direct government support to students has been growing.

State Grants

All but two states, New Hampshire and Wyoming, awarded grants to students for the 2012–13 academic year. Figure 7.3 shows the evolution of state grants per full-time-equivalent undergraduate in constant 2012 dollars.[14] The data are divided between need-based and non-need-based grants. The College Board categorizes a grant as need based if financial circumstances contribute to eligibility and non–need based if financial circumstances have no influence on eligibility. Most non-need-based grants are based on academic merit, but in some states this category also includes grants given to state residents who attend private colleges and universities located in the state.

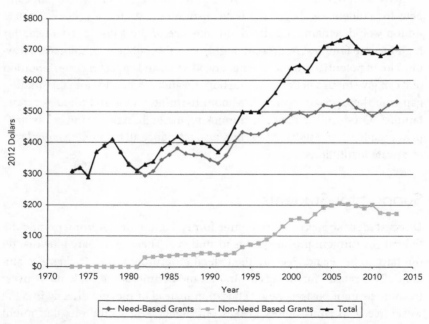

FIGURE 7.3 State grants per full-time-equivalent undergraduate student in 2012 dollars, 1972–2012.

The average state grant to students grew in real terms until the beginning of the financial crisis at the end of 2007. Until the early 1980s, state aid was need based. Since then, merit grants have become popular in many states and an increasing proportion of state aid is not need based. In the 2012–13 academic year non-need-based grants accounted for 25% of all state grants. Despite the rising importance of state-based merit aid, the average need-based award also grew from the early 1990s until that growth was interrupted in 2007. The states, however, are far from uniform in giving direct tuition assistance. In 2012–13, the average full-time student in Arizona got $40 in tuition assistance while the average student in South Carolina got $1,890.[15]

Federal Grants

The federal government has been giving student financial support since the National Defense Education Act was passed in 1958. This support was originally directed at particular fields, including mathematics, science, and foreign languages. Grants available to college students across the board started with the Higher Education Act of 1965. The preliminary data for 2013–14 in *Trends in Student Aid* put federal grants in four categories: Pell Grants are the largest program with 9.2 million recipients, an average grant of $3,678, and total expenditures of over $33 billion. Grants to veterans and the military are next with expenditures of over $12 billion. The vast majority of the military and veteran spending flows from the Post-9/11 GI Bill, which has 800,000 beneficiaries who receive an average grant of $14,107. Federal SEOGs are next with expenditures of $733 million. These are small grants, averaging $451, spread across 1.6 million recipients. An "other" category with expenditures of $316 million completes the picture.[16]

The Pell Grant and the SEOG programs are both need based. A student's Pell Grant is determined by two factors: the student's expected family contribution (EFC) and the Pell Grant maximum. If the student's EFC exceeds the Pell Grant maximum, the student is not eligible for a Pell Grant. If the student's EFC is less than the Pell Grant maximum, the student will receive a Pell Grant that is the difference between the Pell Grant maximum and his or her EFC. Since the EFC is strongly driven by family income, the size of the Pell Grant declines rapidly as family income rises. Virtually all Pell recipients come from families earning less than 2.5 times the federal poverty line. For a family of four, the federal poverty guideline in 2015 was $24,250. The SEOG program is administered by colleges and universities using federal money, and these funds are used to give grants to students who have unmet financial need. Almost all of the students awarded a grant from the SEOG program are also Pell Grant recipients.

Figure 7.4 shows the evolution of the Pell Grant program from its inception in 1978 to 2013.[17] The data for the size of the maximum grant and the average grant are in thousands of 2013 dollars. The number of Pell recipients is measured in millions. Both numbers are displayed on the vertical axis. In 2013, for instance, the maximum grant was $5,600, the average grant was $3,680, and there were 9.2 million Pell Grant recipients. In real terms the maximum and average Pell Grants were very generous at the beginning of the program, but the number who used them was rather small. As college enrollments soared, the real value of the Pell maximum declined and then stagnated for twenty years. The recent financial meltdown and recession saw substantial increases in the maximum and average Pell Grant, and in the number of Pell recipients. Congress allowed the Pell maximum to increase, and the forces of recession and rising income inequality drove up the average Pell Grant received and the number of students who qualified. As a result, the total expenditures on the Pell Grant program grew dramatically. As the economy recovered the number

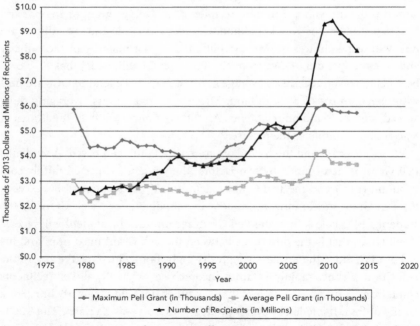

FIGURE 7.4 Maximum and average Pell Grant in 2013 dollars, number of Pell recipients, 1978–2013.

of Pell recipients has leveled off, but it has not declined. The economic recovery from the financial crisis has reduced unemployment but has seen little in the way of wage gains, and this may account in part for the fact that the total number of Pell recipients has not returned to prerecession levels.

The Bennett Hypothesis

The dramatic expansion in federal higher education expenditures over time has generated its share of controversy. Although political support for aid to needy students remains strong, there is a point of view that is deeply skeptical of the efficacy of government financial aid programs. In his oft-cited 1987 *New York Times* op-ed titled "Our Greedy Colleges," former secretary of education William Bennett gave voice to this view when he said, "If anything, increases in financial aid in recent years have enabled colleges and universities blithely to raise their tuitions."[18] The idea that direct student financial support simply pushes up tuition is widely believed and has become known as the "Bennett hypothesis." This argument has become an integral part of the politicization of higher education policy despite the weak and conflicting evidence about it. In the rest of this section we lay out why we believe the theoretical foundation for this view has very little traction at traditional nonprofit four-year institutions and why the best evidence suggests that any aid–tuition links seem much clearer in the market-driven for-profit sector.[19]

The Bennett hypothesis often is justified as simple textbook supply and demand. Government aid is a subsidy. Subsidies increase demand. Rising demand pushes up price, end of argument. Since the authors of this book come from the economist tribe, we want to take some time to challenge the notion that Econ 101 is the only tool needed for understanding the higher education "market." First, this simplistic use of supply and demand does not use the correct supply curve. Over any reasonable time horizon, seats at colleges and universities in the nation as a whole respond rather elastically to changes in demand, so rising demand doesn't necessarily push up price. Over any reasonable time horizon, rising demand increases the number of admission slots in the university system. Second, simple supply and demand isn't even the right lens through which to view the price-setting behavior of mission-driven nonprofit colleges and universities.

In the last chapter's discussion of tuition discounting, we introduced our framework for thinking about how selective nonprofit universities set tuition. We laid out a very different process of price setting from the auctionlike market mechanism of homogeneous products such as winter wheat or West

Texas Intermediate crude oil. Unlike most retail vendors, selective institutions turn away some potential customers. And schools can charge applicants who have different characteristics different prices. Instead of profit maximization, many nonprofit schools try to attract the highest-quality group of students while filling the seats available and hitting a necessary target level of revenue per student. Figure 7.5 allows us to analyze the claim that the Pell Grant program, or any other need-based aid, would cause tuition increases. To refresh the reader's memory: list-price tuition (LT) is determined by the subset of accepted students who have the highest willingness to pay. The average net tuition per student (AT*) times the number of students enrolled (E*) generates total revenue that meets the institution's target for providing the desired quality of education.

Suppose the federal government now raises the maximum amount a Pell recipient can receive. Pell Grants go to the students with the lowest capacity to pay. For many of these lower-income students a higher Pell Grant maximum will increase their willingness to pay for a chance at a degree. In Figure 7.5, the cross-hatched portion of the willingness-to-pay bars shows the increased willingness to pay of students whose maximum Pell Grant has grown. Notice that these bars are all on the right side of the diagram, reflecting the fact that the lowest-income families are the only ones eligible to receive these grants.

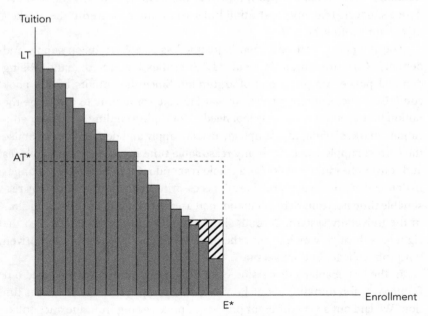

FIGURE 7.5 The effect of an increase in the Pell Grant maximum.

After an increase in the Pell maximum, a school that enrolls these students has many options, and they're all good. Some of them are less good for the average student who relies on Pell Grant support to pay the bill. The best thing this institution could do for its Pell Grant recipients is to subtract the full increase in the Pell Grant from the amount the student needs to borrow. If they do this, the extra Pell money would reduce the student's cost of attendance. By reducing the average student's loan burden, the school's default rate likely would improve over time as well. Thus, universities do have a self-interest motive in fully passing the extra federal support on to students. In this case we would say that the school doesn't tax the federal aid support at all. At the other extreme, the school could cut the institutional grant aid it was prepared to give these students dollar for dollar with the increased federal support. The cross-hatched bars then become a tuition windfall above what the school needs to cover all its immediate costs of producing a given level of educational quality. In this case, we would say that the school has assessed a 100% tax rate on the extra federal aid.

A 100% tax rate is not 100% bad news for students. That extra revenue could be used to improve programming that benefits all students, Pell recipients and full-paying students alike. It could be targeted to student support services that are of disproportionate benefit to students from a disadvantaged background and to students who are the first in their family to experience the college world. Lastly, the extra revenue could be "spent" on lowering the existing list price faced by all students, rich and poor. This would be the opposite of a Bennett effect, but rather perversely it would give some of the federal aid money to well-off families in the form of lower tuition. The federal government might prefer a zero internal tax rate, but schools get to set the tax rate. They know the Pell Grant award their students will receive before they make their own decisions about how much institutional aid to give. The government award is "first dollar." The schools give the last dollar, and the giver of the last dollar has broad options.

Whatever the chosen tax rate our hypothetical nonprofit university chooses to set, it has no incentive to raise list-price tuition. This enrollment management framework applies to most colleges and universities in the four-year nonprofit sector. These schools can find a way to repurpose some of the federal aid by adjusting their own aid packages without fiddling with the list price. Unless the policy change affects students with the highest willingness to pay, there is no reason to adjust the list price. Moreover, schools cannot force up a student's Pell Grant by raising the list-price tuition. The size of the Pell Grant is determined by the difference between the Pell maximum and the EFC. Congress controls the Pell maximum, and the EFC is a formula based on family income, family assets, and the number of children the family is supporting in college.[20] High-income families aren't the ones on the borderline between getting some Pell support and getting none.

Bennett may have suggested a link between government aid and list-price tuition, but his broader worry, we think, is about the tax rate. And this is a sensible concern. His error was in suggesting that most universities would tax federal aid via tuition increases when in fact the more plausible mechanism at nonprofit institutions works through reduced tuition discounting instead. But to see what schools actually do, we have to look at the data. Leslie Turner measures the tax rates that schools impose on the Pell Grant program through changes in their own internal grants.[21] Overall, she finds the tax rate is a modest 12% to 16%. Government grants to students primarily do what they were intended to do. They help students pay for college expenses by reducing the net cost of attendance. This is an average, and there is considerable variation around the average. Selective private nonprofit schools have an estimated tax rate of 79%. Public universities, by contrast, impose a tax rate close to zero. Turner finds that for-profit schools have a tax rate of around 18%.

The low tax rate at for-profits may seem counterintuitive at first, but this is a measure of how strongly federal aid displaces internal grants the schools would otherwise have given. This sector does not use tuition discounting to craft the incoming class like their more selective nonprofit brethren, so there is little institutional aid to displace. Setting the list price at these schools is a profit maximization decision that fits the supply-and-demand model much more closely. For-profit schools do face some constraints on their selection of students. To keep their access to Title IV programs such as Pell Grants and federally backed student loans they need to ensure—like all institutions—that their three-year cohort default rates on student loans remain within federal limits. However, unlike public and independent colleges, they need to get at least 10% of their revenues from non–Title IV sources (i.e., money from students and their families, or from the GI Bill). But this only sets a bare-minimum-quality standard for students. For-profit schools do not carefully sculpt the incoming class of students to improve the learning environment for everyone, and they have no particular incentive to offer scholarships to attract needy or particularly talented students to the residential mix. A quick look at the "net-price calculators" for several for-profit institutions shows that most students pay a set price with no internal discount. The financial aid that is available to students at for-profit institutions is almost wholly made up of federal Pell Grants and loans.

There is strong evidence for a Bennett effect on list-price tuition at for-profit schools, so the effective tax rate assessed at for-profits is higher than

18%. Cellini and Goldin find that for-profit institutions whose students qualify for federal Title IV aid (Pell and SEOG) charge a 78% premium over for-profit institutions of similar quality whose students do not receive federal aid.[22] Lau confirms this finding about for-profit institutions, whose students use a surprisingly large fraction of federal aid.[23] In the 2008–09 academic year, students at for-profit schools made up only 11% of the total population of postsecondary students, but they received 24% of Pell allocations, 28% of unsubsidized Stafford loans, and a quarter of the subsidized Stafford loans. Lau estimates that for-profit schools absorbed as profit 57% of Pell Grants that their students received, and 51% of extra loan amounts, passing through the remainder to students. For-profit schools assess a modest *internal* tax rate because they put less institutional grant aid on the table. But they take their pound of flesh by raising list price in response to federal subsidization.

If the higher education market were perfectly competitive, the Bennett hypothesis would make no sense at all. We would expect new startups to drive tuition back down. But for-profits likely have local market power that could allow them to push up price in the event that the federal subsidy grows. The empirical work on the Bennett hypothesis (at nonprofits and for-profits alike) usually presumes that schools can exercise some form of market power.

This story of how policy affects access is complex. Slogans about the magic of the market are simplistic and do not offer a response to fundamental questions of affordability and access in an industry as complex as US higher education. As we have shown, the most market-responsive sector has benefited greatly from aid programs designed to open doors for financially constrained students. The spectacular growth in the size and reach of the for-profit sector is due in large part to the federal programs that have made postsecondary education, especially short-term certificate and two-year programs, more affordable to lower-income students and to older nontraditional students who seek a marketable credential. We will return to the story of older nontraditional students in the next chapter. The fact that the market-driven for-profit institutions seem particularly subject to the Bennett hypothesis is ironic, though predictable, but that is not evidence that the sector is guilty of high crimes and misdemeanors. The for-profit sector itself is a complex mix of high-quality programs and more questionable ones. There is mileage in thinking about ways to reduce high loan default rates and low completion rates at many for-profit institutions without condemning all for-profit institutions because there may be a positive linkage between federal aid and list-price tuition within this sector.

In our view, the most important questions we face are about program design and achieving targeted results. If the social goal of federal financial aid policy is to make higher education more affordable to many low-income families, there is ample evidence that it does so, despite the fact that some of this aid displaces grant aid the schools might otherwise have given. There is also good evidence that federal aid programs can help persistence (reduce drop-out rates).[24] Yet defects in the design of our aid programs are also well established. For instance, our aid programs are largely one size fits all. But the best program for an eighteen-year-old full-time degree-seeking student from a lower-income family may be quite different from the optimal program for a thirty-two-year-old who seeks a short-term certificate to boost his or her wage and who has to juggle family responsibilities in the process. Likewise, we have good evidence that the complexity and lack of transparency of the current aid system is a real barrier that limits the effectiveness of the Pell program. In a recent controlled experiment by Bettinger et al., high school seniors who received clear information about available aid, and real assistance in completing the Free Application for Federal Student Aid, were eight percentage points more likely to finish two years of college.[25] We do need to know how much of the higher education funding provided by the federal government reaches its target. Most studies conclude that financial aid improves access. The overall amount of the federal support that winds up diverted, or taxed away, by nonprofit colleges and universities seems quite low. And cash-starved public institutions pass virtually 100% of federal aid on to students in the form of a lower net price.

Government Aid for Research

Federal support for research is an important source of funds for many universities. These funds go to the faculty and other research scholars in salary support, to pay for new equipment, or to support graduate students. Some of the funds go to the university to pay for overhead. These overhead recoveries are a significant source of funding for major research universities. The grants that generate these monies are usually awarded on a competitive basis. Researchers have to write compelling proposals that are independently judged, and they have to show that previous grants have been productive.

Figure 7.6 shows how federal research grants to colleges and universities have evolved from 1974 to 2015. From the early 1970s through 1998, federal research funding grew steadily. The growth then accelerated into the early years of the twenty-first century, particularly in funding from the Department of Health and Human Services. This growth halted in 2005, except for a temporary surge that was part of the federal stimulus package

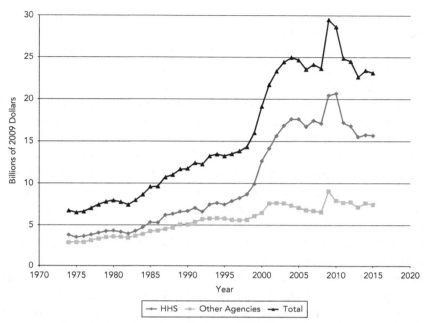

FIGURE 7.6 Federal basic and applied research obligations to colleges and universities, 1974–2015.

following the financial meltdown of 2008. The real value of federal spending on research and development at colleges and universities is lower today than it was a decade ago. If one draws a trend line through the earlier years, however, one could claim that federal research funding has returned to its longer trend. That is deceptive, since flat funding is seemingly the new norm. As the figure indicates, changes in funding have been dominated by the Department of Health and Human Services, which includes the National Institutes of Health. Medical research is the driving engine of the substantial rise in federal support for university research spending. The "other" category combines agriculture, defense, energy, homeland security, and a catchall category that includes the National Science Foundation. Perhaps surprisingly, the department of defense is not a major player in university research spending.

There are consequences of the slowdown of federal research grants to colleges and universities. First, the partnership between federal agencies and colleges and universities has been a critical part of US leadership in many STEM (science, technology, engineering, and mathematics) fields. To the extent that this funding stimulates basic research that complements product-specific research by firms, federal support generates positive spillovers that push up the rate of innovation. This innovation is a primary source of long-run growth in a mature economy. Our leading national universities also rely heavily on federal research grants to fund the training of the next generation of researchers in these fields.

Second, as the growth in federal funds slowed and reversed, industry funding has taken on a larger role in the research undertaken at many universities. This shift can alter the kind of research that takes place in university laboratories. Private firms are more interested in funding applied research and product development than they are in stimulating basic research that doesn't lead to specific patents or new products. As we just noted, basic research tends to have the greatest potential for social spillovers, and universities are uniquely positioned to do basic research. Basic breakthroughs are the meat of journal publications and faculty fame. There are also social risks of allowing too close a connection between faculty research and industry priorities.[26] Many businesses place conditions on the free dissemination of research findings that they sponsor. This creates a potential conflict between the donors' interests and one of the main objectives of the college or university, which is to follow the evidence wherever it may lead.

The Big Picture

We subtitled this chapter "public disinvestment." That was a bit of deliberate provocativeness. Hyperbole is rife in public discourse about the government role in financing higher education, and the disinvestment term is a good example of a buzzword. This chapter has provided some nuance. Through much of the twentieth century public investment was growing in all the ways we have outlined in this chapter. That changed in the 1980s and the landscape of public higher education support became more complex.

The notion that public support for higher education is withering away is not entirely accurate. The real value of federal funding of university research is indeed lower as of this writing (early 2016) than it was in 2004, but it is 3.5 times as high as it was in 1975. The federal government has not abandoned its support for basic research. Yet the abrupt decline after 2004 has caused severe problems for research universities that overinvested in laboratories and human resources during the period of rapid funding growth. This will force painful changes at many research universities, though it will leave the majority of America's undergraduate-oriented colleges largely unaffected. Faculty and staff funded through research grants at some research institutions may be cut, and many schools will be forced to aggressively seek other funding sources, often in the corporate sector. The social consequences of this change will play out over the next generation at research institutions that grew dependent on the federal gravy train.

Trends in direct financial support for students offer a mixed picture, but there is no evidence of federal or state disinvestment in this form of aid. The maximum Pell Grant and the average Pell Grant received have both gone up recently, as has the number of students receiving them. Likewise, the average direct state grant has risen in real value over the last thirty years. On the other hand, the real value of a Pell Grant is roughly the same today as it was when the program was founded in the 1970s, despite the rise in college cost. Federal grants cover a much smaller fraction of the average recipient's bill. As a result, colleges themselves have become a major source of income redistribution. In the post–New Deal world, this is an odd switch of roles between the government and the nonprofit sector.

The most consequential disinvestment is the substantial and long-term falloff in the real value of state appropriation per student in the vast majority of states. This is the fundamental reason that net tuition is growing more rapidly at state universities than at private nonprofit institutions. And it is a major threat to the quality, if not the survivability, of the institutions that serve the bulk of America's students. Equality of opportunity is not enhanced if the US higher education system continues to bifurcate into a well-funded set of selective private schools and a less selective and underfunded public sector that serves the most vulnerable groups in our society.

This discussion is moot if a technological storm sweeps the landscape clean of a substantial portion of America's traditional four-year colleges and universities. To that question we now turn.

Technological Threat

THE ONLINE REVOLUTION

WE HAVE IDENTIFIED a series of internal and environmental challenges that have had a significant and ongoing effect on how a college education is produced, on how it is financed, and on who goes. The trio of technological cost-push forces has not abated, so we would expect continued upward pressure on inflation-adjusted university spending per student.[1] At schools that can find extra revenues, the pressure will be met with some combination of higher price or higher subsidy. Schools whose revenues are more constrained will see a decline in the quality of traditional programming. We have seen how a falling state budget effort on behalf of higher education has already had a significant effect on the real price of public education and on the quality of programming, especially at nonselective schools that serve a large portion of the less privileged population enrolled in four-year programs. Changes in the distribution of income have increased the need of needier students, and this has contributed to rising discount rates that are part of accelerating list-price tuition. Rising inequality also has contributed to rising debt levels for student borrowers. And changes in demography will stress the system further as the proportion of students in college who come from an economically disadvantaged background continues to grow.

Now imagine a future of almost limitless potential for high-quality and individualized online learning. Improvements in artificial intelligence enable software platforms to adjust instruction to accurately match each student's learning style and learning speed. The software also learns each student's current strengths and weaknesses, adjusting assignments and problem solving individually for maximum comprehension gains. By knowing how to optimally trigger each student's capacity to master complex concepts, online learning becomes a joy and a game. By comparison, face-to-face coursework is a boring succession of thrice-a-week lecture hall note-taking sessions, or web surfing instead, as many professors complain. Imagine also that this online information transfer process can be produced and sold at a fraction of the cost of face-to-face coursework on a traditional campus. Students would no longer be forced into rigid semester-based classes, and they would no longer need to buy an expensive bundle of ancillary services they think they do not need.

In this new world the whole concept of time to degree becomes fluid and unmoored from the overly slow four-year progression of a 120-credit bachelor's degree. Furthermore, the accredited degree itself will become obsolete. We move instead into a labor market dominated by narrower knowledge proficiencies, each with its authenticated online credential or badge. The new world of "HP accredited integration specialist" and "Oracle certified expert" is already here. This process supposedly will continue, siphoning off a substantial fraction of the student population that now attends today's universities simply as a tradition. The signaling value of going to college is replaced by the actual value of learning something, and the unintelligible college transcript gives way to the individualized Internet résumé that offers employers clear proof of conceptual mastery.[2]

Questioning such a bright future must sound positively antiprogressive. To many it may seem downright churlish for two tenured professors to express skepticism about a future in which professors are largely displaced by technology, or they are repurposed as graders and answerers of email questions. But there are many ways that the rapid entrepreneurial development of digital learning can change how higher education is provided, and there are many ways that online education may work in the labor market of the future. The revolutionary displacement argument that sees the end of college is but one potential path, and it's one we do not think is particularly likely over any reasonable time horizon.

The Growth of Online Education

Over the last twenty years online educational options have changed the higher education marketplace in many ways. The number of students who have taken at least one online course nearly quintupled between 2002 and 2012, from around 1.6 million to over 7 million.[3] Put another way, over one third of the 22 million students who enrolled in some form of higher education in 2014–15 have taken at least one online class. In 2013, over 6% of the undergraduate students at public universities were enrolled in fully online programs.

The current pattern of online higher enrollment varies substantially across schools of differing types and levels of selectivity. Table 8.1 shows this variation by Carnegie Classification of schools.[4] Fully online coursework has extensively penetrated the for-profit sector, while it has barely scratched the nation's liberal arts colleges.

The growth in online college coursework has been bolstered from below in the K-12 system. Increasing numbers of high school students are familiar with the online learning environment, though the numbers remain lower than for college coursework. Some states require high school students to do some form of online work as a graduation requirement.[5] In part, this mandate is a response to the idea that both college and workplace training will increasingly utilize online methods. At present, thirty states have fully online high school programs, and 315,000 students are enrolled. "Virtual schools" in twenty-six states collectively served over 740,000 course enrollments in 2013–14.[6] These numbers are small compared to university enrollments, but they are growing. Some online high school options are elite, like Stanford's online high school.[7]

As the volume of online coursework has risen over the last fifteen years, some clear patterns have emerged about who attends what kind of institution. The students enrolled in fully online programs are very different from the student populations at campus-based four-year universities. To illustrate this we gathered data from three prominent online providers who also offer

Table 8.1 Prevalence of Online Offerings 2013

Carnegie Classification	All Online	Some Online	No Online
Community college	10%	18%	72%
Four-year public, nonresearch institutions	8%	17%	75%
Public research universities	4%	17%	80%
Private nonprofit research universities	2%	5%	93%
Private liberal arts colleges	0%	2%	98%
For-profit institutions	34%	6%	60%

Table 8.2 Characteristics of New Students, Online and On Campus

New Students 2013–14	Arizona State		Penn State		Southern New Hampshire University	
	Online	Campus	Online	Campus	Online	Campus
Percentage of first-time full-time students who are freshmen	2%	56%	1%	93%	27%	76%
Age twenty-two and under	15%	80%	14%	98%	15%	80%
Average age	31	21	31	19	32	22
Began with >75% of credits	16%	3%	27%	2%	12%	2%
Began with 50%–75% of credits	44%	24%	33%	6%	19%	5%

traditional on-campus programs. Table 8.2 gives the demographic characteristics for online and on-campus students for Arizona State, Penn State, and Southern New Hampshire University (SNHU).

Many nonprofit universities are developing online degree programs. Most of them are quite small at present. We chose Arizona State University (ASU), Southern New Hampshire University, and Penn State's "World Campus" because they are examples of schools that are further ahead in this process. These three institutions have grown large enough for a demographic profile of their online programs to have real meaning. Arizona State is a large public university whose main campus in Tempe, Arizona, serves roughly 40,000 undergraduates. ASU has over 10,000 students in its fully online undergraduate degree programs. Penn State's World Campus served 4,361 students in its BA programs in 2015. And in the 2016 *US News & World Report* rankings, Penn State's World Campus is the top-rated online program. The main Penn State campus in University Park, Pennsylvania, serves 40,500 undergraduates. Southern New Hampshire is a private university. SNHU's main campus serves only 3,000 students, while its online school enrolls roughly 36,000 students in BA and BS programs, and another 24,000 working on associate's degrees and graduate degrees.

The students who seek out an online education at these schools are quite different from the students who choose to go to the traditional campus. The likelihood that a first-time full-time freshman will choose an online program instead of a residential or local commuter program is very low. Likewise, the percentage of students in these large online programs who are in the traditional undergraduate age range (eighteen to twenty-two) is very low. As a result, students on a traditional campus are much younger on average than their online counterparts. As a large public university, Arizona State serves a lot of students who transfer from the state's community college system. Over a quarter of its campus-based students begin with at least half of the credits necessary to complete a four-year degree. But 60% of its online students come with at least sixty credits finished, and those students are mostly older than the students who transfer from the state's community colleges to the main campus. Likewise, the students who attend Penn State's campus-based programs are much younger than the students who sign up for Penn State's online World Campus. And the World Campus students tend to transfer in many more credits than their campus-based counterparts. Most of the students at these online programs are employed while in school. Despite the fact that Southern New Hampshire is private and much smaller than either Arizona State or Penn State and serves more first-time full-time freshman in its online program, the same patterns hold. The online students are older and are much more likely to have previous experience with college-level work than their on-campus counterparts.

Liberty University and the American Public University System (APUS) also offer large online undergraduate degree programs. Over 40,000 students are enrolled at Liberty, while APUS's BA program serves over 60,000 students. In many ways the profile of online students at these two institutions looks very much like the online programs in Table 8.2. The average student is over thirty, the number of first-time students who choose these programs is very low, and most students arrive with lots of credits already earned. Liberty and APUS enroll a very large number of active and retired members of the military, and this is their niche.

The students who attend highly selective public and private institutions are quite different from those who seek out online degrees. At the University of Virginia, for instance, only 3% of the undergraduate population is over twenty-five. This is what one would expect at a university where 97% of the first-year class returns for the second year, which graduates 87% of its students in four years, and which has a very small population of transfer students. At our own institution (William and Mary), the percentage of first-time full-time students who are freshmen is over 86%, and 97% are age twenty-two or younger. Only 3.5% of our first-time students arrive with half of the credits needed to graduate. At Williams College, the percentage of the undergraduate student body over the age of twenty-five is precisely zero.

A Stable Division

Digital platforms and techniques are indeed having a significant effect on the higher education industry. The quality of online coursework, and of the digital components of traditional face-to-face classes, has improved over time. We expect that the impact of online learning on how people obtain skills and credentials will continue to broaden and deepen. Yet the outline of a stable division of labor between the digital and the personal increasingly is visible. The rising wage gap between high school degree holders and those with more training has increased the demand for education among students both in the traditional age cohort and among the large group of older workers who could benefit from additional education. The online option offered at for-profit and nonprofit schools has expanded the set of choices for these returning and older students. To this point, however, it has not affected how the vast majority of students in the traditional college-going age range behave. Of course, this could all change as artificial intelligence continues to improve, but many features of the current educational landscape convince us that the growth in online programming complements the existing traditional campus more than substitutes for it.

For years, traditional nonprofit universities have reached out to older nontraditional students with evening classes, weekend sessions, and part-time pathways to a formal degree or certificate. But the model remained campus based and person to person. This is an extreme disadvantage to older and returning students who have to juggle a lot of life responsibilities to obtain a degree or a useful credential. These large disadvantages of physically going *to* a school at a specific time have created a sizable niche that the online world is readily filling. Global outreach offers yet another growth area for online programming. Traditional institutions and profit-making corporations alike could respond to this demand. At present, however, this opportunity is largely untapped. At Penn State's top-ranked online World Campus, for instance, only 1.1% of the degree-seeking students are international. By contrast, 9.8% of the residential students at Penn State are international.

The bulk of first-time full-time students likely will continue to seek out a campus experience for the advantages that a campus-based education offers, while a substantial fraction of returning and nontraditional students will be pulled toward online options. The rationale for this stable division lies in the nature of online coursework, in the different needs of the two groups, and in the particular advantages the traditional campus bundle retains. We will address the first two in the remainder of this chapter, reserving the (un)bundling question to the next.

Market Niche of Online Courses and Degrees

Fully online coursework tends to work better with students who are older and more mature. One line of evidence for this proposition comes from the growing experience of massively open online courses (MOOCs). This type of course offered the true hope of very low-cost online learning. Labor is the primary variable cost in education. If the amount of human interaction in online work can be kept quite low, the marginal cost of adding additional students is essentially zero. Sebastian Thrun's very first Stanford artificial intelligence class offered online revealed the problem. To Thrun's astonishment, 180,000 people signed up to participate in his class. Every age range and continent was represented. But most of the students who signed up did not finish, and even fewer learned the material well enough to receive a minimally passing grade. This early MOOC was not asynchronous like most of today's online versions. You had to watch the lectures in real time. While that is a disadvantage in many settings, it does force concentration in the moment, just like a standard lecture. Nonetheless, the dropout rate was high. The low completion rate contains important information about how best to utilize online education. When students are anonymous they can leave at the first struggle or frustration. And the ones who succeed well in this environment tend to be those who are mature and motivated.

The completion problem also plagued the initial collaboration between Udacity, the corporation Thrun founded to commercialize online education, and San Jose State University. Udacity helped to develop a set of remedial courses like college algebra and basic introductory courses like introductory statistics, computer programming, and psychology. These courses are well matched with the strengths of online provision. The class material is mostly static—learning how to do a "*t* test" in statistics is not going to change next month, or next year, or next decade—and the courses are primarily about straightforward information transfer. Successful learning means the student can calculate the correct answer or remember the correct name or argument in a multiple-choice format. Yet pass rates in these classes were abysmal. The highest pass rate in any of the online courses was 51%. This was much lower than the success rate in similar face-to-face classes at San Jose State, classes that also enrolled significant numbers of at-risk young students. Thrun has claimed that San Jose State's students were not a good fit for this new medium. "These were students from difficult neighborhoods, without good access to computers, and with all kinds of challenges in their lives."[8] Yet San Jose State is today what much more of the American higher education system will look like in twenty years. It is ethnically diverse. It serves a student population that lacks the technology-saturated and -enriched background of the average Stanford or Berkeley student who studies a few miles to the north. And lastly, like many of the nation's minimally selective public institutions, it is underfunded, with all the consequences that go along with resource poverty.

This completion problem was not restricted to Udacity's set of MOOCs. A 2013 study by researchers at the University of Pennsylvania examined a million users in seventeen MOOCs offered by Penn using the Coursera online platform.[9] Persistence rates capture the percentage of students who are still accessing course material in the last week of the class. Persistence ranged from a high of 14% to a low of 2%. Courses with high persistence tended to be short (six weeks) and directly occupational (mostly health sciences). In the two college-oriented classes (calculus and microeconomics) only 1% to 2% of registrants achieved a grade of 80% or better. Both of these classes were longer (nine to thirteen weeks), used more videos per week, utilized regular problem sets, and had a final exam. Another study of twenty-four Coursera courses offered through Penn's Open Learning Initiative surveyed users directly.[10] The authors found that students who persisted in these MOOCs were more educated than the general population. Almost 80% of the respondents held a bachelor's degree or more. This is a big problem for any MOOC platform in dealing with the young and less mature undergraduate population that currently attends traditional institutions. The Coursera MOOC population was also more likely to be male and employed than the typical group of undergraduates. These older Coursera users tended to take social science– and health-related classes for job advancement, and humanities for curiosity.

In the spring of 2013, Abhijit Banerjee and Esther Duflo taught a MOOC titled "The Challenges of Global Poverty" on MIT's EdX platform. They analyzed their experience the following year in the *American Economic Review: Papers and Proceedings*.[11] For an economics class, their global poverty course is relatively nontechnical, and this likely boosts interest and enrollment. Over 42,000 students officially registered. The students were very diverse internationally, and 82% held bachelor's degrees already. Despite that enriched background, the retention rate in their class was 14% of registrants. Banerjee and Duflo found an imaginative way to understand one aspect of the problems of completion and performance seemingly inherent in the MOOC format. Although there is a formal deadline for signing up, in practice the deadline isn't enforced. Twenty-seven percent of registrants signed up after the deadline. The striking result they uncovered is that students who registered one day late were over sixteen percentage points less likely to score well enough to get a certificate than students who signed up on the day of the deadline. Enrolling a few days late had no effect on a student's ability to complete the course material, and their evidence suggests that late enrollees had the same academic potential as students who signed up within the deadline. They believe instead that the drop-off in performance of those who were late in signing up reflects a different "type" of student, one who is more disorganized and less capable of committing to complete work on time. These are problems that are also prevalent in younger, less mature students.

The MOOC completion problem is well understood and MOOC purveyors like Coursera are very good at sending helpful email reminders to students. They sound like this: "DAVID FELDMAN, you have already completed 65% of Introduction to Philosophy. With only 35% left, keep going." We are happy to report that David has indeed completed the Coursera philosophy class and found it quite enjoyable. The philosophy faculty at the University of Edinburgh have produced a fun set of short videos that introduce students to important questions, and David can now talk about "brains in a vat," Gettier problems, and constructive empiricism. But with a total of five hours of video presentations, no required readings, no writing, and a set of sixty-eight multiple-choice questions as the total evaluation, this is a dilettante's pastime, not an education.

Udacity has seen the same evidence about completion and motivation, hence its pivot to a more vocational focus for the company's online products. Gone is the earlier and bolder Thrun who claimed, "In 50 years there will be only ten institutions in the world delivering higher education and Udacity has a shot at being one of them."[12] Older students who see a direct value in receiving specific forms of training are more likely to set aside the time to work methodically through to completion without the personal interaction or "hand holding" of labor-intensive face-to-face programs. Existing online techniques work best at conveying specific chunks of information and easily measured skills to older, more mature learners who know exactly what they want and why they need it.

The completion issue remains a problem for online BA programs that are "academic" in focus as opposed to vocational. And this is one reason the demographic profiles of students in online BA programs remain quite different from the typical eighteen- to twenty-two-year-old age range of most traditional campuses. This points to a stable division between programs that primarily offer skill acquisition or other forms of "training" and institutions whose mission is about broader education, lifelong learning, and the development of critical reasoning skills in young adults who are still unsure of their goals and whose personalities are not yet fully formed.

Cost and Quality

The great hope for a technological transformation of higher education ultimately rests on issues of cost and quality. The cost of producing and selling online coursework may come down dramatically in the future, but current market prices for online coursework do not give these programs distinct financial advantages over easily accessible traditional programs at most state universities. And this is true despite the cutbacks in state support that have led to rates of tuition growth at public institutions far in excess of tuition growth at private colleges and universities.

Table 8.3 shows a comparison of tuition for online programs versus on-campus equivalents for the same schools as in Table 8.2. We have also added the tuition costs for the online APUS program that serves mostly active military and veterans, and we give the average list-price tuition at public four-year institutions nationwide. Prices at online programs are usually expressed per credit hour, while tuition at traditional universities is given

Table 8.3 Tuition for Online and On-Campus Programs

Institution	List-Price Tuition on Campus	Online Price Per Credit Hour	Annualized: Thirty Credits Per Year
Arizona State	$10,428	$490–$550	$14,700–$16,500
Penn State University	$17,514	$535	$16,050
Southern New Hampshire University	$30,006	$320	$9,600
American Public University System (military)		$270	$8,100
Average public four-year	$9,139		

for "full time" participation. A student is usually charged the same price, for instance, if they take 12 credits or 16. To graduate in four years, however, 120 credits is the usual standard. This amounts to 15 credits per semester or 30 per year. Our price comparison is for a year of school on campus versus 30 online credits.

Existing online programming is not cheap. A thirty-credit year at an accredited public university's online program often costs a student as much or more than the list-price tuition of the same school's traditional campus. For Southern New Hampshire, which is private, the full list price is substantially higher than the online price. But like most private institutions, good students from median-income families receive substantial discounts. Using the net-price calculator at SNHU, the net tuition could easily be half of the list-price tuition, or less. This is still larger than the online price, but the gap between the online price and the list price is deceptive. Even at APUS, which serves thousands of current and former members of the US military, and which is the least expensive online program in the table, the cost of thirty credit hours is roughly comparable to the national average list-price tuition of taking a year of classes at a public university as an in-state student. For the full residential experience there are added costs of room and board, but these are costs of living, not of schooling. The most important reasons students study online are the ones that predispose the typical online student to be older. These students often are fully employed and have many other responsibilities that preclude the full-time cloistered experience of studying in a residential environment with peers who are part of the educational process.

Online degree programs are expensive because the MO part of MOOC is gone. The courses are online, but at most accredited institutions they are neither massive nor open. In fact, many online programs advertise the limited number of students in a class and the amount of human interactivity available to the online participants. This shows how much the quality of the program (perceived or real) remains tied to human contact, interactivity in real time, and exclusivity. At Arizona State the online program employs 260 full-time professors, 53 part time professors, and a full-time technical development staff of 395. The average class size is forty-six. Twelve percent of the classes have fewer than twenty students. Penn State's World Campus employs a whopping 315 full-time instructional faculty and 285 part-time professors. As a result, their average class size is twenty-seven and 17% of the classes are smaller than twenty. Only 15% percent of their classes exceed fifty students. For comparison, at Penn State's residential campus it's also the case that only 15% of the classes exceed fifty students.

One can easily imagine a future in which richly interactive online "adaptive learning" tailors coursework to each student's needs. But the current development cost of sophisticated digital courseware is eye popping. Carnegie Mellon's highly regarded Open Learning Initiative (OLI) courses are not yet fully adaptive and the estimates of their development costs are in the $1 million range. The future may see these costs fall, but the future also will likely see the demand for additional features and quality grow as well.[13] And purely online education will have to compete with face-to-face instruction that is rapidly assimilating the best of digital programming into the structure of traditional instruction. In fact, much of the experimentation and innovation is taking place within the ivied halls of traditional nonprofit colleges and universities.

This experimentation has produced a raft of hybrid or blended courses that combine labor-intensive interaction and evaluation with the current state of the art in digital components. As a result, traditional classes are now sometimes "flipped," with students watching lectures asynchronously, completing online modules to learn basic material and problem solving, and then going to class to work intensively on the details and extensions of the subject matter. In theory, putting the more passive mechanical and memory learning online increases the portion of the class that is devoted to active learning. This approach may work best in STEM (science, technology, engineering, and mathematics) fields and in some social sciences, since problem solving is crucial to mastering those disciplines. In other disciplines, and this may include many of the humanities, the traditional lecture may retain some significant advantages. The synchronous fifty- to eighty-minute lecture may force digital-addicted students to focus in the moment to grasp and summarize a carefully crafted extended argument. Yet even in these disciplines, online course components will allow teachers to enrich the value of the educational package.

Online coursework can be good, and in some cases distance learning may shave off some fraction of the cost. The evidence about quality and cost, however, is mixed at best. Beginning with quality, current evidence from primary and secondary schools is not at all encouraging. A recent study from Stanford's Center for Research on Education Outcomes (CREDO) evaluated reading and math performance of students at online charter schools in seventeen states and the District of Columbia relative to a set of demographically and academically identical "twin" students who attend traditional brick-and-mortar schools.[14] Online education offers great potential for many atypical students since learning is potentially asynchronous. The student can access course material at will, in small chunks, and with easy repetition. And the social distractions of a typical school are removed. The results for typical students in these programs, however, were not good. On average, students in online programs experienced significantly lessened academic growth in both reading and mathematics relative to what their in-school peers achieved. The results were even worse for students from an economically disadvantaged background and for students whose native language is not English. Lastly, synchronous tools like audio conferencing significantly boosted math and reading performance, while digital contact in online chat rooms had a negative impact on math. This strongly supports the idea that effective online learning works poorly with younger learners who are not well organized or motivated, and the deficiencies of online work are mitigated somewhat by expensive labor-intensive interventions that mimic face-to-face instruction.

At the college level many studies have found that students in purely online classes do worse than their peers in traditional face-to-face classes. But most of this evidence comes from nonexperimental comparisons that don't adequately control for the bias that comes from students or teachers who self-select into various types of schooling. If the population of students who take online classes is less talented or motivated, for instance, outcomes from online courses will naturally appear worse. On the other hand, if the instructors who choose to pilot online courses are selected from among the most digitally savvy and most enthusiastic about online education, the results would overestimate the potential efficacy of spreading online courses more widely. Gold-standard studies that randomly sort students into treated and untreated groups are few and far between. Three of these randomized controlled studies illustrate the real possibilities of online coursework while also showing why online education isn't a panacea of superlative outcomes at low cost. Many more studies are underway, so the evidence will continue to accumulate.

Figlio, Rush, and Yin randomly sorted students into two versions of a single introductory class in microeconomics.[15] In one the lectures were live and in the other the lectures were only available online. The students who were sorted into the live lectures did not have access to the video lectures for later review. The students who had the lectures made available on the course website were not allowed to attend the actual lectures. The class was a very large introductory course taught by one instructor to groups of 1,900 to 2,600 students per semester. All of the exams in the class used multiple-choice questions and were machine graded. The experiment used 327 student volunteers from the broader class, 112 of whom were randomly assigned to the live lectures and the other 215 were assigned the online version. All of the class materials and exams were identical for both groups. Students in the online-only group scored roughly two percentage points lower than students in the live group, despite having access to the recorded lectures twenty-four/seven. Studies of this sort cannot identify causally why live lectures might retain some advantages, though "focus in the moment" is a possible reason. The gap in favor of live was larger for Hispanic students, for males, and for lower-achieving students.

In a slightly different test, Joyce et al. randomly assigned 725 students to one of two different types of hybrid introductory microeconomics class at Baruch College of the City University of New York.[16] This is a large and ethnically diverse public university. The classes were hybrid because both types used live lectures and had a full set of online tools available to students. Those tools include lecture slides, online study materials, and videos prepared by the professors. Lecture time was the sole difference between the two types of class. One had a single 75-minute live lecture per week, while the other had two 75-minute lectures per week. Highly regarded tenured professors taught both types of class, and all classes used the same text. The authors understood that frequent assessment and immediate feedback improve performance, so they mandated weekly online quizzes using software from Aplia to deliver and grade them. In this structured format within a traditional university, student retention was not a problem as it is in MOOCs. Students in the two-lectures-per-week format scored 2.5 percentage points higher than students who received only one live lecture per week. Unlike the study by Figlio, Rush, and Yin, in the study by Joyce et al. they do not find that less talented students do worse in the one-lecture format. On the other hand, they do find that working students do worse, perhaps because the reduced lecture attendance means less time spent working on the class.

In perhaps the best outcome for hybrid "blended" learning, former Princeton president William Bowen and three coauthors tested new "interactive learning online" software on 605 students in statistics courses at six public universities. The statistics class was developed as part of Carnegie Mellon's OLI. The software uses machine-guided learning to replace some of the face-to-face instruction common in traditional classes. The OLI classes did have one live lecture per week as a supplement. The control classes were traditional face-to-face classes. The students in the OLI sections performed statistically the same as the students who received a more standard treatment.[17] The study, however, could not fully control for all differences across campuses. The teachers were not the same, and the exam questions were not all the same. Since teachers were aware that they were part of an experiment, that also could have affected grading.

These three studies share important features. They use courses that are introductory and built around elementary tools of analysis. In addition, evaluating student performance in these classes is objective. Problems have correct answers. All three studies looked at hybrid courses that blended classroom instruction with digital components.[18] They compared classes that offered a bit more face-to-face instruction time with classes that offered a bit less. They do not compare online with offline, and the digital components of each case study are different. The studies also examine courses that are all taught inside traditional universities. This is arguably the best-case scenario for online components to perform well. And the online componentry gains much of its power by being embedded in a rich human support network.

Because blended learning can work well in some circumstances does not tell us that online education will work as well as traditional instruction in all or even most situations. Teaching effectiveness across a complex curriculum can't easily be reduced to a simple comparison of which format achieves a higher score on multiple-choice tests of fact recall and calculations. We should be wary of generalizations and grand forecasts about how new technologies will transform the quality or the cost of education. The hype about educational television in its early years reads very much like the initial enthusiasm for disruptive digitalization.[19] Yet the technology is new. Intense experimentation is ongoing, and much of it is taking place inside traditional universities. We should expect gains as we learn more about what kind of online components add value and which kinds of human interactions (if any) can be replaced. And we will also learn more about the cost effectiveness of moving away from the well-worn technology of "chalk and talk."

The barriers to making fully online classes pay for themselves are higher than many people presume. To overcome the disadvantages for many students of an online format, you have to build in a lot of support services, and this erodes cost advantages that flow from reducing one form of labor—the professor in front of the class multiple times per week. The scale advantage of recording lectures for large numbers of students to view goes only so far if you need a substantial support staff to provide the personal connection to students that they want or need. This is one reason that online degree programs likely will continue to appeal mostly to older students. For them the convenience benefit is large, so they are willing to pay the significant cost for existing online programming so they can continue with their work life and family responsibilities.

Updating an online class, though possible, is expensive. A professor in a traditional class can add new material to the syllabus at will. She can change the day's lecture to reflect a new research result she read the night before, and she can integrate current events into the structure of the class with ease. This new information can also appear in the class's digital repository of information. In the three studies of blended courses that we presented, the subject material is mostly (microeconomics) or completely (statistics) unchanging over time. For the finances of digital learning to make sense, this static nature of the material is important. If a substantial investment is sunk in an online course, changing the course is very problematic. Evaluating the potential financial savings from going hybrid is as complicated as trying to measure the quality effects. Figlio, Rush, and Yin conclude that replacing lectures could only make financial sense (ignoring the educational consequences) at schools with very low faculty teaching loads and in fields with very high faculty salaries.

Is the cup half empty or half full? The experience with MOOCs points to real problems that need to be overcome if truly low-cost, purely online education is to make real inroads into the traditional university's market among young first-time students. In hindsight the disruptive initial hope of low-cost asynchronous learning looks more like hype. On the other hand, there is a sizable and growing market among nontraditional students and international students for fully online coursework and training. Yet there are important technological, practical, and legal issues to be worked out. Who owns the intellectual property inside online courses or course components, the professor whose lectures are at their core or the university or company that produces and markets them? Who can make changes to the courses? The answer to questions of this sort will affect how courses can be customized for different users. These issues will take time to resolve. And how will faculty and students alike view the changed relationship between students and teachers? That issue may affect which kinds of online components schools will adopt and the amount of cost saving, if any, that can be passed on.[20] Bending the cost curve may be possible. Revolutionizing the delivery of higher education is more speculative.

The Future of Online Higher Education

Our portrait of the current state of online higher education is a picture of what economists call segmented markets. We have identified a stable division between the online and on-campus worlds. Online programs appeal to older students who have complicated lives and fractured educational experiences. They have jobs that take up large blocks of time, and/or they have families that are similarly time consuming. For them, making the time commitment that on-campus enrollment entails is simply impractical. In many cases these students have tried the traditional education model and for some reason were not able to complete a degree. As a result these students can transfer a considerable number of credits to an online provider who offers courses that fit into their busy lives. The online option represents a second chance, and this is one of the great virtues of the American system. Also, these older students come back to higher education with more self-control and more motivation. As more mature adults, they are able to succeed where they had previously failed.

Students who move directly from high school to college are much younger emotionally and chronologically. Often they are living away from home for the first time. They are still growing up and discovering themselves as individuals. The most common academic major of first- and second-year college students is "undecided." Many of these students were very successful in high school, and they adapt quickly to the rigors of college work and the pressures of college life. Others struggle academically and socially. With 20/20 hindsight, many of these young people might have benefitted from delaying their move into the hothouse environment of a typical university campus. Without the formal national service that many other nations require, American colleges and universities have evolved over the years to serve this younger population. Counseling centers, academic advising centers, and career centers on campuses have been developed to help students cope with the many transitions they are experiencing. This is a topic we will explore more thoroughly in the next chapter on the enduring bundle of services the American university offers. In addition, there are advantages of collecting students of similar ages together on a campus. Much of the learning and maturation that takes place on a college campus comes from living and learning together with peers.

The online and on-campus markets are segmented largely because they serve very different clienteles. We do not discount the possibility that the future might be quite different. Online courses could become dramatically better and substantially cheaper. But we don't see much evidence that the basis for segmentation is eroding. Improvements in online education may prove cost neutral or cost increasing, and there is a distinct risk that adopting an online curriculum may contribute to the further bifurcation of American education into quality tiers. Improvements in online coursework may help reach seventeen-year-olds where they are, though current evidence is not encouraging. But the basic nature of the late teen years will remain a constraint on educators, and purely online work is not a lock to become best practice. If anything, the digital revolution may reinforce many of the benefits of face-to-face encounters in the lecture hall, the professor's office, seminars and research labs, and dorm room chats.

PART THREE

Summary and Policy

9

The Enduring Bundle

A RECENT DOONESBURY cartoon shows the president of Walden University reciting the list of amenities and educational opportunities his school makes available as a variety of package plans.[1] Students can choose options like the stripped-down "supersaver plan," featuring "limited access to online offerings" and "off-peak gym privileges," or the "platinum plan" with live lectures and valet parking. The pinnacle is the "all-access pass" to everything from the student spa to the science center's particle accelerator. In the last panel the scene shifts to two graduating seniors in the audience. One of them says to his classmate, "Wait. We had a particle accelerator?" The classmate responds, "I unbundled it—never used it." This bit of sarcasm envisions a world that many people might find appealing. A traditional college offers a bundle of services for a fixed price. Few students avail themselves of all parts of the bundle. Wouldn't it be sensible for students to pick the parts of the bundle they plan to use and forego the parts of the bundle they do not think they need? This is not too far removed from the technological optimist's vision of the unbundled future that we laid out in the last chapter. In that world, courses would be offered online, and students could pick and choose the courses and programs they wanted from the provider they favored. All of the other services offered by colleges and universities could be purchased individually on the open market.

As we argued in chapter 3, the set of services currently on offer at most American colleges and universities did not spring forth fully formed in the fall of 1955. It arose over a long period of evolution and experimentation at schools of all types and sizes, and the growth and development of each part of the bundle can be tied to certain historical processes buffeting the United States along the way. The bundle is not an immutable all-or-nothing package. We have certainly seen that items can be added to the menu. The research part of the primary bundle grew and developed from the late nineteenth century as the German research university was grafted onto the rootstock of the exist-ing American liberal arts college. Many of the ancillary services that make up the secondary components of the bundle—things like counseling, career serv-ices, and academic resource centers—grew and blossomed after the explosive growth in higher education following World War II. Parts of the bundle can also be reduced, sliced off completely, or priced differently. The history of ath-letics, which we classify as tertiary, offers examples of explosive growth and occasional reversal. The University of Chicago, for instance, was a Big Ten powerhouse in the early twentieth century. Yet the school consciously decided to abandon big-time football in 1939, motivated in part to focus more on rig-orous academic pursuits as the cost of athletic success began to rise. Chicago isn't alone in abandoning football and other sports, yet we have seen schools add big-ticket sports at roughly the same time as others close them down. We need to assess what parts of the existing bundle are most likely to persist in our world of internal, environmental, and technological threats. And we need to evaluate how changes to the bundle might ripple through the wide diversity of institution types that make up the higher education landscape.

We'll give our bottom line first. The bundle offers the greatest value to the traditional-aged college-going population. As a result, the basic shape of the bundle is unlikely to change precipitously. Technological changes that allow students to unplug completely from traditional institutions' curricula and accreditation structures may shave off a percentage of that age cohort, but that fraction likely will be small. Among those of the traditional college-going age, students who migrate to a completely or substantially online environment and abandon campus life are likely to be one of two types. The first are intellectu-ally more mature students who are surer of their plans. These young people are less likely to need the guidance and the organizational structure available on a traditional campus. This group also is likely to be quite a bit wealthier than average. Students who seek out the highly selective Minerva Project rep-resent that group, as do the talented and motived students who take up one of Peter Thiel's $100,000 awards to leave college or not to attend at all.

The other group of traditional-age students who may migrate into a more unbundled environment may be pushed to do so rather than pulled. This group is financially more insecure and academically more vulnerable. The institutions they attend are mostly public and less selective. These students currently attend institutions that are most under pressure from resource insufficiency. Online programming and competency-based credentialing do have the potential to bend the cost curve, and the attractiveness of these alternatives is highest for students and institutions alike whose financial con-straints are the tightest. But current evidence suggests that this approach may trade off a lower price for lower quality and a diminished likelihood of successful graduation or credentialing.

For the most part, we believe these vulnerable students will remain within the traditional higher education sector. Some will trade down from four-year to two-year programs, and this shift may have social and personal consequences. The evidence strongly suggests that students who have the capacity to begin in a four-year program are less likely to graduate if they start in a two-year program. Others will stay at four-year institutions. All will participate in a national experiment as these universities explore ways to do more with less, or less with less. Many resource-poor institutions already are well down the path of replacing full-time faculty with adjuncts. Schools will examine the rest of the bundle, looking for less expensive alternatives that could limit student access to mentors and support networks.

The students most likely to face this tradeoff are precisely the group for whom that tradeoff is the most risky. For them, most of the items in the bundle retain great value. These are the students who most need a nurturing environment rich in face-to-face instruction and mentorship opportunities. This is the group that can benefit most from the ability to change academic or career interests three times without having to start the higher education process over. These are also the students who most need the ancillary counseling, advising, and remediation services of a modern college or university. For them, this is not a hopeful vision of the future. Our policy recommendations are focused around this possible trajectory for an important component of the nation's higher education system.

It's time to revisit the bundle of services we first discussed in chapter 3. What explains its staying power when many students clearly don't use all of its elements? Why do we think that the wholesale unbundling of the traditional college experience is unlikely?

The Option Value of the Academic Bundle

In chapter 3 we assigned the bundle's usual components to three broad categories. In addition to instruction, which is the primary activity of a college or university, all students in traditional institutions use a substantial portion of the bundle that is provided. Things like advising, information technology services, and the library are ubiquitous and unavoidable. Other services, like counseling, team sports, mentored research, and the panoply of group and cultural activities of a modern campus, are used quite intensively by some students but are largely avoided by others. Yet every student has the option to use every service, and as they enter the ivy-covered quads most students don't know which set of services will prove useless and which might prove transformative. Many items in the bundle could be worthless, or priceless.

If you have ever bought a put or a call, you know about options markets. If you haven't, don't worry. The concept is quite simple. If today's price of Apple stock is $100, I can plunk down $100,000 to buy 1,000 shares. That's a lot of money tied up in one asset, and therefore lots of risk. Alternatively, if I think Apple stock will rise to $120 fairly soon, I can buy an "option" today that allows me to purchase Apple stock at $105 at any time in the next three months. This "call" contract will cost me only a few dollars per share, so the total amount of money I have to commit is relatively small. If I'm right, and Apple zooms to $110 or higher, my "call" becomes quite valuable. I've only risked a few thousand, but I can make ten or twenty times that amount in fairly short order. What's the risk? Apple stock could go in the other direction. In the end, however, I don't have to exercise the "call." I could simply write off the small amount of money I paid for the option. But that's small potatoes in comparison to risking $100,000 to buy Apple stock directly.

Reasonable people are now scratching their heads wondering what this has to do with the decision to attend a traditional four-year college or university, or with how this option idea might be related to the technological forces that many are forecasting will soon sweep away the traditional college experience. The simple answer is that it's a rare eighteen-year-old who has enough self-awareness and worldliness to build a complete intellectual path to his or her future.

In addition to providing classroom instruction, the traditional college offers a set of experiences and opportunities that are built on the premise that they just might alter a life trajectory. Outside of the formal classroom, students can meet one on one with a professor to iron out concepts and to make midcourse corrections in how to learn. They can work with teaching assistants and peer mentors. At the higher academic end, some students work independently with a faculty mentor. Some work collaboratively on research, which gives students specific skills and experience, and which sometimes leads to published output. Some students avail themselves of these opportunities daily, while others rarely take advantage. But for all, the option value exists. Ex post, it's worth more to the ones who use it, but ex ante it is valuable to all. But this set of options does have a price tag, and it remains an open question whether or not the bulk of the college-age population will continue to see the value in buying the traditional bundle with its option component.

In chapter 8 we gave clear evidence that older students are much more likely to seek out online options than traditional-aged students. We argued that family and work responsibilities likely played a role in this preference.

In other words, it's more costly for older students to choose the traditional on-campus learning option. But it's also likely that the option value of the traditional college bundle is far lower for older students. Their personalities are more fully formed and they are surer about their needs. On average they're likely to want a sparer group of services from any educational provider. For most of these older students, they just need specific courses or skills. They can dispense with the remainder of the services.

In this chapter we will examine in depth three particular items in the bundle, counseling, independent research, and intercollegiate athletics. Counseling is a student service that we have grouped in the secondary component of the bundle. Mentored research is in the primary category. Both are examples of a college activity that can change lives or save them, and many students who use these services did not forecast that they would walk that path when they arrived on campus. Intercollegiate athletics is in what we classified as the tertiary part of the bundle. For those who participate on teams, intercollegiate athletics will be a very important part of their experience. Competitive team sports also contribute to college life more broadly, and for many students in the stands this is a real benefit. Yet many students know from day one that that they will never be on a team and they have no interest in that aspect of college life. For them, "Rah" is unimportant. A college or university is still a bundle of related services even without intercollegiate athletics, as most European universities demonstrate. This is why we placed it in the tertiary part of the bundle.

Psychological Counseling and Mental Health

In techno-optimistic visions of the future, stripped-down and targeted information acquisition will displace the bundle of services students now receive at "full service" colleges and universities. We will focus on counseling as one particular ancillary service that is often considered disposable. Psychological services, after all, are available in the private sector. Does it follow that university counseling centers and other mental health services are wasteful extras that will disappear when cloud education allows students to individualize their education at extremely low cost? Claims about waste in the provision of ancillary services usually flow from one of two presumptions. The first is that the administrative machine that produces college services follows the bureaucratic imperative. Once two professionals cluster together in an office, they will find a way to persuade the university's leadership that they need to add a third position to do the job well. This is the idea that Robert Zemsky, William Wenger, and William Massy have called the administrative lattice, and it's a standard part of the argument that American higher education's cost problem reflects bureaucratic mission creep and administrative bloat.[2]

The second presumption is more normative and provocative. The cost engine is stoked because universities coddle students by providing unnecessary services based on the preferences and the pathologies of wealth. Like many aspects of American life, some components of the college bundle have been drawn into the left–right political battle. Worse, they have become exhibits of the culture wars. College counseling services offer up a fitting example. On the op-ed pages of major news outlets we hear that "students' needs are anticipated by a small army of service professionals—mental health counselors, student-life deans and the like. This new bureaucracy may be exacerbating students' 'self-infantilization.'"[3]

Claims of waste largely sidestep the historical narrative about the growth and development of counseling programs and other ancillary services. And they are hard to maintain in the face of real evidence about cost and effectiveness. The professional staff at most colleges and universities has indeed expanded, along with the range and quality of the services provided. The cost of counseling has gone up no more rapidly than the average of all service prices in the US economy. The demand for mental health services is demonstrably rising among the age groups most represented in college. In other words, it's not an artificial demand created within colleges. And the pricing model generally used to provide counseling is a perfectly sensible way of targeting insurance on a broad population. It spreads risk in ways that lower the cost and it achieves a product that is generally unavailable in the private market.

American colleges and universities have offered psychological counseling for much of the postwar period. With millions of World War II veterans using the GI Bill to move into higher education, President Truman's Commission on Higher Education recommended that colleges and universities "make growth in emotional and social adjustment one of its major aims."[4] Lessons learned about the long-term effects of stress on the battlefield informed the development of mental health services on campus. These focused services grew out of a hodgepodge of what were called "mental hygiene" programs that evolved in the early twentieth century to help "with educational, vocational, financial, moral, and personality problems that interfered with students' academic progress."[5] From the start, colleges understood that psychological and academic needs were intertwined.

The role of mental health and counseling programs has expanded on campuses over time. Counseling centers now offer a wide range of mental health services using professional staff trained in the developmental issues and clinical concerns common to college students.[6] The staff at a university counseling center is capable of handling crisis situations requiring immediate intervention and stabilization, as well as dealing with temporary stress-related problems and ongoing needs if they can be met with college resources.[7] Counseling centers also serve the college community as a whole. This would include group therapy (in response to grief, for example), as well as consultation to friends, faculty, and parents/guardians concerned about a student in distress.

We will highlight two rationales for why counseling services fit comfortably in the bundle. First, the needs of a student population are at the intersection of mental health and academic support. The lens of a university perspective leads to different modes of assessment and treatment. As a result, either many of the programs schools provide are not available in the community or the campus-based organizations are more effective at treating the combined academic and psychological issues that students are likely to face. College counseling centers are built to support both mental health and academic success, so the staff have specialized skills that are not usually present in private counseling. In part, this reflects the community mental health model in higher education, which puts a major focus on the need for preventative programming. In addition, some of what counseling centers offer to the campus community is a public good.[8] Like most public goods there are no private suppliers. Despite the value of the service to many people, there is no way for private producers to capture a profit from it. Public provision by the college spreads the cost and makes the service generally available.

Second, a service like counseling in a university environment is an insurance policy with an option value. Some students know they will need help from the counseling center, and for them the benefit is both high and certain. But many others who never contemplated a need for counseling when they arrived on campus wind up using the services during their time as a student. Some students discover that they need one-time or episodic help with time management and with controlling stress—around exam time, for instance. Others experience acute crises or need help dealing with serious emotional issues at the nexus of family, relationships, and a more demanding academic environment than they had experienced in the past.

The insurance parallel is reinforced by how these services are funded. Most institutions cover a substantial portion of the costs of running broad programs like psychological services out of general school revenues instead of charging a full fee for specific services. At some universities counseling is an "auxiliary enterprise" that must be financially separate from the rest of the university and funded entirely from a mandatory fee that covers all costs of operation. The auxiliary enterprise model is common at state institutions, and it's the model at William and Mary where we teach. In either model the service is broadly available both to students who use it and to those who never cross the doorstep of the counseling office. This system works because the funding system is essentially a mandate for all students to buy the service. No one is allowed to opt out. Because everyone pays, the cost per person is quite low.

Insurance markets can fail if only the riskiest people want the insurance. This well-known issue is called adverse selection. To use a health insurance example, if those who think they won't get sick opt out of getting health insurance, then the pool of people buying insurance becomes sicker and thus more costly to serve. This raises the insurance premium that is needed to make the system solvent. The higher premium then discourages the least risky among the sickest group from getting coverage, and we can enter the insurance death spiral that ends with an extremely high-risk pool that is uninsurable because no one can pay the necessary premium. For all insurance markets, the trick is to have a large risk pool to dilute the risk and spread the cost. In the health care case, this isn't too hard to accomplish because healthy people generally have something to lose. A single bad health event can drain even a wealthy person's finances. But for the poor, if the young take their chances, then the older and sicker can't afford even modest plans. This is the origin of the subsidies and the "mandate" in the Affordable Care Act (Obamacare).

Returning to a college's counseling center, a funding mechanism that spreads the cost to the entire student population enlarges the risk pool and lowers the cost per student. Ex post, some students will have "bought" a policy that they never use. For those who entered the school with preexisting conditions, however, the benefits likely outweigh the costs many times over. For the majority, it's a relatively low-cost insurance policy whose value can become quite large if their situation changes and they need to use the counseling option. The cost per student at William and Mary was $186 during the 2014–15 academic year. This fee is higher than the cost per student at many schools because William and Mary opts for a higher-than-average ratio of full-time professional caregivers per student than the national average.

Counseling services are quite well utilized. For the 275 institutions covered by the American College Counseling Association's 2014's national survey, 11% of students sought individual or group counseling during the academic year. Around a third of any given cohort of students will utilize the resource during their time in school.[9] At William and Mary, roughly 13% of students use the center annually, so we're well within national norms. Likewise, roughly a third of William and Mary students will use our counseling services during their time as students at William and Mary. We're not aware of national data on the number of students who get psychological care for the very first time during their college years. From internal surveys of users at our own counseling center, 48% of the students who responded say that they had never received any psychological counseling before arriving at the College. This is a proxy for the proportion of students in counseling who did not necessarily expect to use the service, but who found that they needed some form of counseling help while in school. At William and Mary, that proportion would be around 15% of a class (roughly 48% of one third).

As this counseling example shows us, the potential unbundling of higher education is not a pure saving for students. Colleges and universities actually can do a very good and cost-effective job of meeting real needs for large numbers of young people at a crucial time in their intellectual and emotional development. Hara Estroff Marano put it this way: "increasingly, colleges are the first best hope for rescuing the minds of America's future. But what no one ever imagined is that colleges would also find themselves the last best hope of mental health care in America."[10]

Independent Research

In chapter 3 we made the case for research as part of the primary bundle, and we introduced the argument that a research-active faculty can be a component of good teaching. By temperament and by training, teacher-scholars want to discover. Their own search for new knowledge models the lifelong learning behavior they are trying to develop in their students. Good teachers teach by example, and one possible way for professors to impart their knowledge and their values is to assist undergraduates in learning how research is done. One could argue that mentored student research should be reserved for the relative handful of students who progress to graduate school. What is the rationale for supporting undergraduate students in their own research projects?

We have spoken at many small private colleges since our first book appeared toward the end of 2010. This is no surprise, since many small colleges are in the crosshairs of the threats we have laid out in earlier chapters. Returning from one of those trips in 2012, one of us (Feldman) paid a visit to his alma mater (Kenyon College). Like many colleges, Kenyon has added to its physical plant to do a better job of meeting the changing educational standard of care. Since the school has not added students, the extra facilities are a factor pushing up cost per student. One of the major additions to the physical plant is a relatively new science quad.[11] As I walked through the buildings that did not exist when I was a student there in the 1970s, I noticed glossy posters covering many of the hallways. Each was a formal presentation of student

research given at professional conferences. I also noticed the physical connections between the three buildings. All of the sciences were physically linked
together, along with mathematics, so that interdisciplinary contact between
students and faculty of different fields was unavoidable. Faculty offices, labs,
and classrooms were intertwined in ways that made personal student–faculty
research relationships a natural part of the undergraduate environment.

This emphasis on undergraduate research is by no means restricted to
highly selective liberal arts colleges or to major research universities with elite
graduate schools. We searched for "undergraduate research" at four public
institutions that are only similar because they are not the state flagship institution and they all have "north" in their name—Northern Illinois University,
University of Northern Iowa, University of North Florida, and Northern
Arizona University. All four public universities value undergraduate research
and put resources behind their efforts.[12] This is not a scientific sample by any
stretch, but it represents a broader reality that most colleges and universities
are indeed encouraging their students to become engaged in undergraduate
research.

As these examples suggest, terminology can be deceiving. Places like
Kenyon and Amherst are not "research universities" by any stretch of the
imagination. The faculty at these colleges teach more classes than the norm
at places like Yale or the University of Texas at Austin, and they interact more
with undergraduates. "Compass Point" public universities like the "norths" do
research and often have sizable graduate schools, but they are very different
places than either liberal arts colleges that lack graduate programs or better-
funded research elites like Berkeley, Stanford, Ohio State, or Princeton. What
links them all is the shared value they place on research experiences for their
undergraduates. At powerhouse research universities, students may have the
capacity to work with the most sophisticated equipment, and they can interact
with PhD students. But highly successful undergraduate research can be carried out at institutions that do not have doctoral programs.

We frequently encounter first-year students who have great plans to "start
doing research" right away. We never discourage initiative, but we do tell them
that they need to walk before they run. To do research anywhere near the frontier of knowledge, a student has to pay the proverbial dues by learning the
core ideas and methods of a discipline, or of more than one. In hierarchical
subjects like economics, students must master a set of theoretical and math-
ematical tools that includes higher-level microeconomic and macroeconomic
theory, and courses in pure mathematics, statistics, and econometrics. Only
then are they fully prepared to learn how to formulate a researchable question and how best to use models or data to evaluate it. Other disciplines have

different dues to pay. In history, for instance, in addition to learning the basics of the era or events that interest the budding undergraduate historian, a student must learn archival research methods and how to construct a convincing narrative analysis from many types of complex evidence. In addition, they must often be able to decode primary source documents fluently in a foreign language. In many STEM (science, technology, engineering, and mathematics) fields, students can at least get into labs and get their hands dirty in the mechanical processes of research at an early stage in their undergraduate career, and many universities do push their STEM students into research in this way, often leading them to more substantial research projects as part of their graduation requirements.

Once the dues are paid, undergraduates can work successfully on the frontier of knowledge and present work at professional conferences. They also can publish in the same professional journals as their faculty mentors. Another example allows us to brag a bit. In September of 2015 at the iGEM (International Genetically Engineered Machine Foundation) Grand Jamboree, a team of eight William and Mary students won the grand prize in the undergraduate division.[13] This competition featured more than 250 teams from all over the world, and it is one of the most prestigious science competitions. The event is also built to be interdisciplinary. The team's faculty mentor, biology professor Margaret Saha, said, "Synthetic biology is right at the cutting edge of biology, medicine, neuroscience, math, engineering—a wide range of fields." With one exception, the William and Mary team members came from departments that have no PhD program.

As we noted in chapter 3 when we introduced the college bundle, this convergence of behavior at very different institutional types often is depicted in a harsh light as a wasteful prestige competition with hapless undergraduates and their families footing the bill. In our alternative story, even though the higher education system as a whole remains extraordinarily diverse, Harvard, Kenyon, William and Mary, and Northern Illinois University share an understanding about what skills and experiences are important parts of an undergraduate curriculum. Some of these curricular components are long-standing. Others are new. The list includes promoting interdisciplinary linkages in coursework and research, small group experiences, first-year writing-intensive seminars, student–faculty collaborative work, and close mentorship relationships. Mentored research is an increasingly important part of the curriculum at a wide variety of schools precisely because it is a form of active learning that works.

In addition to being a widely recognized best educational practice, the rationale for offering undergraduates the opportunity to do high-level independent student research also includes the same option value argument we provided for psychological counseling. Most students don't publish papers coauthored with faculty mentors. And many do not choose to engage in serious independent research. For many first-year students the notion of working on a research project is not something they think is even remotely possible. But institutions are doing the right thing when they include it in the bundle and give a large number of students the option of doing independent research.

Intercollegiate Athletics

Big-time intercollegiate athletics is a peculiarly American phenomenon. The amount of money spent on intercollegiate team sports at some schools is mind-boggling. Coaches of successful college football and basketball teams make millions of dollars. The annual data reported on the highest-paid individuals at colleges often include coaches whose salary is many multiples of what the college president earns. The highest-paid public employee in forty of the fifty states is a college coach.[14] Assistant coaches regularly make a multiple of what the average assistant professor earns. If you strip away all of this athletic activity, the primary mission of an institution of higher learning is unaffected. Why, then, is the business of intercollegiate sports included in the bundle at all, and how likely is this part of the bundle to wither under the pressure of the threats creating turbulence for the higher education system? The topic of intercollegiate athletics contains grist for many a complete volume. In the next few pages we cannot cover the full ground. Yet we can use our particular lens to examine the economic rationale (or lack thereof) for intercollegiate athletics and how the long-intertwined history of sports and American higher education may evolve.

The option value argument we made for psychological counseling and independent undergraduate research doesn't apply to intercollegiate athletics, at least at the highest level. The National Collegiate Athletic Association (NCAA) Division I teams are largely filled with students on scholarships, and the few "walk on" players often are recruited by the coaches. Even in the NCAA's Division III, which is composed largely of small colleges that do not award scholarships, the coaches recruit a large fraction of the players.[15] With very few exceptions, athletes knew they were going to be involved in sports well before they arrived on campus.

In the absence of an option value benefit, how can colleges and universities justify charging the entire student body for something that only a portion will ever use?[16] At many larger universities, only a small minority of students participate in intercollegiate athletics. As usual, the answer is complex, and provides another good example of the point we made in chapter 2—the diversity of the US higher education system makes blanket generalizations highly suspect.

Our first task is to explore the relationship between revenue and cost. If a program pays for itself, then there is less of a case for dismantling it as a needless fee driver. Despite the very high costs of producing "big time" sports, revenues can be high as well. "Big time" isn't a precise term, but athletics programs in the Football Bowl Subdivision (FBS) of the NCAA's Division I, and particularly those in the so-called power five conferences (Atlantic Coast, Big Twelve, Big Ten, Pac-Twelve, and Southeastern), earn millions of dollars from their sports programs. These earned revenues come from the sale of tickets, radio and television rights, and clothing and other paraphernalia. Athletics programs also receive funds from donors and allocations from revenues taken in by NCAA contracts. Most of the funds the NCAA allocates to member institutions come from the sale of television rights for the men's basketball tournament and the FBS football playoffs. In 2010, the CBS television network signed a fourteen-year $10.8 billion contract with the NCAA for the rights to the basketball tournament. This contract generates about $740 million each year for the NCAA.[17] In 2012, ESPN signed a twelve-year $5.64 billion contract with the NCAA for the rights to the football championship. This contract generates about $470 million annually for the NCAA.[18]

At many public institutions, intercollegiate athletics operates as an auxiliary enterprise much like the dormitories and the food service. Auxiliary enterprises generally operate as stand-alone entities. They have costs, and they produce revenues. If in one year the dormitories do not generate enough revenue to cover their costs, they can tap small auxiliary balances that are maintained to smooth year-to-year fluctuations. But in the next year the university will raise dorm rates so that its auxiliary housing enterprise breaks even over time. Most institutions would like to operate their intercollegiate athletics programs in the same way, but very few are able to pull it off. The 2014 NCAA report on intercollegiate athletics revenues and expenses showed that only 20 of the 126 FBS schools had an operating surplus in 2013.[19] The other 106 FBS institutions, the 122 Football Championship Subdivision (FCS) institutions, and the 103 Division I institutions that do not play football run annual deficits. They cover these deficits by using institutional revenues, and this revenue often comes from a mandatory student fee. To break even, the student athletics fee is set at the per student difference between the expected costs to run the athletics department and the expected revenues, including donations, earned by the athletics department.

The vast majority of intercollegiate athletics programs do not generate enough revenues to cover their operating expenses. Moreover, James Shulman and William Bowen show that with any reasonable accounting for the capital costs of the stadiums, gymnasiums, and playing fields required to run a Division I athletics program, even the programs with an operating surplus do not cover their full costs.[20] Yet colleges and universities require all of their students to pay athletics fees of various sizes for a set of programs that do not provide most students with any option benefit, and which some never even use as a spectator. Arguably this is just an income transfer from the majority of students to the minority who participate. It's also a gravy train to all of the ancillary personnel (like the coaching staff) who earn tidy sums from the revenue stream.

Before we wrestle with our fundamental question of why, we want to note an intriguing regularity about college athletics. The big-time programs that spend the most are not the ones with the biggest athletics fees. Some may find this surprising, but there are two clear reasons for low student charges at large power-conference universities. First, the big-time programs do generate large amounts of revenue. They play in huge stadiums to full audiences with lots of paying fans who don't necessarily attend the university. They attract large donations from ardent alumni. Many of their games are televised. The distribution of NCAA funds from the NCAA basketball tournament is based on the success of teams from a university's conference, and more teams from the big-time conferences qualify for the tournament and win games. The second reason for low fees is about size itself. Institutions with big-time athletics programs generally have large numbers of students. Even if they have an operating deficit that has to be covered by a student fee, the fee will be small because it is spread over a large number of students.

The Commonwealth of Virginia offers a good source of data to help us see the forces at work. In Virginia, public university athletics programs are auxiliary enterprises and state appropriations cannot be used to support them. This means that an explicit student fee must cover any expected operating deficit of the athletics program. At one end of the spectrum, Virginia Tech competes in one of the power five conferences (the Atlantic Coast Conference). Virginia Tech raised $8,992,512 from a student athletics fee of $288 in 2015–16. By contrast, Virginia Military Institute (VMI) plays in a much less powerful conference. VMI raised $5,325,000 from a student athletics fee that is more than ten times as large ($3,090).[21] The difference is explained by the fact that Virginia Tech spreads its athletics deficit over 31,224 students, while VMI only has 1,700 students paying its much larger fee.

The relationship between student population and the size of the athletics fee is very strong. Figure 9.1 plots the athletics fee against the student population for all fifteen of Virginia's public four-year colleges and universities during the 2015–16 academic year. In a linear regression with fifteen data points, statistical significance usually is hard to obtain. But this relationship is very clear.[22] The black line is the predicted relationship, and the probability that this negative relationship is a spurious accident is only 2.2%.

The institutions on either side of the predicted relationship tell a useful story. VMI is the smallest college in the system, and that alone pushes up the athletics fee. But VMI also maintains a full set of Division I sports. That's expensive and it's a choice that mandates a huge athletics fee. Mary Washington is very different. The "Eagles" do not play football and the university is part of Division III. The fiscal footprint of athletics is correspondingly smaller. William and Mary is a midsized institution that competes in Division I, and this drives up cost. William and Mary also does not play in a power conference, so the revenue stream from sports is lower than at places like Virginia Tech or the University of Virginia. The result is a higher athletics fee than would be predicted by the school's size alone. The comparison between

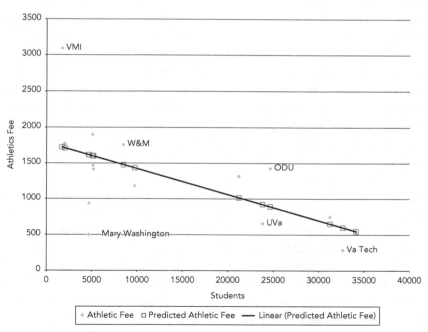

FIGURE 9.1 Student population and athletics fee, Virginia.

Old Dominion University (ODU) and the University of Virginia (UVA) is revealing. The two institutions are roughly the same size, but Virginia plays in a power conference (the Atlantic Coast Conference), while ODU does not (mostly in Conference-USA). Lastly, the state's two power conference universities, UVA and Virginia Tech (VT), both have fees that are substantially below the level predicted for schools of their size.

Allen Sanderson and John Siegfried offer six arguments for why the fiscal footprint of big-time athletics has grown over time, and why spending on athletics has maintained such a deep well of support.[23] These reasons are worth a brief review. First, other things equal, simply having a Division I football team on campus increases a public university's state appropriation.[24] This is an important motive in an era of declining state support for higher education. Second, athletics may be a magnet that pulls in private donations and philanthropy. If these private gifts do not simply generate more spending on athletics, this giving could potentially reduce the athletics fee all students must bear. This is a big if, however. These donations usually are tied to more athletics spending, so we don't see much if any beneficial effects of this giving for the average student.

The presence of a big-time sports program also may help boost applications to the university. The potential applications bump comes from doing well in championships or winning high-profile televised games. This is often called the Flutie effect, after quarterback Doug Flutie, who led Boston College to a stunning victory in 1984 over the University of Miami on a Hail Mary pass with no time on the clock. Applications to Boston College surged over the next two years. Researchers noticed the same effect in other situations and became interested in understanding the process more generally. There is now some evidence that the applications bump includes both low- and high-talent students, and that schools can use this additional interest to improve the number and the quality of admissions.[25] These advertising benefits can persist, especially with higher-ability students. Pope and Pope found that this effect was two to four times larger at private universities than at public universities.[26]

Fourth, much like the merit aid scholarships that we discussed in chapter 6, spending on big-time team sports is likely to have the characteristics of an arms race. Recruiting excellent players is crucial, so a university cannot let practice facilities and team amenities fall behind its competitors. Since the pool of star athletes is fixed, the facilities competition is primarily about rungs on a ladder. Spending ratchets upward merely to maintain an institution's position. Like most arms-race stories, this adds to cost without necessarily changing any socially useful outcome. The average team, after all, will have a .500 winning percentage no matter how much the entire system spends on facilities. A "bare bones" athletics department would indeed be cheaper, but financial restraint usually produces a losing team.

Fifth, athletic events offer a way to tie alumni to their alma mater and might well lead to donations not specifically tied to athletics. This is one reason universities pair homecoming festivities with big games. Keeping the school's name on the sports pages is also part of an overall strategy to keep a faithful alumni base. Lastly, big-time sports are part of the image and identity of many institutions, and this is reinforced by a conference affiliation that groups schools together. In many parts of this sports-obsessed country, schools cannot easily ignore the historical links between sports success and university image, and this may be especially strong for publicly supported institutions. The past conditions the institution's options in the present, and this shapes the outlines of the future. But the future isn't fully determined. The role of athletics on American campuses may well change in response to strong incentives, and in ways that reflect the diversity of institutions within the system.

These six arguments largely apply to universities with aspirations of sports greatness. But many other colleges and universities maintain significant sports programs while avoiding the allure of big-time athletics. The Ivy League plays in Division I but chooses not to offer scholarships or to participate in the FCS tournament. Also, a large number of institutions play in Division III, which does not offer scholarships, play games in big stadiums, or earn large sums from television contracts. With almost 450 members (40% of the NCAA membership), Division III is the NCAA's largest grouping. The average enrollment at a Division III school is only 2,700, and over 80% of Division III schools are private.[27] The rationale for maintaining a large set of intercollegiate team sports at these institutions is not about hitting an elusive revenue jackpot or about national publicity. The reason has much more to do with enlarging the applicant pool by meeting a clear student demand. This is a different cost/benefit calculation, and it suggests why trimming a college's sports program isn't simple.

Other things equal, active participation in high school team sports can signal important noncognitive skills like perseverance and cooperativeness that are correlated with success in college. These are desirable traits that also show up in high school students who have long-developed skills and interests in things like music or theater. Athletic "talent" is as much a honed skill as many other desirable extracurricular attributes students bring to the table. And like students with other extracurricular interests, high school students who have excelled at a sport often want a continued outlet for their long-developed skills, so attracting true student athletes requires fielding teams.[28]

The statistics about this are clear. In 2013, the NCAA reported that student athletes made up 21% of the student population at Division III colleges. The average figure for the entire group of Division I schools is only 6%, and at very large powerhouse schools like Alabama and Florida State, it's only 2.7% and 2.3%, respectively.

An additional issue hangs over college athletics, especially at the big-time programs. The NCAA represents an unusual organizational structure in higher education. It is a membership society that enforces rules on its members, much like the Overlap Group we discussed in chapter 6. The Overlap Group was designed to mitigate an unproductive merit aid arms race by credibly constraining each school's scholarship-giving behavior. The Overlap Group set rules about evaluating need and about the maximum amount of financial aid a member institution could give. This process ran afoul of the antitrust laws, so it no longer exists. The NCAA, which enforces rules about the maximum amount of financial aid a member institution can give a student and about the number of scholarships an institution can grant, still very much exists. Several suits have been filed arguing that restrictions on the size of scholarships that Division I institutions can award athletes amount to price fixing, which would be a violation of the antitrust laws.[29]

The most important issue in the suits brought against the NCAA concern proper compensation for athletes in football and in men's basketball, the two sports that bring in the vast majority of the revenues. This issue has been brewing for quite some time. Many have argued that players are not fairly compensated out of the revenue flows they generate for the NCAA and for their universities. In a test case, members of the Northwestern football team argued that they should be treated as university employees, and they voted to form a union. A regional director of the National Labor Relations Board (NLRB) agreed with the players. In a narrow ruling in 2015, the full NLRB declined to accept jurisdiction, which temporarily upheld the status quo.[30] Nonetheless, the pressure has pushed the NCAA to raise the amount of money student athletes can be offered in scholarships. Scholarship athletes now can receive scholarships that cover the "cost of attendance," which includes items like transportation that go beyond the usual tuition, fees, room, and board. The universities set the maximum value of these additional items individually, so an arms-race competition in athlete compensation remains possible.

The legal issues regarding the NCAA are not settled, and the momentum for change is growing. The change to paying college athletes more than a full scholarship might have profound consequences in a system where only twenty Division I schools earn more than they spend. The others have to tax students in some way, typically by charging a student athletic fee. Raising the compensation of football and basketball players at the big-time programs will have one of two consequences. First, schools could raise the student athletic fee to cover the added expense. Since many of the schools that play big-time athletics are very large, their current athletics fees are relatively small, so there is room for fee increases. Second, schools might reduce the number of sports they offer. Typically football and men's basketball actually earn surpluses, and these surpluses subsidize deficits in other sports. Smaller schools, which cannot spread their athletics fees over as many students, might find it better to reduce costs by eliminating some sports.

These sports programs come at a cost to the average student, and the benefit isn't spread as an option value, so one can envision changes in the economic environment that might induce schools to shrink the size of their athletics programs. But any changes in the strong bond between US colleges and universities and their sports programs must recognize two facts. The larger big-time programs are the ones who "tax" their students the least for sports programming. On the other hand, the schools where the fiscal footprint of intercollegiate athletics tends to be the highest (small colleges) are the ones where athletics programs reach a much greater fraction of the student body and whose student recruitment is most heavily influenced by this.

We have identified two sets of schools that are most in the crosshairs of financial stress today and whose financial prospects are most at risk from economic turbulence over the next generation. The first are underfunded public universities who serve disproportionate numbers of at-risk students. Many of these schools are in Division I of the NCAA and they maintain a full range of team sports. The second is composed of small private colleges in Division III that serve a mostly local clientele within regions of demographic decline. At these two types of institution we would expect the debate about athletics spending to have the most salience.

Football could be the first casualty since it is by far the most expensive sport to maintain. On the other hand, it may have the most entrenched backers. And football can't be reduced in size smoothly. For starters, there is the arms-race nature of team competition that forces schools, even in Division III, to look for good coaching and to provide competitive facilities. Small changes in these details can cause large changes in program success. Second, to be competitive, teams must have multiple players at each position, and there are limits to how much one can economize. At a small college, the football team alone is a meaningful fraction of the student body. In downsizing a sport, at some point you reach an all-in or all-out point. For this reason alone, the debate about dropping football is always contentious and bitter. Eliminating a sport as encompassing as football is a rupture in the fabric of institutional life, not a slow shrinkage. This debate may play out on many campuses over the next quarter century, and the decisions will be consequential at each one. Forecasting the outcome in any particular case is fraught.

We think intercollegiate sports are here to stay on college campuses. As long as high school team sports have very high participation rates, a certain number of college students will want to have a chance to pursue their sport at a higher level or be aligned with a school that has high-profile teams with which they identify. This is yet another reason that large numbers of students in the traditional age range of four-year colleges and universities are unlikely to be pulled to a no-frills online education. But the debate about the role of athletics on college campuses likely will intensify, and schools may continue to drop sports. This debate may swirl around football most particularly, since it is by far the most expensive sport. We may also see some shrinkage in the range of sports offered, with more club sports displacing NCAA-level competition. But few, if any, schools are likely to drop intercollegiate athletics entirely.

Bundling: The Big Picture

We have dived deeply into three specific parts of the traditional bundle of services on offer at most colleges and universities. Undergraduate research is an activity we included in the "primary" part of the bundle, along with teaching and the network of services that make research and teaching possible. Psychological counseling is one of the secondary components of the bundle. And intercollegiate athletics is what we called a tertiary activity. There is a significant price tag on the bundle of services colleges provide, so the individual and social case for maintaining any particular component of the bundle is strengthened if that service contributes in a meaningful and measurable way to goals that are central to the academic mission and to the institution's ability to thrive.

There is an increasing body of evidence that spending on student services is linked to clear gains in first-year retention (the fraction of a first-year class returning for a second year) and ultimately to improvements in the six-year graduation rate. Ronald Ehrenberg and Douglas Webber, for instance, used Delta Cost Project data from 1,161 four-year colleges and universities to show that spending on student services is strongly related to positive academic outcomes. Their category of student services includes everything from the admissions office and supplemental tutoring programs to counseling and psychological services of the sort we explored earlier.[31] Moreover, the effectiveness of spending on student services is more pronounced at schools that serve high-risk populations. This includes schools whose existing graduation rates are low, schools whose student population comes in with lower average test scores, and schools whose students depend more heavily on Pell Grant dollars to support their education.

Ehrenberg and Webber also calculate the effect of a budget neutral shift of $100 per student *away* from "instruction" to student services. Overall, they show that this reallocation of spending is associated with a higher graduation rate. Again the effects are strongest at schools that serve higher-risk student populations. They note wryly:

> This finding is one that neither faculty around the country worried about declining funding for faculty positions nor critics of higher education who point to the wasteful growth of expenditures on non-instructional uses are likely to be happy about. At highly selective institutions, the budget shift produces no change in graduation rate, so if graduation rate were all one cared about then these schools had roughly the right balance between spending on students services and spending on instruction.[32]

The graduation rate is not the only thing a college or university cares about. The quality of the education is also an important consideration, and some things that are done to improve quality—like allocating scarce resources toward small-group experiences—may siphon money away from other uses that could have had a noticeable effect on graduation performance. The fact that some schools might be able to raise the graduation rate by reallocating spending does not tell us that their current model is somehow inefficient. The work done by Ehrenberg and Webber, and by others who find the same positive relationship between spending on student support and graduation rates, confirms that instructional spending isn't the only important part of the higher education bundle.

Schools like Harvard and William and Mary don't need to talk about how spending on the wider bundle boosts first-year retention and graduation rates. Their retention and graduation rates are quite high. For very sensible reasons, schools that are under increasing financial pressure, and which serve many more at-risk students, do need to justify spending on seemingly extraneous things like research and "student services." Financially secure institutions can do these things more richly, at a higher level, and for a greater fraction of their students. All schools, however, see these approaches to learning and student support as "best practices" and adjust them to fit their own circumstances. These circumstances differ by selectivity, by the institution's resource base, and so on. All traditional colleges and universities are seeing the same evidence. We should not be surprised that they all want to support things like student–faculty research within the set of constraints they face.

These measurable effects likely underestimate the total value that various parts of the bundle provide. The option value of things like counseling, advising, and mentored research—perhaps using the unbundled particle accelerator of the Doonesbury cartoon—is not captured in measured effects on things like retention rates or graduation rates. But the option value is a real component of the private and social value students receive when they buy the traditional bundle. Likewise, universities are designed to subsidize activities that often cannot support themselves, but whose existence enhances the whole enterprise. The English major subsidizes the physics major or business major since the cost of providing a course of study in English tends to be much lower than offering a state-of-the-art physics education. And we all know how much a business faculty member costs! Likewise, the university symphony, or its gymnastics team, tends to benefit small groups intensely, but the whole is improved because the symphony and the gymnastics team bring to campus students whose talents and interests help to produce the education of their peers.

The bundle of services provided to students at a traditional four-year institution is not immutable. We have suggested that the historically entrenched role of athletics may change abruptly at some colleges and universities under financial strain, though this is a complex issue that is easily misunderstood and often oversimplified. Likewise, some programs may be forced by financial pressures to reduce or do away with options or support services that are highly correlated with student success. Yet the value proposition of the bundle will persist for the vast majority of potential students in the traditional age range of college students. Our fear is that the unbundled world envisioned by some will provide an impoverished education to this group, and especially to the most at risk.

10

The Evolutionary Future

WE HAVE SPENT the better part of nine chapters identifying the major challenges the next thirty years will throw at the diverse set of nonprofit colleges and universities that offer traditional four-year degree programs. We have focused separately on how the internal workings of colleges and universities, the environmental changes that affect the entire industry, and the digital technologies transforming the economy all may threaten the traditional model of college education. Some of these threats are more apparent than real. We have, for instance, made a case that the new digital technologies working their way through the global economy are unlikely to sweep away traditional higher education institutions. In purely online formats or in blended settings, the new learning methods likely will augment what takes place on campuses and continue to enlarge the higher education market by appealing to older students. On the other hand, demographic processes, rising income inequality, and long-term changes in state support for public higher education have placed, and will continue to place, great stresses on the system as a whole. The reactions to these stresses have been the primary subject of our study.

A one-sentence summary of our findings would go something like this. Each university or college is a rich mix of characteristics—selectivity, location, size, mission, endowment, and connection to the state, to name a few—and that mix goes a long way in determining whether that institution will thrive, tread water, or sink in the years ahead. For some institutions the waters ahead will be very turbulent. This message is quite different from oft-heard forecasts that disruption and revolutionary change soon will ripple through the entire industry, laying waste to the extravagantly wasteful traditional model of student–faculty interaction. We think the traditional model of higher education remains a resilient economic ecosystem offering individuals and society substantial benefits. Its diversity is a source of its resilience and a contributor to its social productivity.

The system's likely resilience, however, is not a sign that everything will work out just right in the end. Dr. Pangloss may have believed that we live in "the best of all possible worlds," no matter what horrible events overtook him, but our outlook is less consistently sunny. The last thirty years have seen a growing bifurcation of the higher education system into well-resourced institutions (the haves) and underresourced institutions (the have-nots). The turbulence buffeting the higher education system risks worsening this gap and cementing it in place.

Which threats, or combination of threats, will be most daunting? Which types of institutions will be in the worst, and best, shape to handle the threats coming their way? In this chapter we will offer our answers to these questions. In the final chapter we will ask if policymakers can smooth the waters in ways that help the higher education system serve clear national goals for inclusion and social mobility.

We have repeatedly warned against easy generalizations, but there is mileage in organizing our summary into four categories: (1) state flagships and other selective public institutions, (2) less selective public institutions, (3) selective private institutions, and (4) less selective private institutions. Schools are arrayed along a continuum of selectivity, so these four boxes are imperfect. Some institutions are on the boundary. Our analysis and our conclusions have more traction for institutions solidly in a particular selectivity group.

Before we dig into the details of these four categories, we offer some general observations about all colleges and universities regardless of selectivity and funding source. First, a four-year college degree will continue to be a highly desirable credential. We may well see growth in certificates or badges in some fields where assessing competency in a discrete skill is easy. This kind of certification already exists for mastering competencies like geographic information systems or Microsoft programming. In our view, skills of this sort are more likely to enhance traditional degrees rather than replace them. Second, the payoff to a four-year degree will remain large despite rising tuition and possibly higher levels of average student debt. Of course there is a distribution around this average, so earning a BA is not a guarantee of economic success. Then again, it never has been a magic elixir. We do not foresee significant changes in the economics of earning a degree that will substantially shrink the demand. Those who do not pursue a college education will face limited opportunities in the future, just as they do today.

State Flagships and Other
Selective Public Institutions

As we developed and explained the many threats facing the US higher education system, the pressures confronting flagships never rose to existential. These institutions always seemed to have more options for adjusting to shocks and unfortunate trends, and in some cases even to prosper. Generally flagship public institutions are large. The vast majority of state flagships have more than 20,000 students. In most cases these schools have loyal followings in the state population as a whole. The members of the state legislature, many of whom are graduates, share this devotion. In a number of states there are other publically supported institutions that are also highly selective. These institutions have attributes that set them apart from less selective state-supported institutions. They're often older and have large alumni networks. The fiscal footprint of their research establishment is bigger, and their athletic prowess powers a valuable brand.

There are no reasons to believe that the factors driving college cost upward will be different at state flagships and at other selective state institutions than they are at their less selective public brothers and sisters or at private institutions. As long as these institutions rely for the most part on face-to-face education and have a large group of students living on campus, the same cost factors we identified in chapter 4 will be at work. What sets these institutions apart is a superior revenue base, not any particular cost advantage.

Demographic trends favor flagships over their less selective public brethren. Public institutions are place bound, so if they are in the Northeast or Midwest where demographic trends are less favorable, they may face pressures to dip their standards to fill their classes. But the state flagship often is the preferred in-state school for many students who wind up enrolling at another institution within the state. The less selective institutions will feel the brunt of the challenges from declining numbers of high school graduates. Where demographic trends are more favorable, flagships will see increasing demand, and this will give them a set of good options for crafting the incoming class, and in pricing.

State flagships and other selective institutions also are better positioned to attract out-of-state students and foreign students if the number of in-state high school graduates declines. These institutions have been favored by their legislatures over the years, and it shows in their facilities and programs. These advantages allow them to tap into sources of demand from higher income families elsewhere in the United States, and their name recognition is an advantage in recruiting students from burgeoning higher education markets abroad.

Similarly, the threats from stagnating family income are less likely to cause serious financial difficulties for state flagships than for less selective private colleges that must offer large tuition discounts to "make" their class and whose revenues are most at risk if they miss their target enrollment. State flagships do discount tuition for some students, but this discounting has more to do with sculpting the class than with making the class. In other words, selective public institutions generally are less concerned with attracting a sufficient number of students and more concerned with attracting the right set of students.

The most compelling threat faced by state flagships and other selective public institutions comes from reductions in state support. This threat is not new, as we documented thoroughly in chapter 7, so flagships have a store of experience in how to absorb cuts. Public institutions have begun to rely more heavily on tuition revenue and on private philanthropy. The evidence on list-price tuition increases at public universities is clear. As allergic as governors and state legislators might be to allowing tuition increases, they have indeed permitted tuition revenue to replace lost state appropriations. As a result, tuition has risen far more rapidly in the public sector than it has at private colleges and universities. Selective flagships have some advantages over less selective public universities in the tuition-setting process. As the first choice of many students, the demand for places at the flagship likely is less sensitive to price changes than is the demand at other public universities. Flagships also compete for students with private institutions whose list-price charges often are three to four times the flagship's list price. Private institutions tend to discount more, yet public flagships still tend to offer a lower net price for most well-off students.[1]

These advantages allow flagships more leverage both to raise list price and to price discriminate more effectively without losing many students to other alternatives, public or private. The political process within each state, however, determines how easily flagships can use these advantages. In states that allow public institutions more autonomy, or which bend more easily to lobbying for tuition increases from flagship presidents, selective public institutions will have an easier time weathering future budgetary belt tightening emanating from the state capitol.

Private fundraising has become critical for state flagships and other selective public institutions. These institutions have recognized the political realities. The state is exceedingly unlikely to return to funding them generously, and they have shifted their fundraising focus away from the state legislature toward private donors. More selective public institutions have become quite successful private fundraisers. Table 10.1 provides data from the Council on Aid to Education (CAE) on voluntary contributions per student to public colleges and universities in the 2014–15 academic year, grouped by the admissions selectivity categories from Barron's Profiles of American Colleges 2015.[2] The CAE data include all types of gifts: for current operations and for capital support, current gifts and deferred gifts, and gifts from individuals and gifts from foundations. The data are quite clear. Public universities in higher-selectivity categories are better at attracting larger gift totals.

In an important sense, the finances of public institutions are slowly being privatized. This is clearly true if one looks at funding sources. As we showed in chapter 7, state universities increasingly rely on direct tuition payments from students and their families to cover a rising fraction of the bill, and this is strikingly apparent for flagships. Likewise, as fundraising efforts at public flagships come to resemble the philanthropic efforts at major private institutions, the more the distinctions between them begin to blur.

On the other hand, public institutions face constraints that their private competitors do not. Selective state-supported institutions often face binding limits on the number of out-of-state students they can matriculate. Out-of-state students pay considerably higher tuition on average than in-state students, so these constraints limit the revenue the institution can earn. Since out-of-state tuition helps subsidize the experience for in-state students, there is a tradeoff between the economic benefits of enrolling another out-of-state student and the political costs of seeming to limit the opportunities for state residents.

In addition, public institutions have to follow state regulations for how they can use state-appropriated funds, and this can include tuition revenue.

Table 10.1 Per-Student Voluntary Contributions to Public Institutions by Selectivity, 2014–15

Barron's Selectivity	Average Voluntary Contribution Per Student
Most competitive	$7,610
Highly competitive	$3,719
Very competitive	$2,579
Competitive	$1,215
Less or noncompetitive	$724

State institutions often face restrictions on their discretionary spending that limits flexibility and raises cost. The rules often aren't very defensible. At William and Mary, for instance, we must buy our office furniture from Virginia Correctional Enterprises (VCE). At some point in the past, Virginia's prison population did make most of the office furniture on offer, and state agencies were a captive buyer. Most of these items now are sourced from places like China, but colleges and universities remain a captive market. VCE acts as a monopoly middleman and collects the markup. For state legislators, this may be a convenient way to fund one state bureaucracy out of the revenue stream of another. But students see some of their tuition dollars siphoned away to support another state agency when higher-quality items may be available from Staples or Home Depot at lower cost. Rules and restrictions of this sort make public institutions less financially nimble than their private counterparts.

For state institutions that have a private foundation in control of the endowment, spending private money typically is less constrained by rules that needlessly absorb administrative time and diminish flexibility. Some states have recognized the benefits of relaxing some of the constraints faced by their universities, but others continue to micromanage the way institutions spend public money. Often this micromanagement politicizes basic economic decisions on college campuses, like how best to design and construct a building. In states that continue to impose burdensome restrictions on how universities use funds, and especially if they continue to classify tuition collected from students and families as state revenue, their public universities will have more difficulty transitioning to a world in which institutional revenue sources are increasingly privatized.

The end of the era of rapid growth in federal research support will have a significant effect on state flagships. Graduate programs are a vital part of the academic life at a large majority of flagship institutions, and federal research funding is a critical component that makes those programs work. With the exception of programs that focus on medicine and biological science, graduate departments and schools have been living with stagnant or falling federal research support for quite some time. Many graduate programs only enroll students who are supported by grants, so any tail-off in funding can directly impact the number of funded students. This creates difficulties for universities that rely on graduate students to be lab assistants and instructors in many undergraduate courses. The results could include retrenchment in graduate programs that cannot pay for themselves in other ways, even if the advanced training of more chemists or geologists pays social dividends the school cannot capture in grants or in tuition. The rising cost of undergraduate education could be another consequence as schools are forced to hire more expensive labor to staff labs and introductory classes.

State flagships and other selective public institutions will have an interesting relationship with new technologies. They offer the complete bundle of college services to a clientele that is predominantly of traditional college-going age. Most of these students are unlikely to find fully online programs very appealing even if the quality of online learning improves. Leading public institutions likely will be suppliers in this market rather than demanders. Many state flagships currently sponsor massively open online courses (MOOCs), and many of them are experimenting with blended learning courses that incorporate online components often developed on campus. These services and products could have a market value, and other institutions might be the willing buyers. As we discussed in chapter 8, the business models needed to transform these innovations into valuable intellectual property are at best nascent, and there are real risks involved in moving quickly given the sizable up-front and unrecoverable costs involved. Yet for selective public institutions, these new technologies could be more of an opportunity than a threat.

Finally, many state flagships and other selective public institutions have relatively successful athletic programs that do not burden students with large athletics fees. The public image of most flagship schools is intimately tied to athletics, especially in high-visibility sports broadcast nationwide. This allure extends to students and to supporters in the legislature alike. We do not foresee any large changes in the athletics programs at most of these schools, even as elite-level competition becomes more expensive, as long as the rising cost is mostly supported by athletic revenue and student fees remain fairly low.

Less Selective Public Institutions

The future of less selective state-supported institutions is cloudier and full of hard-edged choices. These institutions will have more difficulty navigating the turbulent waters created by many of the threats we have outlined. If they continue to rely primarily on face-to-face instruction using full-time tenure-track professors, and if they strive to offer most of the student services found at their more selective counterparts, they will not be able to escape rising costs. They can limit some of these cost increases by switching more heavily to part-time and non-tenure-track faculty and by cutting student services, but these changes are likely to reduce the quality of the student experience in ways that are easily measured (like falling retention rates) and sometimes hidden in multicausal processes (like how education translates into what someone earns in midcareer).

Less selective public universities often are a student's second (or third) choice within his or her state. As a backup or safety school for so many potential applicants, these institutions are less able to adapt to many of the shocks they will face. They are more fragile in many ways. Some of the weaker state institutions in demographically challenged regions may not survive in their current form. These institutions often draw students from surrounding communities, so demographic decline can hit them particularly hard. Demographic problems may be compounded if other regional schools (private and public) can poach a significant number of potential applicants. This decline is likely to be more pronounced among the students the weaker institutions would most like to attract, and this includes students from well-off families who can afford to pay full freight, as well as poorer students who are pulled to slightly better programs that offer something distinctive, or just a better financial deal.

Less selective state universities have borne the brunt of reductions in state funding. As we showed in chapter 7, spending per full-time student at public universities has fallen relative to private colleges and relative to more selective flagships. This is evidence of the weaker relative political power of these institutions, and absent major political changes there are few reasons to believe this situation will change in the near term. Like flagships, less selective state universities also need to find other revenue sources. The dual strategy of pushing the envelope on in-state tuition and going after private gifts also is available to them. Yet their comparatively low tuition is one of the few remaining competitive advantages they possess. Also, they are late to the private fundraising game and, as the data in Table 10.1 indicate, not very successful to date.

Nonetheless, we expect that many of these schools will try to push both levers. Tuition increases will work best if coordinated with other less selective in-state schools, and if done as part of a strategy to discount more aggressively to keep net price down for the most economically disadvantaged students. Yet the potential revenue gains for less selective schools are much smaller than for their flagship peers because the family of the average student at less selective schools comes from lower down the income distribution. And accomplishing a coordinated tuition increase would require a compliant or tolerant state legislature. This is not at all guaranteed. On the fundraising side, these schools may find some low-hanging fruit among alumni they can locate, but they are confronting serious headwinds. Their alumni base has not been trained in the art of giving back, and in comparison to flagships and to many private universities their alumni base likely has much less giving capacity.

Underresourced public institutions disproportionately enroll students from lower-income families, and these students often have a weaker academic background. The poorer resource base of these schools then contributes to low retention and graduation rates. Many at-risk students accumulate loan debt for a time in school that does not provide any significant economic benefit.[3] If the chronic underfunding of these institutions continues or worsens, progress toward increasing college completion rates or decreasing student loan default rates will be difficult to achieve.

New technologies that promise to reduce costs will be very appealing to these institutions, and they are much more likely to integrate fully online offerings than are state flagships and other highly selective public institutions. Flagships and private universities will try to do digital right, often in blended face-to-face settings, while nonselective public institutions will face strong incentives to adopt online alternatives simply to shave off some cost. Rather than pay the often substantial up-front costs of building online components, they are more likely to use materials from other institutions or from for-profit vendors.

We have shown that this kind of digitalization is no panacea, and it's far from a risk-free strategy. The students who attend less selective state universities still want—and in many cases really need—the hands-on services that are an integral part of the traditional bundle of services on offer at schools that focus on the needs of students in the eighteen- to twenty-two-year-old age range. Less selective public institutions that move too aggressively into online course delivery will find that they are less attractive to these students. Some of the smaller state institutions may recognize this tradeoff and adjust their recruiting accordingly. They may move more aggressively into predominantly online programming with smaller campus-based offerings designed around serving local students' vocational and professional needs while taking advantage of some location-specific strength. You will recognize this as a variant of North Central State from our introduction. Barring some major change in federal aid programming or in the way state support is distributed, the resource gap between flagships and less selective state institutions may widen further, and this will be an existential risk to some state universities, especially if they have no neighbors they can cannibalize for enrollment. This set of schools faces very hard choices.

When the college-age population was expanding and state support was steady or growing, many less selective state institutions added graduate programs. In a world of diminishing state support and fewer traditional-age students, some of these graduate programs will be difficult to maintain. Many of the graduate programs at these institutions are not highly ranked. Some are populated mostly with foreign students lured to the program with graduate assistantships of some kind. In most cases these graduate programs do not generate enough in tuition revenue or in research funding to cover their costs. Professional programs pose some different issues. For many schools, post-BA professional training programs have been a good financial investment. This is especially true of skills-oriented vocational training programs. As we mentioned in chapter 6, some professional programs—like lower-ranked law schools—are no longer cash cows for their universities, but careful invest-ment in professional training programs still can produce a surplus for the institution. Careful strategic planning should guide any new or expanded graduate programming. Overall, less selective state-supported schools are likely to prune back their graduate offerings, starting with their most expen-sive nonprofessional graduate programs.

Many of the less selective public institutions compete in the NCAA's Division I and play football in the Football Bowl Subdivision (FBS). These institutions tend to inhabit the conferences outside the Big Five (Atlantic Coast Conference, Big Ten, Big Twelve, Pac-Twelve, and Southeastern Conference). They have football teams that are seldom, if ever, in the hunt for national championships or in the running for a place in a big-money bowl game. These institutions rarely have athletic programs that break even. Since these institutions generally have a smaller enrollment than the Big Five conference schools, the athletic deficit is spread over a smaller number of students, and this leads to sizable athletic fees on top of tuition. If the athletic arms race continues to intensify among the major Division I institutions, the fiscal con-sequence for the less successful public institutions will grow. The politics of athletic downsizing won't be pretty, but many less selective public institutions may well find it fiscally prudent to downsize their most expensive athletic endeavors.

The problems less selective institutions face are exacerbated by the fact that they are so heavily dependent on state appropriations. As we showed in chapter 7, state budget swings can wreak havoc on appropriation-dependent schools. But even during relatively stable economic climates, they are subject to the vagaries of state politics. We are writing during fairly stable economic times. Employment is growing steadily, and inflation is well under control. In many states, the budget picture is stable or improving. Yet the March 11, 2016, *Chronicle of Higher Education* contained three stories of state higher educa-tion systems in crisis. Since 2008, Louisiana's support for higher education has fallen 40%, and large cuts are expected to continue in the next two years. A governor and his state legislature deeply believed in the restorative power of tax cuts just as oil prices were collapsing.[4] At Louisiana's public universities, faculty and staff layoffs are planned and some schools worried they could not meet their May payroll. In a second example, a political stalemate in Illinois left the state without a budget, and public colleges have not received any state appropriations in the past nine months. Chicago State University has sent out 900 notices of possible layoffs because it could not meet its March payroll.[5] Lastly, the governor of Kansas announced a $17 million cut in spending over the remainder of the fiscal year.[6] This kind of financial turbulence is particularly destructive at appropriation-dependent public universities.

The bottom line for less selective state colleges and universities is that the waters will be very turbulent. Following World War II public higher education was in expansion mode. States created many new schools, and existing schools grew dramatically. Many a large state university can trace its origins to a very humble state teachers college or an equally humble branch campus of a state flagship. In most states the days of rapidly expanding state higher education systems are over. In an era when the number of high school graduates has plateaued and state appropriations continue to decline, less selective state institutions are at a disadvantage in finding new funding sources. The survivors will be the ones that are most clear headed about finding or creating new revenues and who can identify a market they can serve even if state appropriations continue to decline. Many high-cost graduate programs may fold, replaced by more vocational-oriented programs that have a ready audience willing to pay. Schools that successfully ride out the turbulence may be those that refocus on nontraditional students and their distinctive needs, which often are quite different from the mix of services in the bundle offered to younger students in traditional four-year degree programs. Many schools already are well down this path, so our forecast is not a big surprise.

Selective Private Institutions

In most respects our forecast for private institutions mirrors the likely trajectory of the public sector. The most selective institutions will have to react to changes in the economic and policy landscape, but their resources and nimbleness will allow them to adjust successfully, and in many cases to thrive. A significant slice of the nation's less selective private colleges will struggle.

There are a large number of selective private colleges and universities. When we explored the diversity of America's colleges back in chapter 2, the data from Figure 2.5 showed us that close to 13% of students enrolled at a private four-year institution attended one that admits fewer than 30% of its applicants. Only 2% of students at public universities attend schools with that level of selectivity. These very selective private institutions include the elite universities of the Ivy League and universities like Duke, Stanford, Rice, MIT, and the University of Chicago. The group of highly selective private institutions also includes a sizable selection of liberal arts colleges as varied as Amherst, Williams, Wesleyan, Swarthmore, Carleton, Kenyon, and Pomona. These selective colleges and universities are the schools that returning alumni in the 2040s will still recognize, despite the changes that will mark the technological and social evolution of the nation over the next thirty years.

Demographic trends will touch these institutions more lightly, because they already draw their students from a national pool. Colleges in demographically declining regions will have to work harder than similar institutions in regions with growing numbers of high school students. Bowdoin College in Maine, for instance, currently draws around 40% of its students from New England. It is less national than Harvard or Duke, so Bowdoin's admissions team has some work to do. But with an endowment of around $1.4 billion, elite private institutions like Bowdoin have crafted the distinctive experiences that will allow them to adjust their recruiting to expected changes in the regional population of qualified applicants. Selective schools that lack such deep pockets may have to practice need-aware admission for a larger portion of their class so that they can offer competitive financial aid packages to other students needing financial aid.

As we move down the selectivity ranking to private institutions that are merely selective instead of elite, the problems will be more acute. But they will not be insurmountable. Selective institutions often have large endowments that provide a considerable fraction of their operating revenue, and their selectivity means they have ways to avoid substantial fluctuations in tuition revenue. These institutions aggressively discount for desirable students, and they are likely to be need aware in admission. If state flagships and other selective state institutions are forced to move further down the path of aggressive tuition hikes, this will improve the competitive position of even modestly selective private institutions.

The undergraduate programs of these selective institutions are likely to survive intact. They will change with the times and with the moving target of current best practices. Students will continue to attend these institutions, particularly the liberal arts colleges, because they offer small classes and lots of interaction between students and full-time faculty. These schools are firmly in the business of offering a personalized education rich with mentorship opportunities.

Like state flagships and other selective public institutions, selective private institutions are much more likely to be suppliers of digital course components and courses than demanders. The open-source EdX courseware begun at MIT, for instance, is a platform for the kind of MOOCs that might displace some face-to-face coursework at less selective colleges.[7] Although these institutions develop MOOCs, they tend not to accept them for credit at their own institutions. These schools are firmly in the business of offering face-to-face education.

The universities in this group often have extensive graduate offerings, and many of the top graduate programs in the world are found here. Even though the economics of providing graduate education is not as promising as the economics of undergraduate education, particularly with federal research support stable or declining, most graduate programs at highly selective private institutions do not face existential cuts. These institutions have the resources to cross-subsidize money-losing but important programs, at least for the time being. The professional schools at some of these institutions are prestigious enough that they remain mostly self-supporting, and some even provide a small surplus to the rest of the institution. These schools also support a large number of stand-alone research institutes. Some have their own endowments, while others depend on federal and foundation grants. The grant-dependent research institutes could run into trouble on occasion, and downsizing or eliminating some of them will be a source of institutional drama. These "crises," however, will not radically change any of these institutions.

One of the great strengths of selective private institutions is their continued capacity to raise funds from a wide set of donors. Students are educated about the importance of giving back from their first days on campus. Buildings, sidewalks, classrooms, professors, professors' offices, and whole departments are named after benefactors. This culture of paying forward is deeply embedded in the undergraduate experience. One of higher education's unfortunate ironies is the fact that the wealthiest institutions also are the best at engaging private philanthropy while the need is much greater elsewhere. But the evidence is as clear for private institutions as it is for public universities. The wealthiest ones dominate the rankings of the most successful fundraisers each year. This prowess allows them to promise the same personalized education remembered by the alumni making the current gifts.

Lastly, the world of big-time athletics treads more lightly on highly selective private institutions. There are exceptions, like Duke, Stanford, and Notre Dame, but they are unusual. Only eleven of the sixty-two schools in the Big Five conferences are private. The Ivy League teams are in the next category down, and most of the other highly selective private colleges compete in Division III, so they have no expenses for athletic scholarships. Few private universities are heavily invested in the arms races to get the highest-priced coaches, to expand their football stadium, or to make their locker rooms into spas. These universities often do have large athletics programs. Many of them field more athletic teams than the much larger schools that compete in the so-called big time. Yet they tend to spend much less on athletics than do the FBS schools.[8]

Most of our predictions in this book are hedged. We respect the complexity of the industry we study. Yet without any qualifiers we will humbly predict that all of the currently elite private schools will be around and thriving thirty years hence. Their current wealth, their fundraising ability, the quality of their programming, and the national and international reach of their student recruitment efforts will allow them to survive the general turbulence buffeting the higher education system as a whole. The threat of a disruptive online tsunami remains speculative, and the experience and trajectory of digital education to date tells us that its "threatening" aspects are unlikely to trouble the basic foundations of higher education within the traditional age group. For the elite private colleges and universities, the digital revolution will only enhance their advantage over other schools.

Less Selective Private institutions

Highly selective private institutions educate a sizable fraction of the students enrolled in private colleges and universities. On the flip side, the data from Figure 2.5 also tell us that over 35% of students enrolled in private nonprofit colleges and universities attend schools that admit at least 70% of their applicants. Over 68% attend schools that accept more than half of the applicant pool. A lot of students in the private four-year sector go to minimally selective schools. The future of less selective institutions is much less secure, especially if they are small, tuition dependent, and in regions of demographic decline. This is not a new observation, and the pressures on these schools are well reported in the mainstream press.[9] Here we'll unpack those pressures systematically.

Small nonselective schools do not have large endowments, so they are very tuition dependent. A story from a conference we attended a few years ago illustrates the precarious situation of this type of school. While we were talking to the president of one of these colleges, a fellow president of a similar institution came up to greet him. After exchanging generic pleasantries, the presidents asked each other, "Did you make your class?" This is a fundamental question. Did the school attract enough students to fill the seats, with a subtext of bringing in enough revenue to avoid the death spiral of falling quality? One of the presidents answered that he had indeed met his class, but he had to give a lot of deep tuition discounts. The other president replied that he fell a few students short. His admissions office decided against giving the really big discounts required to attract the last few students. If a school is willing to discount tuition by enough, it can easily fill the class in any particular year. But to be financially stable the school must have the resources to educate the group over the full time they are in school. Deep discounting for one class can eat into potential future revenues in many ways.

Our tuition model in chapter 6 laid out the rationale for discounting and showed how it can be used effectively. To survive, a school must have a sufficiently large pool of students who can pay a net tuition above the level the school must earn on average to keep program quality from declining. These wealthier families get at best a small discount, and this enables the school to discount more aggressively to fill out the class. If it cannot hit the revenue target and program quality slips, the school risks a vicious circle of declining quality causing further revenue problems.

One might ask why a college would ever choose to leave places unfilled. An empty seat generates no revenue, while most of the costs of serving the extra students are fixed and must be paid nonetheless. The reason is that a student admitted on deep discount is a four-year revenue problem. The school may prefer to hold the spot open and hope for a better, higher-paying admission outcome next year. The school is playing an intertemporal guessing game about expected revenue. If each episode of "next year" brings a worse outcome, that defines a school on the financial ropes.

Small, tuition-dependent, nonselective private colleges face all of the same threats faced by other institutions. If they provide a personalized education in a face-to-face setting using full-time faculty, then they have no get-out-of-jail-free card that exempts them from cost disease and from the responsibility to provide a technologically up-to-date education. Most of these schools already have gone through painful rounds of cost cutting. Further cuts would find little fat, and cutting away muscle would threaten the death spiral of quality cuts and loss of distinctiveness. These national problems are compounded for schools in regions of demographic decline, and they are multiplied if the school draws its students from a narrow geographic radius. The Northeast and Midwest contain many of the colleges most at risk.

Finally, the curricula of many of these institutions focus on the liberal arts. As more and more information is revealed about the relatively low starting salaries of college graduates in many liberal arts disciplines, particularly those in the humanities, many of the less selective "liberal arts only" institutions may experience more trouble recruiting students. This may be mostly a public relations issue. As we have shown, the value added of becoming a good

English major can be higher than the return to scraping by as a bad STEM (science, technology, engineering, and mathematics) major, especially if a student's interests and abilities lean toward nonprofessional or nonvocational subjects. Nonetheless, people tend to focus on averages, and public relations problems can have real consequences.

The key to survival for these colleges in the cross-hairs involves solving or shedding one or more of their current impediments—they are small, tuition dependent, nonselective, and poorly located; only offer liberal arts majors; and lack some competitive programmatic distinction. For some, this task may prove impossible.

Let's begin with the problem of size. There is reasonable evidence that cost per student falls until an institution reaches a "midsize" of roughly 5,000 students. A college of 1,500 students may be inefficiently small, but a college of 500 has a much higher cost per student because of its choice of smallness. Yet that nonselective school cannot charge a price premium just for its smallness, so its quality suffers relative to what it could achieve if it were a bit larger. Growth is a potential savior, but that's a solution easier said than done. For many colleges "small" is a vital part of their identity. The cost of remaining small is easier to bear if a sizable endowment cushions the effect on price, or if elite status perpetuates high demand from families that can afford to pay. For schools on the financial edge, growing from 500 to 1,500 or from 1,500 to 2,250 may be the margin between survival and failure. Achieving growth may demand a change in a college culture that is often deeply conservative. Second, it may require taking real risks. One way to grow is to use the campus during the summer as intensively as in the traditional academic year. That too is a culture change. Growth may require investing in new facilities and programs whose upfront cost must be set against the future benefit of lower cost per student, if they come. New patterns of student recruiting, including recruiting abroad, must take root. In some cases, growth may mean lower admissions standards. In other cases, recruitment may be simplified by the failure of other local competitors.

Tuition dependence is a more difficult problem to solve. Although the presidents of all small colleges are unceasing in seeking donations, small institutions often lack a significant formal development effort. As a result, progress on fundraising often depends on luck as much as skill. A transformative gift is a *deus ex machina* truly to be desired, but waiting for J. R. R. Tolkien's eagles to rescue an underendowed institution is not a plan. Smaller, less selective colleges often have no tradition of aggressive philanthropic campaigns, and they underinvest in seeking private gifts.[10] Schools that fail to change that tradition are at great risk of financial failure.

Tuition dependence is less of a problem in states that pay a portion of tuition. In many states, small private colleges benefit from fairly generous tuition assistance plans for state-resident students who attend a private institution within the state. These tuition assistance grants reduce the net price to students who receive them while increasing the revenue stream to the college from any given list price. Private college associations fight hard to maintain these grant programs. If they were to decline over time as part of squeezing more higher education spending from state budgets, the financial health of many small nonselective private colleges would become even more precarious.

If economic turbulence falls disproportionately on less selective institutions, they have two related ways to become more selective. They can expand their reach geographically, or they can change their programming to appeal to a greater share of students from their existing geographic region. Just as growth is an investment that requires upfront cost for uncertain gains, expanding a college's appeal to potential students from a broader geographical area is a similar investment in the future. An admissions staff has to make connections and travel more, and do this with an eye on pockets of demand that fit the school's mission, attributes, and strengths. The school must invest in the human resources, physical materials, and digital presence to make this happen. Foreign students who can pay a high net price are attractive, even if their needs may push up support costs in a number of ways. The foreign market for the US residential experience is not yet fully exploited. Done well, recruiting a more national and global student body can help an institution become more selective, even in its own region.

The other alternative involves innovative or distinctive programming that makes the institution more attractive to students in its traditional recruiting area and beyond. Many schools have been able to successfully change their image and have enjoyed recruiting success as a result. A school could add new programming at the edge of the traditional liberal arts, or beyond. Small business schools, for instance, or programs that are clearly more career oriented (like nursing and other medical assistant training) can be grafted onto the rootstock of a liberal arts college. This too is a culture change, and like all culture changes is likely to produce a backlash. Instead of (or in addition to) new schools or departments, a college can build semesters in Washington, internships on Wall Street, or wholly owned programs in Madrid that give students opportunities not available at competing local institutions. On campus, a college could invest in a new and distinctive core curriculum. All of these examples come at a cost and have no guarantees, but they may be the difference between growth and failure in some cases.

Lastly, we have the problem of location. Although location may be fixed, its implications are malleable. The difficulties of location and selectivity naturally are related. Expanding a school's geographical reach is essential for all colleges in a region of demographic decline or in a local area whose historically rural clientele has urbanized. Colleges that cannot easily do this will have to find ways to cut cost that do not initiate the death spiral of collapsing quality. One possibility is mergers and shared facilities. This makes a virtue of the large number of these institutions clustered in the most demographically challenged regions of the country. Merging two or more institutions that are close together could lead to considerable savings and expanded opportunities. The merged campuses could have one central library, one football field, one advanced science facility, and perhaps one administration. Mergers needn't be complete. They might just involve some sharing of facilities or programs. Expensive science programs offer a good target for cost savings, but sharing can be more encompassing.

Current examples abound. The New College of Florida shares library facilities with University of South Florida Sarasota Manatee. Georgia Tech and Emory opened a joint facility to share their collections of printed books. The Georgia Tech and Emory partnership, known as EmTech, is intended to jumpstart many other potential collaborations between the universities. Few universities today would consider building a large telescope or observatory, but many would pay a fee to share one. The WIYN Consortium of schools, for instance, uses the .9-meter Cassegrain telescope on Kitt's Peak. One member of the consortium is called the Five College Astronomy Department, and it is a department shared between the University of Massachusetts at Amherst, Amherst College, Hampshire College, Mount Holyoke College, and Smith College. The "Universities of Shady Grove" campus in Rockville, Maryland, is an example of a large cooperative venture. Nine of the state's public universities offer their own career-oriented programs in one physical space to an audience of mostly older students. Mergers of this sort require rethinking old habits of autonomy, and perhaps changing cherished traditions and symbols, but the gain from sharing resources can be substantial. It can open new opportunities and make existing institutions more cost effective. These are all examples of how the existing institutional structure of higher education is capable of adapting.

The experience of Sweet Briar College in Virginia might foreshadow the fate of many small nonselective private colleges that fail to adapt successfully. In 2015, the Sweet Briar board decided to close the institution before exhausting the endowment because they saw no likelihood that the institution could ever meet its annual budget.[11] A group of alumni and other supporters have taken over and they are going to try to resurrect the college and put it on a sustainable financial path. We will not venture a guess about that particular institution, but we can forecast that many of the nation's small, relatively non-selective private colleges may go through a similar struggle.

The Bottom Line

For much of the past century, education was a clear pathway of upward economic mobility. The first seventy years of the twentieth century saw the near completion of universal high school education and the robust expansion of higher education opportunity to a mass audience. This was also a period when the income gap between the top 20% and the bottom 20% narrowed substantially. A greater fraction of the nation enjoyed a middle-class standard of living that was growing rapidly by historical standards.[12] Rising education levels contributed to both of these trends. The last forty years have seen the nation move rapidly away from the middle-class world of the 1940s to 1970s. Rising income and wealth inequality also is one of the fundamental forces of turbulence reshaping the landscape of higher education.

Just as rising income and wealth inequality is splitting American society, many of the forces of turbulence we have explored also are bifurcating the higher education system into the haves and the have-nots. Instead of an engine of economic mobility, the higher education system could become inequality's enforcer. This is a gloomy scenario for anyone who values higher education as a source of social mobility and economic opportunity. We end this chapter with a review of some facts that should undergird any serious discussion of how the landscape of higher education is likely to change. Those facts also propel us into our final chapter's brief review of the policy options available to states and the federal government. Using those tools, however, will require a political will our system hasn't mustered in many years.

As we noted in chapter 5, the fraction of a high school cohort that enters a four-year degree program has risen from roughly one in three to one in two between the high school class of 1972 and the class of 2004. But the fraction of attenders who complete a degree has not improved. This is the first fact. From census data, the overall completion rate in 2011 conditional on attendance (45%) is slightly lower than it was in 1970 (46.7%). For men, the completion rate has fallen from 47.5% in 1970 to 41.8% in 2011.[13] The progressive impoverishment of much of the nation's state university systems is one reason, and this is especially true for the less selective state universities that serve the majority of students.

That is the second fact. Along with community colleges, less selective state institutions educate many of the nation's students from low-income families. Selective institutions, public and private, tend to enroll students who come from families further up the income distribution. Table 10.2 provides data from the Educational Longitudinal Study of 2002 (ELS 2002), which collected information from students in the high school class of 2004. For students in the sample who went to college, the table shows the breakdown by socioeconomic status (SES) of the students who attended institutions grouped by Barron's competitiveness categories. For example, the entry under "Four-Year Most Competitive" and "Bottom SES" is 4.1%. This means that only 4.1% of the students who attend institutions rated most competitive by Barron's are from the bottom quarter of the socioeconomic status distribution. The evidence of economic stratification in the US higher education system is quite clear. The more competitive an institution's admissions standards is, the more likely it is that that college or university will draw its students from the top of the income distribution.

This pattern has not changed over time. Data from three other major education datasets (the National Longitudinal Survey for 1972, High School and Beyond for 1982, and the National Educational Longitudinal Survey for 1994) show the persistence of this economic stratification. In our table, for instance, students coming from families in the bottom half of the SES distribution made up 12.2% of students at the most competitive institutions in 2004. The comparable figures were 12.6% in 1972, 15.2% in 1982, and 7.9% in 1992. For the highly competitive schools our table shows that students coming from families in the bottom half of the SES distribution made up 14.3% of the total. The comparable figures were 19.7% in 1972, 13.7% in 1982, and 17.0% in 1992. Finally, the table shows that students from families in the bottom half of the income distribution made up 22.3% of the students at very

Table 10.2 **Percentage of the Student Body by Barron's Competitiveness Groups and Quartiles of Socioeconomic Status (SES), Education Longitudinal Study: 2002**

SES Quartile	Four-Year Most Competitive	Four-Year Highly Competitive	Four-Year Very Competitive	Four-Year Competitive	Four-Year Noncompetitive	Two-Year Public
Bottom	4.1%	5.0%	7.3%	13%	19.6%	25.2%
Third	8.1%	9.3%	15.0%	19.1%	25.4%	28.7%
Second	18.7%	19.5%	26.8%	30.2%	29.1%	28.2%
Top	69.0%	66.2%	50.9%	37.8%	25.9%	17.9%

competitive institutions in 2004. The comparable figures were 25.2% in 1972, 23.6% in 1982, and 23.6% in 1992.[14] The percentages bounce around as you would expect in any sample, but there is no obvious improvement over a forty-year time span. As you move up the spectrum of school selectivity you find fewer students from lower-income families. This was true a generation ago and it remains true today.

This economic stratification reflects many forces. The influence of family income and parental education on the likelihood a student moves directly from high school into a four-year program actually has diminished over time, and this is a positive force for social change.[15] But this only means that academically qualified students are more likely to attend a four-year program today, despite coming from poorer or less well-educated families. It doesn't tell you about how those students sort into the most selective institutions, or how well they succeed. Highly selective programs have become even more selective over time, and undermatching is endemic. Students from poorer families are far less likely to attend selective colleges and universities that match their academic abilities, and this is our third fact.

Bowen, Chingos, and McPherson studied undermatching among students entering North Carolina public universities in 1999.[16] In their study, undermatching occurs when a student enrolls, for whatever reason, at a university that is less selective than other state institutions for which the student was objectively qualified. They found that 59% of students from families in the bottom income quartile were mismatched. They attended less selective universities than their academic qualifications warranted. Only 29% of students in the top income quartile were similarly underplaced. Likewise, 64% of students whose parents had no college training were undermatched, but only 31% of students whose parents had graduate degrees were similarly mismatched. This evidence of mismatching shows us that differences in student preparedness can't fully explain the skewed income and wealth distributions of students across the selectivity spectrum of the American university system. Many low-income students attend less selective schools because they are financially constrained, but others do so because they lack information about how to navigate the complexities of the admissions and aid processes, not because they cannot succeed at a more selective university.

This is also the message of more recent work by Caroline Hoxby and Christopher Avery. They look at the behavior of high-achieving low-income students.[17] These are students whose test scores (on the SAT or ACT) and grades are comparable to many of their higher-income peers. Using census data, they show that the vast majority of high-achieving low-income students don't even apply to any selective school despite the fact that for most of them a selective institution would cost less than the two-year programs and nonselective four-year universities to which they actually do apply. They call this set of students "income typical," and they explore the characteristics of this group that differ from the "achievement-typical" low-income students who apply to selective institutions and who succeed at the same rate as their higher-income peers. The "income-typical" students who mismatch at less selective schools tend to come from smaller school districts that do not support enriched programming. They are isolated from other high achievers in many ways. Their high schools often lack a sizable group of high-achieving students, and they rarely come in contact with anyone who attended a highly selective college or university. By contrast, low-income students who do apply to more selective colleges come from high schools that have a critical mass of high achievers. These tend to be feeder schools in larger school districts that are in the standard recruiting grounds for more selective colleges.

Here are the facts in brief. Attendance rates at four-year institutions have risen, but completion rates have not. Our higher education system remains highly stratified. Students from economically disadvantaged families go to less selective or nonselective schools, while the children of wealthier families cluster at better, resource-rich colleges and universities. And lastly, this stratification often reflects mismatching. Many of the students from poorer families never even consider better schools for which they are qualified. These three facts bring into sharp focus the problems we will face over the next generation as the forces of turbulence continue to reshape the American economy and the landscape of higher education.

The forces we have identified will force all colleges and universities to adapt. But the three facts mentioned reinforce the point that the schools at greatest risk are those that serve the bulk of the nation's most vulnerable students. Second-tier state universities and less selective private colleges face the greatest threats to their revenues and often have fewer tools to mitigate the problems they face. As the Universities of Shady Grove example demonstrates, there are creative solutions available for institutions that can clearly define their goals and find cooperative partners. But these solutions nibble at the edges of much larger problems.

In many ways our forecast is that the current winners will continue to win, and the current losers will lose even more. The Princetons, Virginias, Amhersts, and Colgates of the world are very good at delivering high-quality education, mentorship, peer relationships, and networking. There are reasons students line up around the block to get a chance to study at these institutions. The market for students is an information-rich market. Prospective students can investigate an ever-expanding number of rankings and guidebooks to help them identify a good match. They can talk to guidance counselors at their schools and in the private sector, and they can talk to current and former students. And because your peers are truly important in higher education, there is real truth to the notion that the most selective schools are the best schools. They can select the kinds of students who make real contributions both inside and outside the classroom.

This is the world that confronts policymakers. Income and wealth inequality remains entrenched. State governments still face hard choices. Lower-income students have weak access to better schools, in part because they are not fully plugged in to the information networks that higher-income families routinely enjoy. The schools they do attend are falling behind better-resourced institutions that disproportionately serve the better off. Yet the traditional high-touch model of personalized education and mentoring remains the best option for helping the most disadvantaged students in our society achieve a meaningful improvement in their life chances. In our final chapter we will explore a few of the internal reforms, experimental programs, and state and federal policy options that could change the trajectory of our troubled higher education system for the better.

11

The Road Ahead

POLICY OPTIONS

THERE IS A certain irony in our analysis of the turbulence buffeting the American higher education system and in our thinking about how that turbulence may affect the trajectory of its diverse institutions. Those who prophesy the wholesale makeover of how higher education is delivered actually foresee a better future ahead. In a brave new world of digital entrepreneurship, new technology and new firms replace an expensive, wasteful, and failing model with higher-quality and lower-cost educational options that target precisely what students supposedly want and need. By contrast, our forecast of the future of the US higher education system isn't apocalyptic. We do not foresee the disruption and dissolution of a substantial portion of the nonprofit higher education sector that currently educates roughly ten million young people in traditional four-year programs. The ancient but adaptable model of the college or university still offers great value to students in the traditional age range of undergraduates, and the bachelor's degree is likely to retain its value as a strong signal of innate and learned skills. Yet we are *not* optimists. The systemic stresses that we have identified point toward a lock-in of many negative features of our current system, features that reinforce income inequality and diminish social mobility.

In our view the problems we face are not easily reducible to poor decision making by university administrations or to bad choices by political leaders in state capitols or Congress. The causes of rising cost, for instance, are mostly found in economy-wide forces that defy simple solutions. Cost disease that afflicts personal service industries can't be "fixed" by price controls without sacrificing quality. Federal and state subsidies to students are not an engine of tuition growth at nonprofit colleges and universities. And the administrative costs of state and federal accountability rules can't be fixed by wishing away a national movement that is much broader than the higher education sector.

We have also argued that technology offers no simple solutions to the problems of cost, quality, and access. The digital revolution is unlikely to spur massive productivity growth in this still artisanal industry, especially where the education of eighteen-year-olds is concerned. And lastly, the causes and consequences of income inequality go well beyond anything that can be remedied by simple tweaks to higher education policy. If we are near the mark in our forecast for the trajectory of the diverse set of traditional higher education institutions, then we are faced with an interrelated set of social and economic stresses that defy easy answers and that cannot be reduced to a narrative of the virtuous against the villainous.

Higher education can contribute to social mobility in many ways. The system can become more inclusive in allowing and encouraging families to move into the system regardless of their means. This is access, and on this score we have done reasonably well over the past forty years, despite the rising cost of providing high-quality programming. But access is only the starting point. Once in the system, students must move through it in a timely fashion, acquire personally and socially useful skills and habits, and exit with a meaningful credential valued in the labor market. Here is where the higher education system increasingly is less successful, and the systemic challenges we have identified may cement social division in place.

We can frame the policy discussion as a need to preserve access while improving attainment. The instruments of access and attainment can be macro policies or micro interventions. Macro policies are the large programs that deliver funding to students and to institutions. This includes the federal programs that provide portable grants and loans directly to students, as well as state appropriations for public university operating expenses and bond funding for capital projects. Micro policy refers to targeted interventions that change incentives for specific groups of students. We will also use the term to describe ways that states could potentially change the balance between flagships (and other selective public institutions) and the less selective state universities that educate the bulk of the nation's at-risk population.

Basic Policy Trade-Offs

Federal need-based aid and state support for public colleges and universities are the two primary portals for helping students access the higher education system. Before we dig into the details of how these portals could be productively reformed, we want to introduce the inherent trad- eoff between simplicity and targeting. Simplicity and targeting each have virtues, but the tradeoff between them often is missing from much of the public discussion.

Federal student aid is aimed at families for whom basic access to college is limited by financial constraints. The primary goal is to increase the num- ber of qualified students from low-income families who seek postsecondary education instead of going directly into mostly low-paying jobs. Means-testing federal student aid changes the incentives of the targeted group without need- lessly subsidizing the broader population of higher-income families for doing what they would have done anyway. Targeting reduces the fiscal footprint of the program, and this kind of financial efficiency generally is a good attrib- ute of any spending program. Achieving this policy parsimony requires pro- cedures that winnow the group and allocate resources based on measurable characteristics of the beneficiary. Rules and procedures, however, have a side effect. They make the program more difficult to understand, and this can reduce the program's potential reach.

To access federal financial aid programs, a family must submit to an information-intensive and complex process. Filling out the Free Application for Federal Student Aid (FAFSA) requires complete tax returns plus a full accounting of all family assets. This information is fed into a black-box for- mula and a number comes out called the "expected family contribution," or EFC. The difference between the EFC and the current Pell maximum (which is $5,815 for 2016–17) gives the amount of assistance the family can get in the form of a Pell Grant. If the EFC exceeds the Pell maximum, the family is inel- igible for a Pell Grant. Most families that make more than $50,000 per year will not receive Pell support, though families earning substantially more will qualify for subsidized federal loans that may facilitate attendance but which do not reduce the actual price of a year in college. Pell dollars are well targeted on the most needy families, and this limits the cost of the program.

Ask most students (or their parents) if they understand how the Pell pro- gram works and you will likely get blank looks. There is now a wealth of evidence that the complexity of the federal financial aid process itself is a sig- nificant barrier to higher education access. Many families that might qualify for federal grant support never apply.[1]

Colleges themselves contribute to the complexity families face. The tui- tion discounting process means the list price loses much of its information value, especially at private institutions. Most families know that the list price often is discounted, but despite the existence of online net-price calculators people systematically overestimate the cost of college. Markets work better when prices contain real information. If families do not believe college is in the cards for their children, they often fail to make important choices about coursework as early as middle school, and those choices and related behaviors then reduce the likelihood of college attendance and college success. The mismatching issue we explored in the last chapter is another consequence of complexity. Families often mistake the lower list price of nonselective state universities for a lower net price, when better deals may be available at more selective schools. Undermatching at less selective institutions worsens outcomes for these students and for the nation as a whole.

State appropriations for public university operating expenses exemplify the alternative approach. The bulk of the appropriation is passed through to students in the form of reduced list-price tuition. In-state tuition is an untargeted subsidy that goes to the well-off and the economically disadvantaged alike.[2] For most students the list-price tuition at public universities contains much better information about the true cost of attendance than does the list price at private colleges and universities. This is especially true for families who earn substantially more than the median national income since they do not qualify for significant amounts of need-based aid at most universities outside of the super-elite.

Untargeted subsidies are a form of entitlement, and one major virtue of an entitlement is simplicity. The politics of entitlements, however, is less simple. Entitlement programs are more expensive than targeted subsidies, and this requires either more taxation or less spending on other things. The case for using state tax revenues to depress tuition for all families isn't open and shut. The state subsidy allows wealthier families to divert their own resources away from funding their children's education toward more consumption or personal saving. This is certainly a provocative way for us to frame the policy. On the other hand, spreading the benefits of a program further up the income distribution builds political support. This is the idea of "targeting within universalism" pioneered by the sociologists Theda Scokpol and William Julius Wilson, and it explains the broad support for programs like Social Security. Making Social Security an encompassing program for most of the elderly population builds broad political support while meeting its goal of specifically aiding the low-income elderly. Similarly, making in-state tuition an entitlement of all state-resident students creates the political support necessary for a subsidy that also benefits the poor. Big entitlements are hard to enact precisely because they cost a lot. State subsidization of higher education, however, began small and grew over time as the demand for higher education expanded.

At present our federal aid programs largely target lower-income families, but they are complex. State university systems offer much simpler subsidies through an in-state tuition "entitlement." These two approaches are complementary. Need-based federal programs address the access problems of lower-income families. And federal programs directly subsidize the student. Pell Grants and subsidized loans are portable to public and private institutions alike. These are desirable attributes and we think they should be maintained in the future. State appropriations that subsidize in-state tuition make college more affordable to all students, including middle- and upper-middle-income families whose children likely would have gone to college anyway. The fact that this form of state subsidy is not targeted on the poor is one reason for the remaining political support for public higher education. Yet that support has been ebbing for years as the demands on state budgets have grown along with enrollment. The sustained substitution of private tuition dollars for state tax revenue that we documented in chapter 7 tells a story of the declining political power of higher education as state budgets tighten and alternative demands on state revenues proliferate.

Policy Options I: What Not to Do

We start with three examples of policy approaches we think are *unhelpful*. Starting in the negative helps us identify important dos and don'ts in changing the policy environment. We will discuss one proposal that has yet to be enacted and two others that are currently very much in place.

Free College

Senator Bernie Sanders's (I, VT) 2016 run for the Democratic Party nomination introduced "free public tuition" as a policy idea and as a slogan to energize many of his young supporters. In his specific proposal, two thirds of the cost of reducing public tuition to zero would be borne by the federal government, while the other third would come from increased state appropriations in any state that signs on to the idea. Supporters of eliminating tuition and mandatory fees often rely on three general arguments. First, public higher education was essentially tuition free in many states in the past, so we can do it again. Second, it's currently free or very low cost in other parts of the developed world, so we should be able to do what other countries do. And third, a partial step in the right direction must be preferable to the status quo. While well intentioned, this is an example of a policy approach that is politically unfeasible and economically unsound compared to many alternatives.

First, consider the political feasibility of the proposal. We will make a big leap and assume for the sake of argument that the proposal passed the US Congress. Will the states sign on? Will they be willing to contribute their one third of the cost of making public colleges tuition free? There is considerable variance in the average tuition at public institutions by state. Some states are low-tuition states, and others are high-tuition states. The per-student cost of the free tuition proposal would therefore not be the same for all states. We very much doubt that the high-tuition states would be willing to participate. These states are high-tuition states because in the past they have not supported their public colleges and universities. These states are the least likely to change their behavior and embrace higher taxation or new priorities.

Second, arguments like "we used to do it" and "other countries do it" are history-free contentions. They implicitly assume that history does not, or should not, constrain current choices. To supporters of tuition-free policies, a critic who contends that history conditions and constrains our current choices simply lacks sufficient will, or worse, has capitulated to established interests. As economists, we're used to teaching about history-free processes, and we do so without apology. If the global reserves of oil within the supply chain decline on March 1, our modeling can offer us a range of likely price increases. If the supply shock is transitory, the economy may very well return to the old status quo. The fact that the market price of oil went up by a few percentage points for a few weeks does not forever change the structure of the oil industry. On the other hand, trying to return the world to its 1973 energy usage patterns is not a serious idea. The massive and sustained oil shocks of the 1970s led to significant changes in technology that permanently altered usage, production, discovery, and the range of alternatives. History matters.

Likewise, the historical arc of the higher education industry raises formidable obstacles to inserting the federal government so forcefully in funding state-supported universities. And the social case for attempting to recreate a long-gone status quo is not at all clear. As we discussed in chapter 7, changes in public university tuition reflect substantial changes in the economy and in the political structure within the states. The 1950s and 1960s were the years of maximal state effort on behalf of higher education. Yet college was not free, even in states that subsidized higher education enough to dispense with explicit tuition payments. For most students of that time, including those who attended private colleges, the primary cost of attendance was foregone wages. In that era when the college wage premium was at its lowest, someone with a high school degree could earn a substantial living. This is no longer true. Foregone wages are now a much smaller portion of the real cost of attendance. Cost disease over the last half century, plus the rising costs of producing a technologically up-to-date education, means that tuition subsidy from all sources is a much larger fraction of the total cost of attendance. Given the massive increase in enrollments over the past forty years, the fiscal consequences of reducing list-price tuition to zero are far larger than in the halcyon years of the post–World War II expansion.

We do have the example of other nations with free tuition. These countries tend to fall into one of three categories. Many are countries with very high tax rates. In others only a very small fraction of students go to college. Lastly, there are free-tuition countries with extremely high dropout rates. The history of the United States puts us in none of these groups. We have chosen relatively low taxes. We send a very large fraction of our students on to college. And while our dropout rate is higher than it should be, it is dwarfed by the dropout rate in some countries with free tuition. Argentina provides an interesting case. In Argentina, college is free and public institutions cannot reject any student. As a result, lots of students attend college, but an estimated 73% of the students who start do not finish.[3] And in many free-tuition nations, college students spend more years in school than in the United States.

More generally, should list price be zero? Using extra federal dollars explicitly to drive down list price doubles down on untargeted subsidies. And it claims tax revenues that have many other potentially better uses. As we have noted, untargeted list-price reductions boost spendable income of wealthier families. The children from families that earn three to four times the median family income are going to college anyway. But like all untargeted subsidies, this approach offers the virtues of simplicity. "Free public college tuition" is a slogan that fits easily on a bumper sticker. And as an easy-to-understand entitlement, free tuition may induce more students to take the steps necessary to move smoothly on to the college track.

Yet the consequences of focusing federal policy on list-price reduction at state universities are far reaching, and many are undesirable. Using federal dollars to cut tuition for students who attend state-chartered universities discriminates against the millions of students who attend private nonprofit colleges and whose families pay federal taxes. Enacting such a policy could drain demand away from many of the smaller and less selective private colleges that have a good track record of educating lower-income and first-generation students who need the high-touch programs they offer. This group of colleges is one that we have identified as at risk from the turbulence shaking the higher education system. Using federal dollars to discriminate against private nonprofit schools may tip many of these institutions over the financial edge.

Another side effect of federalizing the funding of state universities is a change in the locus of control. Proposals of this sort are inevitably a form of price control. And like most price controls, a free-tuition mandate would invest the regulator in prescribing what universities must do and telling them what they cannot do. A quick look at Senator Sanders's proposal (Senate Bill 1373) confirms that it is full of restrictions on what states and state universities must do and must not do. Micromanaging the behavior of local decision makers is unlikely to spur efficient responses to changes or to opportunities. Price controls also would put downward pressure on quality. Most of the forces pushing cost upward over time have not been repealed, so the controls on spending necessary to keep tuition at zero over time are likely to progressively degrade the quality of programming and support services. As a result, federally enforced spending controls are unlikely to improve the retention and graduation rates that are a fundamental systemic problem today and an increasingly important issue going forward.

Performance-Based Funding

The second example of problematic policy comes from the accountability movement. State accountability formulas that tie funding to performance can paradoxically reinforce disparities that disadvantage students who need the funding most. The logic of performance requirements seems simple. Tying funding to performance goals seemingly gives public institutions the right incentives to operate effectively and efficiently, changing an institutional culture steeped in justifying resource use into one that is results oriented. In an era of increasingly tighter budgets, enforcing performance requirements also says to voters that legislators are doing something to ensure that state revenues are used wisely. In higher education, funding traditionally has been based substantially on incremental growth. This year's allocation is the starting point for next year's funding base. Measurable things that differ across universities, like the number of full-time students enrolled, the presence of significant graduate programs, or the square footage of enclosed space, also drives funding. These traditional measures prioritize the status quo and reward universities for their inputs instead of their outputs.

The number of states using performance-based budgeting rose from one in 1990 to nineteen in 2000. A second surge after 2010 pushed the total to thirty-five states.[4] Despite this growth, there is a decided lack of evidence that states using performance measures have experienced better higher education outcomes. Higher education output is inherently difficult to quantify with a simple metric. Almost eighty years ago Clarence Ridley and Herbert Simon identified the problem in their analysis of performance measures for a wide variety of public services where outcomes are difficult to measure.[5]

The expenditures of a fire department, for instance, don't necessarily reflect just the number of fires put out. Performance incentives work better when the production process is simple and tasks are repetitive, as in much of the manufacturing sector. In higher education, we can count the number of first-year students who return for their second year, or the number who graduate within six years, but the process that leads to these outcomes is hardly simple. Using these counts to determine funding can lead to very perverse outcomes.

Some performance measures seem quite defensible in light of our analysis of current turbulence. Encouraging schools to prioritize underserved populations is one such worthy goal, yet even this type of goal doesn't guarantee a good outcome. Lesley Turner (2012) has shown that public universities are willing to "pay" for additional Pell recipients, but one way they attract more Pell recipients who are near the Pell eligibility threshold is to transfer resources away from even poorer Pell recipients. Other common performance measures are even more problematic.[6]

Tying funding to completion rates has obvious negative consequences. Graduation and retention are highly correlated with a university's selectivity, and school selectivity remains strongly related to family income. Linking funding to a school's graduation rate, for instance, favors selective institutions whose students come to school better prepared to succeed over less selective public universities whose students actually need *more* help. Worse, schools can improve graduation rates by taking fewer chances on students with risky academic backgrounds or by lowering their academic standards and graduating students who do not deserve to pass. Likewise, some formulas reward schools for giving out more financial aid. This can perversely lead to a reduction in need-based discounts and a rise in merit aid. It can also induce schools to push up list price more rapidly than they might otherwise have chosen, since a higher discount rate raises the amount of "scholarship aid" they disburse. One of the strongest virtues of the American higher education system is its willingness to invest in giving young people a second or third chance. Performance-based funding can easily erode that characteristic.

As long as mission remains an important set of norms governing how nonprofit institutions behave, adherence to that mission can explain the absence of any large and sustained impact (positive or negative) of vague performance metrics. Yet we must be aware that putting a firm price on bad behavior isn't always a sure incentive to improve outcomes. In an amusing but telling example, Uri Gneezy and Aldo Rustichini ran an experiment at Haifa day care centers.[7] Closing time was 4:00 PM, and by social custom most children were picked up by 4:30 PM. To see if they could reduce the incidence of late pickup, they placed an explicit fine on tardiness. Instead of a deterrent, the fine became a clear price for extra babysitting. The social taboo against lateness disappeared and tardy pickups increased significantly as the social norm was replaced by a simple monetary consequence. In higher education, putting a small price on certain numerical targets could induce schools to meet those goals in ways that harm more important targets. For instance, Hillman, Tandberg and Fryar show that performance targets in Washington State led community colleges to produce more certificates, which are easier and quicker to generate, in place of associate's degrees, which are costlier.[8] The social benefit of this switch is dubious since the long-term earnings gains from an associate's degree tend to be larger than the return to a certificate.

Loan Repayment Options

Our third "don't" is about the set of loan repayment options currently offered. This menu of options maximizes the likelihood of adverse selection as an unintended consequence. For instance, offering students an income-contingent repayment option, especially if it comes with an eventual forgiveness of residual debt, is an invitation to adverse selection. Students who know they are likely to wind up in low-paying positions will opt for income contingent repayment with a forgiveness horizon. Students who think they'll be well compensated will choose a more standard fixed repayment plan that operates more like a mortgage.

At present, our loan system does not rate the riskiness of student loans using any screening process (like grades or entrance test scores). This ignored information raises the riskiness of the overall pool of borrowers. The adverse selection issue arises because the students have private information. Students know more about their noncognitive skills and other attributes that correlate with the likely payoff to a degree. This is private information about repayment risk. Some students know that they are likely to work in lower-paying occupations. Some students also have clear preferences about the kind of work they wish to do upon graduation. Some students *want* to work in low-paying occupations for the nonpecuniary benefits that these low-paying jobs bring to them.

One can argue that we should not have a system that funnels students into higher-paying jobs that they dislike simply because they have student debt to repay. In this view, the wealthier students can indulge in socially productive but privately unprofitable work, while students who are "forced" borrowers must forego that option because they need to repay student loan debt. Some will see this as a deeply unfair attribute of our current system. But a system that allows students with private information to behave in ways that push up the loan system's overall default risk punishes other borrowers and the taxpayers who fund the program. We should not build a system with adverse selection as a feature.

What to do? One solution is to design a system in which all who choose to borrow must use the income-contingent feature (no choice), and it must be actuarially fair. Some "winners" will pay more than the value of their loan (within limits), while others will get a break due to bad luck in the labor market. In a similar vein, students can be charged zero for their education, with full repayment over time in an income-contingent manner. Alternatively, we can maintain the income-contingent option but require full payback over time at a reasonable interest rate. No one should be able to parley their private information into a "heads I win, tails you lose" outcome.

Policy Options II: What to Do

We argue that policy reform should be based on several guiding principles. Seek simplicity whenever possible. Leave important decisions to the lowest feasible level (the student and the institution). Maximize the flexibility of students and universities to respond to incentives and to choose their own path. Lastly, whenever possible, ensure that resources flow toward creating social mobility, not toward established hierarchies that favor the well prepared and the well-off. As a general rule, policymakers should be skeptical of setting simple numerical targets when the processes they are attempting to regulate or affect are complex.

Some of our suggestions require greater government expenditures on behalf of higher education. But we recognize that simply increasing government outlays is not all that is needed. Governments have to spend their money more wisely. Other suggestions do not call for extra spending. They call for changes in the priorities that direct spending. Unfortunately we do not uncover any magic bullets, but we think there are changes that can improve the higher education system of the future.

Improve Information Flows

General information about college is very easy to access. There are numerous books rating and describing colleges. Every college is eager to provide visitors with lots of literature and guided tours. College websites have page after page of useful information interspersed with a certain amount of propaganda. But when it comes to some of the most important information, like the chances a student with certain characteristics will be admitted and just how much it will cost, accurate information becomes much more difficult to obtain. There is considerable evidence that many students make poor choices because this critical information is lacking or is enmeshed in overly complicated websites that amount to informational overkill. We have three suggestions for improving information flows.

Simplify the Needs Analysis System

There is a long-standing debate about how best to target federal student aid. The current FAFSA process attempts scrupulous fairness by factoring in family income, an appropriate measure of family assets, family size, and the number of children in college. It is an exhaustive and information-intensive evaluation of need. Yet its complexity is a barrier to access. We favor simplifying this process substantially. There are many viable alternatives to the traditional FAFSA.[9] The simplest would use some form of easily understood postcard version that focuses primarily on two numbers, adjusted gross income and the number of children in college. Another good alternative involves a check box on a family tax return that would allow this data to be used to calculate eligibility and the EFC. This check box approach also would not consider family assets, although some proposals use interest and dividend income to impute the value of family assets.

Using a postcard FAFSA, it's possible to imagine a wealthy family with a low-reported income qualifying for a Pell Grant. The tradeoff between scrupulous fairness and simplicity, however, is more apparent than real. The fairness gain from extracting family asset information actually is quite small. Taxing family assets also discourages saving for college, while the exemption of the family home from total assets encourages overinvestment in a primary residence. In our view the benefits of simplifying the FAFSA are large and clear, while the costs in terms of cheating the system are hypothetical and seemingly quite small.

Simplify Federal Provision of Information

The federal government can act as a storehouse of easy-to-use, reliable, comparable, and nonpolitical information about colleges and universities. The College Scorecard (https://collegescorecard.ed.gov) does not do this particularly well. The scorecard contains many items that should not be compared across schools in the absence of much more context than is currently provided. Graduation rates provide a good example. As we have noted before, graduation rates are determined by many things that have nothing to do with the school's value added, like the quality of incoming students. We have no easy and foolproof measures of the school's value added in improving graduation rates. No one knows what an appropriate graduation rate would be. Historically black colleges and universities, along with many religious schools, often have higher graduation rates. This fact alone offers no policy advice or clear best practices. The easiest ways to improve graduation rates involve shedding risky students who are disproportionately first generation or underprivileged, or softening standards. Neither of these is socially useful.

Salaries of graduates provide another example. As we showed in chapter 5, starting salaries vary considerably by a student's course of study. Engineering students, for instance, earn higher average starting salaries than students who major in most other fields. Two institutions can have very different average starting salaries because their students have a different mix of college majors. Likewise, the fraction of an institution's graduating class that moves directly into the labor force can vary substantially from university to university. An institution whose graduates move in large numbers into graduate school may see an average starting salary no higher (or perhaps even lower) than another institution whose students move immediately into the workforce. Yet the lifetime trajectory of income earned by students from the two schools may differ substantially. These raw differences in earnings tell us little about whether or not the school will be the best place for a particular student.

What should the government report instead? We would move away from complex net-price calculators. Instead, each college or university could be made to provide a simple table that lists the net price by family income level for enrolled students. As such, it's not a contract for any individual family. But a family should be able to look at that table to see what a student who is roughly in their income range actually pays as a net price at that college. They should see how much institutional need-based aid the school offers and how much merit aid the school kicks in for students at a variety of income levels. This information would be comparable across schools and accessible on one public website.

The current federal obsession with lists and rankings adds little value and is often counterproductive. As an example, the Department of Education publishes shame lists of the most expensive schools, where expensive is defined as the average net price of students who receive aid. This metric immediately disadvantages schools that serve a lot of middle-class students who receive some aid but who also pay a substantial amount of tuition. It favors schools that enroll large numbers of full-paying students who get no discount and whose needy students receive large aid packages. This makes elite schools look inexpensive, though their full-paying clientele actually pays more. Worse, the formula can be gamed. It is an incentive for schools to find ways to bundle more aid on needy students, which pushes down the average net price paid by aid-receiving students, while also pushing out middle-class students in favor of wealthier full-paying students. The federal government has no business creating this incentive.

Provide Information to Improve Matching

One of the most promising areas of current research explores how we might improve the matching process for low-income high-achieving students. These are not students for whom the return on educational investment is in doubt. Instead, these students seem to miss the opportunities that are available to them. The Expanding College Opportunities (ECO) project developed by Caroline Hoxby and Sarah Turner provided individualized information to students about the college application and selection process.[10] The program offered information about graduation rates and available resources at various colleges, and about the true net cost of attendance for students who come from an economic background similar to their own. Students were also guided on how to apply. Lastly, they were offered free applications at up to eight of the nation's most selective colleges and universities. The invitation to the ECO program was mailed to students, and the mailing included web links and passwords to a site that was customized for each student.

The ECO intervention was a randomized controlled trial, which is the gold standard in empirical research. The treated group consisted of 10,000 randomly selected high school seniors from the top 10% of SAT and ACT takers in 2010–11, with a randomly selected control group of 2,500 who did not receive the mailing. An additional group of 15,000 was selected in 2011–12. The results were strongly positive despite the fact that the mailing did not come with the imprimatur of an easily recognized outside group like the College Board or the National Merit Scholarship Corporation.[11] The percentage of treated students who applied to college soared, as did the number who applied to better programs. In follow-up surveys, substantially more of the treated students were accepted into more selective programs with higher graduation rates and higher instructional spending per student. These effects carried over into where students actually enrolled. The cost of the program was an astonishingly low $6 per mailing.

This ECO experiment offers a number of strong messages. First, many students lack good information about colleges and the application process, and that lack strongly affects outcomes. Second, the quantity of information is less important than the relevance. Information needs to be targeted and customized to the particular background of each student, and the information is processed better if it is sent directly to the student. By contrast, on government websites like the College Navigator maintained by the Department of Education, the great volume of information found there is both complex and passive.[12] Students have difficulty extracting personal meaning from it. When confronted by such a mass of information, students often default to the most familiar options, which tend to be the local college or state university branch campus.

With its low cost, this type of micro intervention is both scalable and expandable. It could be enlarged to reach all high-achieving low-income students, and it could be expanded to a broader group beyond just the highest achieving. Doing so requires the active involvement of an independent third party, such as the College Board, and the active cooperation of the government. In addition to the credibility a major third party would bring, an outside sponsor solves a collective action problem. Individual schools lack the information to make the program work, and they have little incentive to undertake information provision that is as likely to benefit their competitors as themselves. The federal government is a necessary partner because the rich data needed to target students geographically comes from federal sources, and some of these sources are not collecting as much information as in the past.[13] Finally, this type of program is an example of how the government can assist what is essentially a nonprofit solution to a significant social problem.

Rethink Federal Student Loans

In chapter 6 we showed that the loan burden of the average college graduate doesn't warrant sensationalism. Finishing college with a debt between $25,000 and $35,000 is not a crushing burden for most degree holders to bear. Much of the sensational media coverage is based on outliers or is driven by the for-profit sector. Nonetheless, our system of student loans falls well short of ideal, and there are productive reforms we might consider. First, some students do incur very high undergraduate debt levels, and paying off these debts is quite burdensome. Second, the reassuring data were for college graduates and for those who earned graduate degrees, most of which pay well enough to support a sizable debt. But students who do not complete a degree owe a troubling amount of debt. These debts are much more difficult to repay since students whose stay in college was short have earned neither the skills nor the sheepskin to command a substantial premium in the labor market.

Prudential Underwriting of College Loans

The total volume of student loan debt has risen substantially over the last twenty years. Some factors that raise student borrowing are of no policy consequence. Other issues are more worrisome. Separating the two is an important step in moving the public discussion forward. Total enrollment at colleges and universities has grown by four million over the last decade alone. Rising enrollment naturally tends to push up total borrowing. If improved access is indeed a force for raising the total level of educational borrowing, this is not a problem to be solved. In addition, if recent increases in the number of degree-seeking students come disproportionately from the ranks of the less well-off, average debt per student will rise. Again, this is not a problem requiring a policy remedy.

Lastly, the economic return from additional schooling has grown almost continuously since 1980. In 1973, a full 30% of college graduates in the twenty-five- to forty-year-old age range earned less than the income of the median high school educated worker in the same age range.[14] Today, that figure is down to 17%. A college degree also creates career options that do not exist for people who stop their education with a high school diploma, and college-educated people switch more easily between jobs at roughly the same pay scale. The extra earning potential of a college degree allows the average student to borrow much more today than in the past without taking on any more repayment risk. As best we can measure, repayment-to-earnings ratios are no different now than in the supposedly halcyon past when college was cheaper.[15]

On the other hand, the difference between the median family's income and the net cost of attendance has shrunk over the last decade. For a growing percentage of the student population, this decline in college affordability increases the need to borrow. Other things equal, declining college affordability could raise the likelihood of default, especially for students who borrow but fail to complete a degree. In addition, the widening gap between incomes at the upper end and the lower end of the income distribution means that needy students come to college ever needier and more likely to use debt to fund a larger portion of their educational bill.

The personal and social consequences of going into default on student loan payments are long-lasting. Large debt can alter a variety of personal and economic decisions about things as diverse as family formation and home ownership. We have shown that the average level of student preparedness for college has not declined over the last forty years. Diminishing student quality, therefore, is not a likely driver of rising nonrepayment rates. On the other hand, the sheer volume of students who are in the bottom half of the high school grade point average (GPA) distribution and who move directly from high school into four-year universities has risen over time. Using data from Figure 5.1 on the size of the high school class and data from Figure 5.4 on the fraction of the high school class that attend a four-year school by high school GPA decile, we estimate that 143,016 students from the bottom 30% of the high school class start at a four-year college each year.[16]

For most commercial loans, the prospective borrower has to qualify. This means satisfying the lender that the prospective borrower has sufficient collateral, a good credit reputation, and the capacity to make the required payments. These conditions are not applied to college loans. Students rarely have sufficient collateral, and an education cannot be repossessed. The borrower is usually a recent high school graduate who has had little time to establish a credit record. Unlike graduate training in medicine or business, individual variance in earnings from a two-year or four-year program is quite high. The return depends on choices (of major and career path) that the average eighteen-year-old has barely begun to make. As a result, a private lender has little way to ascertain whether or not the prospective borrower will have the capacity to repay the loan.

To qualify for a federal student loan, a student who has not previously defaulted on a student loan, and who has not been convicted of a drug offense, only has to demonstrate that he or she is enrolled in an accredited institution of higher education. Federal student loans are given to students, and PLUS loans to families, who would never qualify for any other type of loan outside of the payday lending market.

One plausible way to reduce the frequency of "default" is to limit loan access to incoming students who meet simple and easy-to-understand criteria. The simplest is a GPA cutoff. Many states use a GPA cutoff for scholarship entitlements. The Georgia Hope Scholarship program, for instance, guarantees grant money to all students who have a 3.0 GPA in high school, and all students easily can see their grant amount at any Georgia institution by reading a table provided online by the state.[17] The cutoff for loan eligibility need not be this stringent. It could be set at a lower bound below which non-repayment risk is unacceptably high.

The federal government has deeper pockets and a broader understanding of the social return to education. We would not want the student loan process to follow purely private creditworthiness checks. The American higher education system offers students a large number of second chances. A student with a very poor high school record who also fares badly on standardized tests can still become a college graduate. There are many people who have taken advantage of the second chances offered by open-admission institutions. We do not think this opportunity should be taken away. But our current system does burden many young people who never achieve a meaningful education with unsustainable educational debt that cannot be discharged in bankruptcy. The federal student loan program might work better if students who are very unlikely to benefit from further education did not automatically qualify for large and potentially crippling amounts of student loan debt immediately after completing high school. Yet all students should have a path back to full loan eligibility.

Using some form of student loan underwriting, perhaps by GPA cutoff, offers a number of distinct advantages or social payoffs. First, it would give real information to students and to their families about the consequences of weak preparation while the students are still in middle school and high school. This may lead to some positive behavioral changes early enough to improve the pool of students entering the higher education system. The second benefit of financial "tough love" goes to marginal students who choose to enter the system anyway, even though they may not qualify at the outset for student loans. They will still qualify for need-based Pell Grants, so these students may select lower-cost options like local community colleges. This is not a bad thing. These students will learn about themselves in that first year, and that knowledge will improve the efficacy of the student loan program. Some will learn that postsecondary schooling really is not for them. They will buy this knowledge relatively cheaply, since they will not have accumulated a significant first-year debt. And for students who qualify for Pell Grants, the financial cost of that first learning year may be quite low.

Others in this same group of marginally prepared students will learn how to learn. They will develop the habits of mind and persistence that increase the chances of academic success. For these students, their poor high school performance will become less predictive of their chances to succeed in college. For this group, full loan eligibility can be restored after successful completion of a semester or a year of postsecondary training. Third, some students who otherwise would have racked up thousands of dollars in debt will be deterred from seeking postsecondary education. But these are most likely to be the students who have the smallest chance of success. Without a debt millstone, they will be better positioned financially as they navigate the job market.

Lastly, some schools may be willing to bring in students from this high-risk marginal group, even though those students cannot get loans for the first year. If those students have significant financial need, the schools will be responsible for increasing institutional grant aid to make their program affordable. Those schools will bear the risk of matriculating these students, not the federal loan program. The schools will have skin in the game, and they will have an incentive to provide services to help these marginal students succeed.

Instituting a creditworthiness barrier to accessing student loans is not a perfect solution. There will be some students who might have succeeded in a four-year program despite their weak academic background but who fail in a two-year program and never go back to school. Before instituting such a policy, the costs and benefits must be evaluated thoroughly. The hypothetical costs of inappropriately deterring some weaker students from seeking a four-year degree directly out of high school must be set against the arguments on the other side of the ledger we have articulated previously. And we must recognize the clear negative consequences of saddling underprepared students with substantial educational debts they cannot reasonably repay.

Skin in the Game of Loans

Critics of the student loan program have long focused on the fact that government loan guarantees and direct federal lending often allow colleges and universities to avoid responsibility for their failures. Under our current system of direct government lending, the school gets its money up front as student loans are used to pay tuition. But the school faces no penalty if its students do not repay the loans. There are several proposals based on the notion that colleges and universities should have some financial stake in whether or not their students successfully repay what they borrow from the government. This "skin in the game" could induce better outcomes.[18]

Under these "skin" proposals schools would have to pay a percentage of the government's cost if a student defaulted on a loan. Under current rules schools do face some costs if their overall default rates are too high. They can lose eligibility for federal grant and loan programs if their default rate exceeds 30% for three consecutive years or if it goes over 40% for one year. This rule does affect some schools, but the vast majority of public and private not-for-profit institutions that are our focus operate far below these thresholds. These policies are blunt instruments. It is all or nothing, and the 30% and 40% bars are arbitrarily chosen. If institutions have to pay a percentage of all defaults, even schools not threatened by the current standards would be forced to pay attention to their students' behavior.

Colleges and universities do not have complete control over the behaviors that lead to default, but they can have some effect on their students' choices. Currently there are no direct incentives for them to try. Schools can do more to counsel students about how loans work and how different levels of debt will affect their future. They can do more to steer students to the best loan options. For example, they could counsel students not to rely on credit card debt. Schools can also do more to increase completion rates, which will keep default rates low. And schools can do more to tailor financial aid packages that currently rely too heavily on loans.

One obvious objection to "skin" proposals is that they would cause institutions to do a less socially desirable form of loan underwriting than the GPA cutoff proposal we just discussed. If the schools were doing the underwriting, they would likely add family income to the factors considered. Colleges might prove much less willing than they currently are to admit poor students, because these students likely would have to take out large loans. Combining a skin-in-the-game proposal with a substantial increase in the maximum Pell Grant could mitigate this problem. Another fear is that any skin requirement would push up tuition by adding to a college's costs. A recent paper by Douglas Webber estimates that there would only be modest increases in tuition from this kind of a change. Webber also estimates that by far the largest impact of these programs on total borrowing would come from reduced borrowing at for-profit institutions.[19]

Adding a carefully crafted skin-in-the-game requirement could improve the overall effectiveness of the federal loan program because it would provide all schools with an incentive to monitor student borrowing and to take actions that would reduce default, not just schools whose default rates are near an arbitrary and extreme threshold. Like our prudential underwriting idea, skin-in-the-game proposals currently are hypothetical. The benefits, costs, and possible unintended consequences have yet to be systematically evaluated. Many of the policies schools might initiate to shrink their default rates could be socially undesirable, and schools cannot control default rates precisely. The burden of skin proposals also falls most heavily on the under-resourced schools that are at greatest risk and that serve the most vulnerable populations. We would not advocate for this approach unless it's tied to other policies that replace a portion of the loans students currently take out with larger federal grants that do not need to be repaid. Still there are ways that schools can encourage better borrowing behavior, and the current set of rules provides little incentive for schools to adopt them.

Deepen the Public Investment in Higher Education

We understand the natural temptation to suggest that problems can be solved if we just spend more money. Given the substantial public retreat from investing in higher education, a boost in spending is not altogether a bad idea. Much of the public disinvestment has been unplanned in any long-run sense.

Some of the problems we see in higher education are a result of the fact that government has backed away from its role as a funder of higher education. We can imagine some helpful policies that are based on increased government spending on higher education.

Automatic Increases in Pell Grants

Figure 7.4 showed that the real value of the Pell Grant maximum declined substantially between the late 1970s and the mid-1990s and only returned to its initial 1970s levels around 2010. During that same time period the real value of college tuition has increased. As a result, the fraction of the cost of attendance covered by Pell Grants has decreased considerably. This pattern was not planned. One way to stabilize the value of a Pell Grant is to link the Pell maximum to the price index for services. This would also depoliticize setting the Pell Grant maximum and ensure that any future congressional neglect was more benign. As long as service prices continue to rise faster than the overall consumer price index, the Pell Grant maximum would increase in real terms. We recognize that this proposal could lead the Pell Grant maximum to continue its long-run decline as a percentage of the cost of attendance, but indexing the Pell Grant maximum to some price index of college tuition is fraught with problems. There is currently no index of net tuition. Also, using an index based on tuition would give colleges a role in determining how much subsidy they would get, which is not politically appealing.

With the current arrangement, the Pell Grant maximum is set by an act of Congress. It can be changed any year, but the data are clear that in many years it is not changed. This leaves college students from poorer families in a difficult situation. In years in which the Pell Grant maximum is not increased, a Pell recipient's grant tends to cover a smaller percentage of the student's cost of attendance than it did in the previous year. In years in which the Pell Grant rises, in many cases students get a significant and unexpected (but still desired) windfall as the grant now covers a larger percentage of the cost of attendance than it had in the previous year. There is mileage in eliminating this kind of political uncertainty. Indexing the Pell Grant maximum would reduce the intense politicization of the issue in much the same way that indexing Social Security benefits depoliticized the process of determining the size of annual federal benefit changes to the elderly. We suggest using a price index for services as opposed to an overall price index to preserve the Pell program's ability to cover increases in the costs of providing a college education.

State/Federal Partnership

In 1999, the net tuition and fees the average family in the top (or fourth) quartile of earners paid to attend a private college was 3.5 times higher than the cost to attend a public institution.[20] For a family in the second quartile (the twenty-fifth to fiftieth percentiles of the national income distribution), the cost of private tuition was 4.8 times higher. Roll the clock forward to the 2011–12 academic year and the gaps have shrunk to 2.4 and 3.7, respectively. Net tuition at public universities that educate vast numbers of the nation's most at-risk students is rising relative to net tuition at private colleges. We have argued against an ahistorical push for making public universities tuition free. Yet there are productive ways the federal government could encourage states to restore some of their past effort on behalf of higher education.

Constructive ideas for federal–state partnerships have languished in Congress for a number of years. The key idea is to use federal dollars to induce states to raise their effort on behalf of higher education without micromanaging university spending or setting precise targets for tuition levels. We would identify three essential elements of this partnership approach. The first is to set reasonable eligibility criteria that push the least generous states to spend at least a certain minimum amount per full-time student. In one proposal (Senate Bill 2954), states become eligible for federal matching grants if they spend at least half the value of the maximum Pell Grant in that year. This is a minimalist hurdle that would force only a handful of states to raise higher education spending to qualify.[21]

The second element is some formula for using new federal dollars to encourage *increases* in state higher education spending above the minimum threshold. Such a formula would provide states with predictable federal block grants for higher education based on their level of spending per full-time student. This would reward states that have a deep commitment to higher education and encourage extra effort from states that currently spend less-than-average amounts per student. Requiring states that receive grants to maintain effort would ensure that federal money did not simply displace state spending. Lastly, the program must recognize the power of recessions on state finances. In an economic downturn, state revenues contract. If states need to cut higher education spending as a response, they would lose federal matching money as well. The federal program would become a force for destabilizing state finances. This means that a reasonable state–federal partnership must recognize that recessions happen and offer states a safe harbor exception to reduce higher education spending during an economic downturn. But once the state's macro economy recovers, the provisions of the partnership should be restored in full.

Focusing Funding on Struggling Institutions

In our summary in chapter 10, we argued that less selective colleges and universities would face the most difficulty in the coming years. We also presented evidence that these institutions are the ones most often attended by students from lower-income families. These less selective institutions, both public and private, generally spend less per student than their more selective counterparts. These institutions are at a significant disadvantage in a world in which colleges and universities must rely increasingly on private resources, either from tuition or from private donations. Our last set of policy recommendations directly addresses this concern. We have one policy recommendation for state governments and another for the federal government.

More Autonomous Flagships

In our previous book, we advocated rewriting the financial compact between states and their public universities.[22] We argued that public universities needed more control over their revenue stream. State higher education appropriations tend to follow a roller coaster pattern, rising in good times but falling further in bad times, and trending downward overall. As a result, public universities do not have a stable planning horizon and the weaker among them are increasingly revenue starved. Yet they must compete with private institutions that are not so constrained. If state universities had more autonomy to set their own tuition and then discount like private colleges, their revenues would rise and would become more predictable.

This idea can work most quickly for flagships and other selective public institutions that have the power to behave differently. In the last chapter, we noted that flagships and other selective public institutions can discount more effectively than less selective institutions because places in the their first-year class are in higher demand. And some of that demand comes from wealthier families who are not particularly price sensitive. We also noted that flagships and other selective public institutions are better at encouraging private philanthropic giving. States with strong institutions could recognize these facts and give their flagships and other selective institutions more autonomy in exchange for a smaller appropriation or a smaller share of any increases in appropriations. These revenues could be diverted to the less selective and often woefully underfunded state universities that increasingly serve students from disadvantaged backgrounds. We recognize the political difficulties involved in doing this. State control of tuition setting at flagships ensures relatively low tuition for upper-middle-income families whose incomes have stagnated. Any movement away from using state appropriations to deliver untargeted benefits will be controversial.

Institutional Support Based on Pell Enrollment

In addition to making the portable Pell more generous by linking the Pell Grant maximum to a nonpolitical formula like the service price index, the federal government could use a simple financial incentive to encourage schools to enroll Pell recipients and to devote more resources to their needs. The federal government could pay, for example, 10 cents to the college's operating budget for every Pell dollar its students bring in. This would reward schools that serve a large number of Pell recipients without attempting to micromanage or to judge performance. These schools could use the extra federal resources to maximize the mission. Why not restrict this to schools that perform "well" with those Pell students? That would direct dollars to elite schools that take the cream of the Pell crop. These are well-endowed institutions that don't need extra operating support. Graduation success can be tied easily to things that are innate to students or to resources available at schools. Yet many of the characteristics of "successful" schools aren't easily replicable. We can punish badly performing schools by targeting egregious outliers without imposing unrealistic graduation rate performance on substantial numbers of schools as though federal programs can easily manipulate performance.

In such a program we would *not* want to give resources to schools per Pell student enrolled since that would encourage schools to concentrate on attracting students who have the Pell label but who qualify for very little Pell money (the better-off Pell families). A proposal of the sort we are advancing would reward schools that work with low-income populations, and it responds to our fears that the future will bring a more bifurcated system. A Pell supplement directed to schools' operating budgets would pump resources directly into currently underresourced public and private institutions. These extra resources would be aimed specifically at institutions in the front lines of dealing with diversity in the current system. It might also encourage highly selective institutions to admit more Pell recipients at the margin, and these students would be exposed to the resource-rich environment of those colleges and universities.

Savvy readers will note that we could achieve almost the same outcome if we simply increased the Pell Grant maximum by 10% and mandated that institutions impose a 100% tax rate on the new funds. This might appear odd, but our intent is to increase the operating budgets of schools that serve the most needy students, and we think the Pell Grant program gives us a convenient way to locate just those schools. Also, many people might be inclined to add requirements directing institutions on how they are to spend their Pell

Grant bounty. This is a path we do not want to walk. We trust that the institutions will know the best use for these funds better than a congressional committee. They are in the trenches and they are facing stiff competition.

The Last Word

We have touched on a wide variety of reasons that the stresses on our higher education system may reinforce income inequality and social immobility. Education has the potential to be the great equalizer, except for all the reasons that it isn't. Income inequality itself is driven in substantial part by the rising premium on education, so any factor that stratifies access to the system by family income can deepen and lock in inequality. Lower-income families lack the resources to invest in their children from their earliest years, so these children tend to be less well prepared to succeed in a university environment. Lower-income families also lack information, and this discourages many from applying to programs they could reasonably attend. Many who do go often mismatch at schools that are more expensive and of lower quality. Attending underresourced programs reduces the likelihood that students from lower-income families will complete a degree.

We have identified reasons for deep concern, but we've also identified a set of reforms and initiatives with great potential. Each reform proposal individually may have only a limited impact. As a package, a number of the proposals we have outlined could fit together to solve deeply rooted structural problems that keep education from fully performing its social function.

Notes

CHAPTER 1

1. See Lenzner and Johnson (1997), p. 127.
2. See Blumenstyk (2014).
3. See Carey (2015), p. 36.
4. This low quality of undergraduate teaching is the central theme of *Academically Adrift*, by Arum and Roksa (2010).
5. See Taylor (2010).
6. See Shaffer (2011) for the interview with Theil.
7. See, for example, Frey (2013) and Staton (2014).
8. See chapter 3 of Carey (2015). Joel Trachtenberg served as president of George Washington from 1988 to 2007.
9. On the 2015 list there were actually eleven because Cal Tech and Johns Hopkins tied for tenth. The others were Penn, Duke, MIT, Columbia, Stanford, Chicago, Yale, Harvard, and Princeton.
10. The *US News & World Report* rankings include many quantitative measures that offer targets for ambitious schools. Many of these targets, like the percentage of classes that have fewer than twenty students, accord with most people's sense of quality.

CHAPTER 2

1. The selective liberal arts college is Kenyon College, the less selective liberal arts college is Washington College, the selective private university is Stanford University, the flagship state university is the University of Arizona, and the nonflagship state university is Western Kentucky University.

2. We defined the liberal arts disciplines as area, ethnic, and gender studies (Classification of Instructional Programs [CIP] code 5); computer and information sciences (CIP code 11); foreign languages, literature, and linguistics (CIP code 16); English (CIP code 23); liberal arts/general studies (CIP code 24); biological/life sciences (CIP code 26); mathematics and statistics (CIP code 27); interdisciplinary studies (CIP code 30); philosophy and religious studies (CIP code 38); physical sciences (CIP code 40); psychology (CIP code 42); social sciences (CIP code 45); visual and performing arts (CIP code 50); and history (CIP code 54).

3. The University of Phoenix enrollment was 460,000 students in 2010. In the following five years it fell by roughly 200,000 students (http://money.cnn.com/2015/03/25/investing/university-of-phoenix-apollo-earnings-tank/).

4. These data are from the College Board's 2013 *Trends in College Pricing*, Table 2A, p. 15.

5. The Delta Cost Project uses the Department of Education's IPEDS data. The specific variable used in Figure 2.1 is "fte12mn - Total 12-Month FTE student Enrollment."

6. The data show pricing for the 2013–14 academic year. They come from Figure 2, p. 12 in the College Board's 2013 issue of *Trends in College Pricing*.

7. The Delta Cost Project variable is tuition discount, which is computed as the ratio of institutional grants to list-price tuition. The data are weighted by the variable fte12mn.

8. The tuition variable for this figure was tuition03_tf from the Delta Cost Project data.

9. We constructed our selectivity measure using the Delta Cost Project variables admitcount and applicantcount.

10. See Clinedinst (2014), p. 17.

11. This attendance and completion information comes from US Census data. See Archibald, Feldman, and McHenry (2015).

12. For this figure we used the Delta Cost Project variable grad_rate_150_p (the percentage of first-time first-year undergraduates who graduate within 150% of the normal time).

13. For this figure we used the Delta Cost Project variable tuition_reliance_a1.

CHAPTER 3

1. This epigram is widely attributed to president James Garfield, who studied with Mark Hopkins at Williams College in the 1850s.

2. Virginia Tech's Math Emporium offers a good example. Many of the introductory mathematics courses are offered online through the emporium. See more at its website: http://www.emporium.vt.edu.

3. The movie "The Ivory Tower" does an effective job of pushing the wasteful amenities position, complete with splashy visuals of rock climbing walls set to

dramatic but vaguely sinister music. Here's the trailer: https://www.youtube.com/watch?v=eLdU7uts4ws.

4. See Coase (1937).

5. We use the quotes because in our experience some people are uncomfortable talking about education using the same language applied to mere "business." The logic of economic incentives, however, applies to both.

6. See Panzar and Willig (1981).

7. Coase (1937), p. 387.

8. Coase (1937), p. 390.

9. See Scott (2006).

10. Schachner (1962), p. 151.

11. Cobban (1975) gives a detailed account of the formation of the University of Bologna. See his chapter III (pp. 48–74).

12. Schachner (1962), p. 161.

13. Cobban (1975) also gives a very detailed account of the early days of the University of Paris. See chapter IV (pp. 75–95).

14. Schachner (1962), p. 57.

15. Schachner (1962), p. 71.

16. Panzar and Willig (1981), p. 269.

17. Panzar and Willig (1981), p. 269.

18. See, for example, Cohn, Rhine, and Santos (1989); Laband and Lentz (2003); and Worthington and Higgs (2008).

19. Lewis and Dundar (2001), p. 165.

20. Carey (2015), p. 29. Carey's tale of the creation of the hybrid university brings together most of the major critics of American higher education over the last century, while studiously avoiding any nuanced contemporary (or current) rebuttal. His story is also very light on what most social scientists might regard as evidence. The critics he cites are called "honest observers," so the dissenters must be less honorable.

21. See Christensen and Eyring (2011).

22. This storyline never mentions significant contemporary efforts at major research universities to improve the quality of the undergraduate experience. As but one example, in 1995 the University of Texas at Austin created the "Academy of Master Teachers" to reward teaching excellence among the tenured faculty and to spread innovative teaching methods throughout the curriculum. These master teachers are integrated into the core curriculum and teach "signature courses" to first-year students.

23. Despite the iconic status of disruption at business schools, the whole empirical basis for the disruption argument is open to question. See King and Baatartogtokh (2015).

24. Ask the faculty at Oberlin or Amherst if they are in thrall to Harvard and we're sure you will get many a raised eyebrow. In a quiet corner, away from

microphones, you may even hear some comment that their undergraduates are offered a better, more personalized education (including research) than the average fare at more elite "research institutions."

CHAPTER 4

1. For the 2014–15 school year, tuition at one institution, Sarah Lawrence College, passed the $60,000 barrier. Next year we can look forward to stories about the number of schools that joined Sarah Lawrence.
2. See Ikenberry and Hartle (1998).
3. See Belkin (2013).
4. See Quandt (2014).
5. See Taylor et al. (2011).
6. Figure 2.7 gives data on tuition reliance. Here we are talking about the reliance on subsidies, which is essentially one minus tuition reliance.
7. Data availability limited our sample.
8. See Baum and Lapovsky (2006).
9. Several institutions have reduced or eliminated tuition discounting and have announced dramatic reductions in their list-price tuition. See Scott Jaschik (2005).
10. Leonhardt (2014) also noted the problem with the BLS using list prices.
11. The data for these two series come from *Trends in College Pricing* published by the College Board. The information for net price starts in 1990 instead of 1987. Anyone who has more than a passing interest in higher education should become familiar with this very readable and data-rich publication.
12. This section is a brief reprise of the analysis in our earlier book, *Why Does College Cost So Much?* (Archibald and Feldman, 2011).
13. See Baumol and Bowen (1966).
14. Jones and Yang (2016) use a sophisticated general equilibrium model to demonstrate that differences in productivity growth can explain college cost growth. Their analysis supports our argument. Also, many people think that cost disease requires soaring wages in any industry so afflicted. This is a misunderstanding. Cost disease only requires compensation to behave like national averages. The driver of cost disease is a difference in the rate of productivity growth, not growth in compensation.
15. See Eagan et al. (2014).
16. University of Groningen and University of California, Davis, *Total Factor Productivity at Constant National Prices for United States* [RTFPNAUSA632NRUG], retrieved from FRED, Federal Reserve Bank of St. Louis, https://research.stlouisfed.org/fred2/series/RTFPNAUSA632NRUG/.
17. Hoxby (1997) shows that the fraction of students applying to a college outside their home state grew dramatically, from 23.4% in 1972 to 43.2% in 1992.

18. See Green, Kisida, and Mills (2010), p. 1.

19. Not all of the job titles were as illuminating as one would have liked, but in most cases they were clear. Unfortunately, William and Mary redefined the department variable in 2006, and we found it very difficult to reconcile the two systems. Therefore, we will focus on the data from 1994 to 2005.

20. The growth in professional staff is per 1,000 students, from 43.5 in 1994 to 73.9 in 2005, which suggests a bit faster growth compared to the Delta Cost Project data for public institutions, from 53.0 in 1990 to 73.0 in 2012, but the differences are not large.

21. We could have gone further in this direction by moving staff with computer-related jobs in some academic unit to information technology, but we decided not to do this. In this way we may understate the rise in jobs directly related to increases in support for computing on campus.

22. This calculation assumes a conservative 5% discount rate on the future.

23. Benchmarking Investments in Advancement: Results of the Inaugural CASE Advancement Investment Metrics Study, 2012.

24. In the 1994 data computer science and related was occupational code 25100. We created our 2005 estimate by combining occupational codes 15-1011—computer and information scientists, research; 15-1021—computer programmers; 15-1031—computer software engineers, applications; 15-1032—computer software engineers, systems software; 151041—computer support specialists; 15-1051—computer systems analysts; 15-1061—database administrators; 15-1071—network and computer systems administrators; 15-1081—network systems and data communications analysts; and 15-1099—computer specialists, all other.

25. We are making the comparison under the assumption that the executive secretaries are a relatively small group.

26. The new $85 million leisure project with a lazy river at cash-strapped Louisiana State University offers a prime example.

CHAPTER 5

1. In 1970, only 28% of enrolled students were more than twenty-five years old. By 1990, that number had risen to 44%. Since then, the percentage has fluctuated around 41% to 44%, and forecasts for 2023 show it staying in that range. See Table 303.40 from the NCES (2015) Digest of Education Statistics.

2. At four-year for-profit schools, however, only 30% of full-time students were younger than twenty-five. The nontraditional age range is their bread and butter. See Table 303.50 from the NCES (2015) Digest of Education Statistics.

3. See Prescott and Bransberger (2012).

4. In 2014, full-time enrollment at public four-year schools totaled 5,911,000. The Higher Education Information Survey (HEGIS) forecasts a 2024 enrollment

of 6,669,000. Likewise, overall full-time enrollment at four-year schools (public, private, nonprofit, or profit making) is forecast to rise from 9,739,000 to 11,016,000.

5. Hoxby (2009) discusses the reasons selectivity has increased at the most selective institutions while it has tended to decrease at schools that started out less selective. Writing in 2009 she concluded, "Only the top 10 percent of colleges are substantially more selective now than they were in 1962."

6. Northeast (ME, VT, NH, MA, RI, CT, NY, PA, NJ), South (MD, DE, WV, KY, VA, TN, NC, OK, AR, MS, AL GA, SC, TX, LA, FL), Midwest (MN, WI, MI, NE, IA, IL, IN, OH, KS, MO), and West (AK, HI, WA ID, MT, ND, OR, WY, SD, CA, NV, UT, CO, AS, NM).

7. While high, the number of students attending college close to home is falling. In 1970, 64.6% of students attended college within 100 miles of home. This information comes from the freshman survey conducted by the Higher Education Research Institute at UCLA. See http://www.heri.ucla.edu/monographs/.

8. A good example is Bain's "financially sustainable university" calculations. Any institution that borrows to fund a new building or an expansion of a program will see its equity ratio fall. No matter how much potential the forward-looking investment might have, the school will be tagged as financially weaker. See http://www.thesustainableuniversity.com.

9. See Selingo (2015).

10. Taylor et al. (2011).

11. See Abel and Dietz (2014).

12. Carnevale, Cheah, and Hanson (2015) use census data to show that the graduate degree wage premium varies by undergraduate major. Nonetheless, there is a graduate degree wage premium, and this premium is left out of the analysis done by Abel and Dietz.

13. See Oreopoulos and Petronijevic (2013).

14. See Archibald, Feldman, and McHenry (2015).

15. The first is the National Longitudinal Study of 1972, which tracked the high school class of 1972. The second is the Educational Longitudinal Study of 2002, which tracked high school sophomores from 2002.

16. The college-going rate has increased most dramatically for young women, and young women disproportionately make up the top half of the high school GPA distribution.

17. See Altonji, Bharadwaj, and Lange (2012). The gains over time are largest for the best students and smallest for the least capable, but they are positive throughout the ability spectrum.

18. See Brand and Xie (2010).

19. The data for Figure 5.5 come from the American Community Survey and sample employed graduates of high school and college ages twenty-five to thirty-five.

The shape of the line changes very little if we expand the age category to broader ranges like twenty-five to sixty-five.

20. Abel and Dietz (2014) do a similar calculation using the census's March Current Population Survey and get much the same result.

21. The individual majors used were agriculture and natural resources—general agriculture; architecture and engineering—electrical engineering; arts—fine arts; biology and life sciences—biology; business—business management and administration; communications and journalism—communications and mass media; computers, statistics, and mathematics—computer science; education—general education; health—nursing; humanities and liberal arts—English language and literature; industrial arts, consumer services, and recreation—physical fitness, parks, recreation, and leisure; law and public policy—criminal justice and fire protection; physical sciences—multidisciplinary or general science; psychology and social work—psychology; social science—economics.

22. See Carnevale and Rose (2011).

23. See Ashenfelter and Krueger (1994).

24. See Angrist and Chen (2011).

25. See Card (1995, 2001).

26. Zimmerman (2014).

27. See Oreopoulos and Petronijevic (2013).

28. A claim that has been confirmed by Riddell (2008) using Canadian data.

29. Hungerford and Solon (1987), p. 177.

30. Oreopoulos and Salvanes (2011) survey this literature.

CHAPTER 6

1. St. Louis Fed. https://research.stlouisfed.org/fred2/series/A229RX0.

2. These data come from the US Census Bureau, http://www.census.gov/hhes/www/income/data/historical/inequality/.

3. This section borrows heavily from Archibald and Feldman (2016).

4. Friedman (1968), p. 108.

5. See Archibald and Feldman (2006).

6. Some for-profits do offer small discounts for recent high school graduates who pass a minimal grade point average threshold. This is marketing, not enrollment management of the sort that mission-driven nonprofits practice.

7. Ferris (2013) noted that Colby College, Reed College, Tufts University, and Wesleyan University had recently announced a shift toward need-aware admission.

8. NACUBO (2015), Figure 1, p. 4.

9. At more elite institutions that leave potential tuition revenue uncollected, the competition makes existing *need*-based aid packages more grant heavy instead

of loan heavy. As a result, students may sort into better schools, and access at the bottom may improve as net price falls. But for schools not in the elite, they will see a decrease in revenue from the existing "optimal" group of applicants. As the school does its best in the face of more intense discounting competition, it may reduce the fraction of students with need that it enrolls (become more need aware if it can). Alternatively, it may have to cut the quality of its programming as its revenue base declines or shrink overall enrollment. But it has to adjust.

10. The Third Circuit Court reversed the Philadelphia decision, saying the issue required a more complete hearing. MIT settled with the Justice Department, but the remaining constraint on information sharing meant that aid coordination ceased.

11. This table is extracted from Table 6 in the NACUBO report.

12. If the inflation rate that year was 2%, then the family's money income rose to $55,080, which buys $54,000 worth of goods and services at last year's prices.

13. See Bureau of Labor Statistics (2014).

14. It is easy for us to explain our claim here using the language of microeconomics. What a family can afford is contained in its budget set. If a commodity bundle was in the family's budget set in one period and is still in its budget set after some changes, the changes have not made the commodity bundle less affordable.

15. See Baum and Ma (2014).

16. See Baum and Ma (2014).

17. See Avery and Turner (2012).

18. The data for average debt at public institutions includes in-state and out-of-state students, so the students are facing different prices. This makes direct comparisons difficult. The data are more easily compared for private nonprofit institutions and the 2012–13 average tuition fees and room and board are $33,898. See the College Board's *Trends in College Pricing 2014* (College Board, 2014).

19. This table appears as Figure 14.A in the 2014 edition of *Trends in Student Aid 2014* (College Board, 2014).

20. See, for example, Bronner (2013).

CHAPTER 7

1. At our own institution the figure is roughly 12% (for 2015–16). As recently as 1980 the figure was 43%.

2. Figure 2.8 presents these data.

3. The diagram first appeared in American Academy of Arts and Sciences (2015), p. 15.

4. These percentages come from American Academy of Arts and Sciences (2015), pp. 8 and 10.

5. These data come from the College Board's *Trends in College Pricing 2014* (College Board, 2014). See Table 2.A.

6. These data come from the College Board's *Trends in College Pricing 2014* (College Board, 2014). See Table 1A.

7. See Bound et al. (2016).

8. The state of Texas created the Permanent University Fund (PUF) in 1876 to support the development of higher education. The revenue from a portion of state-owned land funded the endowment. The oil boom of the late nineteenth century ensured the PUF's lasting size.

9. See Anderson (2015).

10. Differences in accounting practices do not allow for accurate comparisons of total E&G expenditures for public and private institutions. There is no problem with the comparisons using "wages and salaries" in E&G categories. The data for these calculations come from the Delta Cost Project.

11. The October 15, 1990, *US News and World Report* only ranked twenty-five schools. Other schools were put in tiers.

12. See Hanks (2015).

13. See Bound, Lovenheim, and Turner (2010).

14. These data come from the College Board's *Trends in Student Aid 2014* (College Board, 2014). See Figure 26A.

15. These data come from the College Board's *Trends in Student Aid 2014* (College Board, 2014). See Figure 27A.

16. These data come from the College Board's *Trends in Student Aid 2014* (College Board, 2014). See Table 1A and Figure 7.

17. These data come from the College Board's *Trends in Student Aid 2014* (College Board, 2014). See Table 22.

18. Bennett (1987).

19. This argument comes from Archibald and Feldman (2016). This paper also contains a more thorough review of the problems with the empirical literature about the Bennett hypothesis. In brief, the existing literature on the Bennett effect is inconclusive and suffers from many defects in experimental design.

20. Some state financial aid programs do increase a student's grant if his or her tuition bill rises, but not the federal Pell program that is the subject of so much of the political rhetoric.

21. See Turner (2012, 2014).

22. See Cellini and Goldin (2014).

23. See Lau (2014).

24. Bettinger (2004), for instance, works carefully through the statistical issues involved in identifying the relationship between changes in Pell support and persistence. He shows that increases in aid do not reduce persistence, as they might if eliminating "skin in the game" caused lower-income students to reduce their work effort. And under many specifications, he shows that extra aid significantly improved persistence.

25. See Bettinger et al. (2012).

26. See, for example, Press and Washburn (2001) and Washburn (2005).

CHAPTER 8

1. Labor productivity growth has been very low since the onset of the financial crisis in 2008, and if it stays low we would expect the push of "cost disease" to abate. This way to slow the growth of college cost, however, is worse than the disease.

2. We have not written a caricature. This view suffuses many recent books that forecast a rupture in the higher education industry. Some prominent examples include *The Innovative University* by Clay Christensen and Henry Eyring (2011), *The End of College* by Kevin Carey (2015), *College Disrupted: The Great Unbundling of Higher Education* by Ryan Craig (2015), and *College (Un)Bound: The Future of Higher Education and What It Means for Students* by Jeffrey Selingo (2013).

3. Grade Change – Tracking Online Education in the United States: http://www.onlinelearningsurvey.com/reports/gradechange.pdf.

4. The data come from IPEDS, and the table is drawn from McPherson and Bacow (2015).

5. In 2012, Alabama, Florida, Michigan, Virginia, and Idaho required students to take an online course for high school graduations. See Kelsey Sheehy (2012).

6. Evergreen Education Group: "Keeping Pace with K12 Digital Learning," http://www.kpk12.com/wp-content/uploads/Evergreen_KeepingPace_2015.pdf.

7. See https://ohs.stanford.edu.

8. See Chafkin (2013–14).

9. See Perna et al. (2013).

10. See Christensen et al. (2013).

11. See Banerjee and Duflo (2014).

12. The quote can be found in many places. See *Wired Magazine* for instance: http://www.wired.com/2012/03/ff_aiclass/.

13. See Parry (2009).

14. By using "twin-like" students as the comparison group, the CREDO analysis avoids one of the pernicious problems of nonexperimental studies that don't randomly assign students to different schools or courses. Some students also may self-select into online programs for reasons we cannot observe or control. To deal with this potential selection issue, the study's authors also compare online students to brick-and-mortar students who had at one time attended an online program. When the data all came from students who were at least familiar with online schooling, the results were roughly the same. On average, students in the online programs lost ground to their peers in traditional schools.

15. See Figlio, Rush, and Yin (2013).

16. See Joyce et al. (2015).

17. Michael McPherson, president of the Spencer Foundation, quipped that the learning gaps were "precisely estimated zeros."

18. Clayton Christensen has derisively likened this mixing of distance components with traditional face-to-face instruction to "steamboats with sails."

19. The transformational potential of educational radio, and of correspondence courses before that, similarly failed to dislodge traditional education.

20. McPherson and Bacow (2015) have written an excellent summary of these issues, and of the costs and benefits of online education more generally.

CHAPTER 9

1. The cartoon is number 13479 and it appeared on May 31, 2015.

2. See Zemsky, Wenger, and Massy (2005).

3. See Shulevitch (2015).

4. *Higher Education for American Democracy*, also called the Truman Commission Report, is a six-volume discussion of the condition of higher education in the United States. This quote comes from p. 53 of the first volume.

5. See Barreira and Snider (2010).

6. These concerns include standard social and emotional development issues, academic and personal stress, and the trendier issues of identity development and personal growth. The staff usually includes people with advanced training in psychology and in medicine (psychiatry).

7. For severe issues that require intensive or permanent care, counseling centers do refer patients to professional care outside of the college environment.

8. Examples include psychoeducational programs and presentations, information sessions, and crisis response to campus emergencies. These services are "public goods" because they don't exclude people, and, with the exception of some minor congestion, adding to the number of people served doesn't reduce the amount of the service available to others. This is very different from markets for "private goods" where people are routinely excluded (for nonpayment) and where one person's consumption leaves less available for others.

9. The American College Counseling Association's annual surveys contain a wealth of information about the nation's student counseling centers. See http://www.collegecounseling.org/wp-content/uploads/NCCCS2014_v2.pdf.

10. Marano (2002).

11. Which you can see and read about here: http://www.kenyon.edu/virtual-tour/locations/science-quad/.

12. See www.niu.edu/engaged learning/research/, www.uni.edu/resources/undergraduate-research, www.unf.edu/our/, and www.nau.edu/undergraduateresearch/.

13. See http://www.wm.edu/news/stories/2015/alert-wm-team-wins-top-honors-at-igem-synthetic-biology-competition.php.

14. See http://247wallst.com/special-report/2015/09/11/highest-paid-employee-in-each-state/2/.

15. See chapter 2 in Shulman and Bowen (2001).

16. The Department of Justice traditionally takes a dim view of firms that try to "tie" the sale of two or more products together. A pharmaceutical firm that sells a blood chemistry medication, for instance, may want consumers to buy its proprietary blood monitoring devices, and it may force the issue by tying the sales together. That firm will find itself in court, charged with violating antitrust law. On the surface, the college bundle seems like a set of tied services. Most of the college bundle avoids the tying issue because the courts recognize efficiency as a reasonable case for tying. In the case of the college bundle, economies of scope offer a clear rationale for joint production, and there are other convenience benefits from the bundle that make it economic for the consumer. The option value argument we have made is one of those benefits.

17. See http://chronicle.com/article/NCAA-Signs-108-Billion-De/65219/.

18. See http://www.cbssports.com/collegefootball/eye-on-college-football/21083689/espn-reaches-12year-deal-to-air-college-football-playoffs.

19. Fulks (2014).

20. Shulman and Bowen (2001).

21. See http://www.schev.edu/Reportstats/TuitionFees/2015-16TFreport.pdf.

22. In addition to student size, we included a categorical (0,1) variable for whether or not football is part of the athletics program. Football-playing schools do have larger athletic fees, but the effect is not statistically robust. You can't ask fifteen data points to tell a complete statistical story, so adding more control variables isn't of much use.

23. See Sanderson and Siegfried (2015).

24. Humphries (2006) and Alexander and Kern (2010) provide evidence of this effect.

25. See Chung (2013).

26. See Pope and Pope (2009).

27. There is also a Division II. It has over 300 members. The membership is a diverse mix of public and private institutions (including one from Canada), and the variation in school enrollment is substantial as well. Division II schools can offer scholarships.

28. At Division III schools, student athletes who have no scholarship to lose often quit team sports at some point if they are simply riding the bench. A quick look at the rosters of the Oberlin and Kenyon football teams showed thirty-four freshmen, thirty-four sophomores, twenty-seven juniors, and seventeen seniors.

29. See"Antitrust Suit Claims NCAA Is 'Unlawful Cartel,'" http://www.cbsnews.com/news/antitrust-suit-claims-ncaa-is-an-unlawful-cartel/.

30. See Farrey (2015).

31. See Ehrenberg and Webber (2010). They break college expenditures into four categories: instructional expenditures, student services, academic support services, and research expenditures. "Instruction" is mostly faculty salaries, and

it includes the portion that goes to departmental research. Academic support refers to everything from the library to information technology services. Finally, the separate research category measures externally sponsored research and separately budgeted research centers. Increased spending on instruction and department research also raises graduation rates, though by a smaller amount.

32. Ehrenberg and Webber (2010), p. 953.

CHAPTER 10

1. One prominent exception is the large "need based" discount that well-endowed elite institutions offer to students in excess of anything their public counterparts can match. Presuming the student can get in, tuition is free at a number of elite institutions even for families earning well above the national median income.

2. The pattern we see in the table still holds if we correct for the fact that an institution has a medical school. Having a medical school clearly attracts large donations, but it does not erase the effect of admissions selectivity.

3. Using two big longitudinal data sets (the NLS-72 the NELS:88), Bound, Lovenheim, and Turner (2010) find that cuts in public funding are the most significant reason for falling graduation rates in the last quarter of the twentieth century. Low graduation rates were a feature of life at lower-ranked public universities but not at higher-ranked flagships.

4. See Kelderman (2016).

5. See "2 Public Colleges in Illinois Announce More Layoffs and Cuts," *Chronicle of Higher Education* LXII (March 11, 2016): A23.

6. "Kansas' Public Colleges to Lose $17 Million in State Funds," *Chronicle of Higher Education*, LXII (March 11, 2016): A23.

7. A quick look at the list of EdX charter members (https://www.edx.org/schools-partners) shows that all of the American members are selective private institutions or state flagships.

8. Using data from 1998, James Shulman and William Bowen (2001) show that the average total expenditures for intercollegiate athletics at Division I institutions in their sample are roughly twenty times the same expenditures for Division III institutions in their sample (see p. 230).

9. See http://www.nytimes.com/2016/04/30/us/small-colleges-losing-market-share-struggle-to-keep-doors-open.html?hpw&rref=us&action=click&pgtype=Homepage&module=well-region&region=bottom-well&WT.nav=bottom-well.

10. The following is an unscientific example of potential underinvestment, but it is suggestive. Swarthmore is a 1,537-student institution rated most selective by Barron's. It lists forty-two individuals in its development office (http://www.swarthmore.edu/giving/development-staff). By contrast, Ferrum College with 1,440 students is rated less selective in Barron's, and we could find only eight

individuals in the Ferrum Faculty and Staff Directory with titles suggesting that they worked in institutional advancement (which combines development with alumni relations).

11. See Reid (2015).
12. Goldin and Margo (1992) have called this time period of relative income equality "The Great Compression."
13. The underlying data come from the Census Bureau. See Archibald, Feldman, and McHenry (2015).
14. These data come from Appendix 6 in Bastedo and Jaquette (2011). The appendix is online (http://www.umich.edu/~bastedo/papers/EEPA-Appendix.pdf).
15. See Archibald, Feldman, and McHenry (2015) for evidence on the diminishing importance of family income and parental education for college attendance.
16. See Bowen, Chingos, and McPherson (2009).
17. See Hoxby and Avery (2013). They define high achieving as having scores in the top 10% of test takers and grades at least at the A– level. High (low) income is defined as being in the top (bottom) quartile of the income distribution of families with a high school senior.

CHAPTER 11

1. See Kantrowitz (2009).
2. Many state universities do discount tuition, and much of the discounting is need based. But discount rates at private universities often are two to four times as large as the average discount rate at public institutions.
3. See Kelly (2013).
4. See Hillman (2016).
5. See Ridley and Simon (1938).
6. See Turner (2012).
7. See Gneezy and Rustichini (2000).
8. See Hillman, Tandberg and Fryar (2015).
9. See Rueben, Gault, and Baum (2015) for an overview of eight options for simplifying the FAFSA process.
10. See Hoxby and Turner (2013, 2015).
11. Almost 40% of the recipients didn't remember getting the mailing. This means that these positive results substantially underestimate the potential of the program once recognizable sponsors back it.
12. See http://nces.ed.gov/collegenavigator/.
13. The Census Bureau, for instance, no longer collects basic information on incomes, house values, and parental education.
14. Authors' calculation from the March Current Population Survey (census data).
15. See Avery and Turner (2012).

16. The data from Figure 5.1 show that there will be at least 3.2 million high school graduates. The data from Figure 5.4 indicate that 8.65% of students in the tenth decile of the high school grade point average distribution attend a four-year school. Combining these students with 13.94% from the ninth decile and 20.08% from the eighth decile gives us our estimate.

17. From the Georgia Student Finance Commission: https://apps.gsfc.org/Main/publishing/pdf/common/FY2017%20Award%20Charts%20Combined.pdf.

18. See Archibald (2002) for an early proposal of this type and Alexander (2016) for proposals currently under consideration in Congress.

19. See Webber (2015).

20. We can't construct a similar ratio for the bottom quartile of the income distribution because net tuition and fees were zero in 1999 and again in 2011. Average grant aid from all sources exceeded list-price tuition. The net cost of attendance, however, was not zero because that includes room, board, and transport.

21. At present, only Vermont and New Hampshire spend so little per full-time student that they would be ineligible under this criterion without ramping up spending.

22. See chapter 15 of *Why Does College Cost So Much?* (Archibald and Feldman, 2011) for a fuller treatment.

Bibliography

Abel, Jaison, and Richard Deitz. 2014. "Do the Benefits of College Still Outweigh the Costs?" *Federal Reserve Bank of New York Current Issues* 20 (3).

Alexander, Donald, and William Kern. 2010. "Does Athletic Success Generate Legislative Largess from Sports-Crazed Representatives? The Impart of Athletic Success on State Appropriations to Colleges and Universities." *International Journal of Sports Finance* 5 (4): 253–67.

Alexander, Lamar. 2016. "Risk-Sharing/Skin-in-the-Game Concepts and Proposals." http://www.help.senate.gov/imo/media/Risk_Sharing.pdf.

Allen, Elaine, and Jeff Seaman. 2015. "Grade Change – Tracking Online Education in the US." http://www.onlinelearningsurvey.com/reports/gradechange.pdf.

Altonji, Joseph G., Prashant Bharadwaj, and Fabian Lange. 2012. "Changes in the Characteristics of American Youth: Implications for Adult Outcomes." *Journal of Labor Economics* 30 (October): 783–828.

American Academy of Arts and Sciences. 2015. "Public Research Universities: Changes in State Funding." https://www.amacad.org/multimedia/pdfs/publications/researchpapersmonographs/PublicResearchUniv_ChangesInStateFunding.pdf.

Anderson, Nick. 2015. "William and Mary launches $1 billion drive, with help from $50 million gift," *Washington Post*, October 23, 2013. https://www.washington-post.com/news/grade-point/wp/2015/10/23/william-and-mary-launches-1-billion-drive-with-help-from-50-million-gift/?utm_term=.631660932deo.

Angrist, Joshua, and Stacey Chen. 2011. "Schooling and the Vietnam-Era GI Bill: Evidence from the Draft Lottery." *American Economic Journal: Applied Economics* 3 (April): 96–119.

Archibald, Robert. 2002. *Redesigning the Financial Aid System: Why Colleges and Universities Should Switch Roles with the Federal Government*. Baltimore: Johns Hopkins University Press.

Archibald, Robert B., and David H. Feldman. 2006. "State Higher Education Spending and the Tax Revolt." *Journal of Higher Education* 77 (July /August): 618–44.

Archibald, Robert B., and David H. Feldman. 2011. "Are Plush Dorms and Fancy Food Plans Important Drivers of College Cost?" *Change* 43 (January/February): 31–37.

Archibald, Robert B., and David H. Feldman. 2011. *Why Does College Cost So Much?* New York: Oxford University Press.

Archibald, Robert B., and David H. Feldman. 2016. "Federal Financial Aid Policy and College Behavior." American Council on Education.

Archibald, Robert B., David H. Feldman, and Peter McHenry. 2015. "A Quality-Preserving Increase in Four-Year College Attendance." *Journal of Human Capital* 9 (Fall): 265–97.

Arum, Richard, and Josipa Roksa. 2010. *Academically Adrift: Limited Learning on College Campuses.* Chicago: University of Chicago Press.

Ashenfelter, Orley, and Alan Krueger. 1994. "Estimates of the Economic Return to Schooling from a New Sample of Twins." *American Economic Review* 84 (December): 1157–73.

Avery, Christopher, and Sarah Turner. 2012. "Student Loans: Do College Students Borrow Too Much – Or Not Enough?" *Journal of Economic Perspectives* 26 (1): 165–92.

Bacow, Lawrence S., and Michael McPherson. 2015. "Online Higher Education: Beyond the Hype Cycle." *Journal of Economic Perspectives* 29 (4): 135–54.

Banerjee, Abhijit, and Esther Duflo. 2014. "(Dis)organization and Success in an Economics MOOC." *American Economic Review: Papers and Proceedings* 104 (5): 514–18.

Barreira, Paul, and Lalorie Snider. 2010. "History of College Counseling and Mental Health Services and Role of the Community Mental Health Model." In *Mental Health Care in the College Community*, edited by Jerald Kay and Victor Schwartz (Hoboken: Wiley), chap. 2.

Bastedo, Michael N., and Ozan Jaquette. 2011. "Running in Place: Low-Income Students and the Dynamics of Higher Education Stratification." *Educational Evaluation and Policy Analysis* 33 (September): 318–39.

Baum, Sandy, and Lucie Lapovsky. 2006. *Tuition Discounting: Not Just a Private College Practice.* Washington, DC: College Board.

Baum, Sandy, and Alice Ma. 2014. "College Affordability: What Is It and How Can We Measure It?" Lumina Foundation. https://www.luminafoundation.org/files/publications/ideas_summit/College_Affordability-What_Is_It_and_How_Can_We_Measure_It.pdf.

Baumol, William J., and William G. Bowen. 1966. *Performing Arts: The Economic Dilemma.* New York: Twentieth Century Fund.

Belkin, Douglas. 2013. "How to Get College Tuition Under Control." *Wall Street Journal*, October 8, 2013. http://www.wsj.com/articles/SB10001424127887324545490045790689928347361 38.

Bennett, William. 1987. "Our Greedy Colleges." *The New York Times*, February 18, 1987. http://www.nytimes.com/1987/02/18/opinion/our-greedy-colleges.html.

Bettinger, Eric P. 2004. "How Financial Aid Affects Persistence." NBER working paper 10242 (January).

Bettinger, Eric P., Bridget Terry Long, Philip Oreopoulos, and Lisa Sanbonmatsu. 2012. "The Role of Application Assistance and Information in College Decisions: Results from the H&R Block FAFSA Experiment." *Quarterly Journal of Economics* 127 (3): 1205–42.

Blumenstyk, Goldie. 2014. "At 2 Conferences, Big Claims Are Staked on Higher Education's Future." *Chronicle of Higher Education*, May 12, 2014. http://chronicle.com/article/At-2-Conferences-Big-Claims/146461.

Bound, John, Breno Braga, Gaurav Khanna, and Sarah Turner. 2016. "A Passage to America: University Funding and International Students." Population Studies Center Report 16-859, March, 2016. http://www.psc.isr.umich.edu/pubs/pdf/rr16-859.pdf .

Bound, John, Michael F. Lovenheim, and Sarah Turner. 2010. "Why Have College Completion Rates Declined? An Analysis of Changing Student Preparation and Collegiate Resources." *American Economic Journal: Applied Economics* 2 (July): 129–57.

Bowen, William G., Matthew M. Chingos, and Michael S. McPherson. 2009. *Crossing the Finish Line: Completing College at America's Public Universities*. Princeton, NJ: Princeton University Press.

Brand, Jennie E., and Yue Xie. 2010. "Who Benefits Most from College? Evidence for Negative Selection in Heterogeneous Economic Returns to Higher Education." *American Sociological Review* 75 (2): 273–302.

Bronner, Ethan. 2013. "Law Schools' Applications Fall as Costs Rise and Jobs Are Cut." *New York Times*, January 30, 2013, p. A1.

Bureau of Labor Statistics. 2014. "Explaining the 30-year shift in consumer expenditures from commodities to services, 1982–2012." *BLS Monthly Labor Review*, April, 2014. http://www.bls.gov/opub/mlr/2014/article/explaining-the-shift-in-consumer-expenditures.htm.

Card, David. 1995. "Using Geographic Variation in College Proximity to Estimate the Returns to Schooling." in *Aspects of Labour Market Behaviour: Essays in Honour of John Vanderkamp*, edited by Lous N. Chistofides, E. Kenneth Grant, and Robert Swidinsky. Toronto: University of Toronto Press, 201–22.

Card, David. 2001. "Estimating the Return to Schooling: Progress on Some Persisten Econometric Problems." *Econometrica* 69 (5): 1127–60.

Carey, Kevin. 2015. *The End of College: Creating the Future of Learning and the University of Everywhere*. New York: Riverhead Books.

Carnevale, Anthony and Stephen Rose. 2011. "The Undereducated American." Georgetown University Center on Education and the Workforce.

Carnevale, Anthony, Ban Cheah, and Andrew Hanson. 2015. "The Economic Value of College Majors." Georgetown University Center on Education and the Workforce.

Cellini, Stephanie Reigg and Claudia Goldin. 2014. "Does Federal Student Aid Raise Tuition? New Evidence from For-Profit Colleges." *American Economic Journal: Economic Policy* 6 (November): 174–206.

Center for Research on Educational Outcomes, Stanford University. 2015. "Online Charter School Study." https://credo.stanford.edu/pdfs/OnlineCharterStudyFinal2015.pdf.

Chafkin, Max. 2013–14. "Udacity's Sebastian Thrun, Godfather of Free Online Education, Changes Course." *Fast Company Magazine*, December/January. http://www.fastcompany.com/3021473/udacity-sebastian-thrun-uphill-climb.

Chokshi, Niraj. 2009. "Education Costs Rising Faster Than Health Care" *The Atlantic*, August 24, 2009. http://www.theatlantic.com/business/archive/2009/08/education-costs-rising-faster-than-health-care/23705/.

Christensen, Clayton M., and Henry J. Eyring. 2011. *The Innovative University: Changing the DNA of Higher Education*. San Francisco: Jossey-Bass.

Christensen, Gayle, Andrew Steinmetz, Brandon Alcorn, Amy Bennett, Deirdre Woods, and Ezekiel. J. Emanuel. 2013. "The MOOC Phenomenon: Who Takes Massive Open Online Courses and Why?" University of Pennsylvania.

Chung, Doug J. 2013. "The Dynamic Advertising Effects of College Athletics." Harvard Business School Working Paper 13–067 (April).

Clinedinst, Melissa. 2014. "State of College Tuition 2014." National Association of College Admission Counselors. http://www.nxtbook.com/ygsreprints/NACAC/2014SoCA_nxtbk/#/0.

Coase, Ronald H. 1937. "The Nature of the Firm." *Economica* 4 (November): 386–405.

Cobban, A. B. 1975. *The Medieval Universities: Their Development and Organization*. London: Methuen & Co.

Cohn, Elchanan, Sherrie L. W. Rhine, and Maria C. Santos. 1989. "Institutions of Higher Education as Multiproduct Firms: Economies of Scale and Scope." *Review of Economics and Statistics* 71 (2): 284–90.

College Board. 2013. "Trends in College Pricing 2013." https://trends.collegeboard.org/sites/default/files/college-pricing-2013-full-report-140108.pdf.

College Board. 2014. "Trends in College Pricing 2014." https://trends.collegeboard.org/sites/default/files/2014-trends-college-pricing-final-web.pdf.

College Board. 2014. "Trends in Student Aid 2014." https://trends.collegeboard.org/sites/default/files/2014-trends-student-aid-final-web.pdf.

Craig, Ryan. 2015. *College Disrupted: The Great Unbundling of Higher Education.* New York: Palgrave Macmillan.

Delta Cost Project. http://www.deltacostproject.org.

Deming, David J., Noam Yuchtman, Amira Abulafi, Claudia Goldin, and Lawrence F. Katz. 2016. "The Value of Postsecondary Credentials in the Labor Market: An Experimental Study." Working Paper.

Eagan, Kevin, Ellen Bara Stolzenberger, Joseph J. Ramirez, Melissa C. Aragon, Maria Ramirez Suchard, and Sylvia Hurtado. 2014. *The American Freshman: National Norms Fall 2014.* Cooperative Institutional Research Program at the Higher Education Research Institute. http://www.heri.ucla.edu/monographs/TheAmericanFreshman2014.pdf.

Ehrenberg, Ronald, and Douglas Webber. 2010. "Do expenditures other than instructional expenditures affect graduation and persistence rates in American higher education." *Economics of Education Review* 29 (December): 947–58.

Evergreen Education Group. 2016. "Keeping Pace with K12 Digital Learning." http://www.kpk12.com/wp-content/uploads/Evergreen_KeepingPace_2015.pdf.

Farrey, Tom. 2015. "Northwestern Players Denied Request to Form First Union for Athletes." ESPN, August 15, 2015. http://espn.go.com/college-football/story/_/id/13455477/nlrb-says-northwestern-players-cannot-unionize.

Ferris, Sara. 2013. "Across U.S. colleges turn toward need-aware policies to manage financial shortcomings," *The GW Hatchet*, October 24, 2013. http://www.gwhatchet.com/2013/10/24/across-u-s-colleges-turn-toward-need-aware-policies-to-manage-financial-shortcomings/.

Figlio, David N., Mark Rush, and Lu Yin. 2013. "Is it Live or is it Internet? Experimental Evidence of the Effects of Online Instruction on Student Learning." In *Journal of Labor Economics* 31 (October): 763–84.

Frey, Thomas. 2013. "Eight Reasons Why More Than Half of Colleges Are Doomed," July 18, 2013. http://www.cobizmag.com/articles/eight-reasons-why-more-than-half-of-colleges-are-doomed.

Friedman, Milton. 1968. "The Higher Schooling in America." *Public Interest* 11 (Spring): 108–12.

Fulks, Daniel L. 2014. *NCAA Division I Intercollegiate Athletics Programs Report, 2004–2013: Revenues and Expenses.* Indianapolis: NCAA. http://www.ncaapublications.com/p-4334-division-i-revenues-and-expenses-2004-2013.aspx.

Gansemer-Topf, Ann M., and John H. Schuh. 2003. "Instruction and Academic Support Expenditures: An Investment in Retention and Graduation." *Journal of College Student Retention* 5 (2): 135–45.

Gneezy, Uri, and Aldo Rustichini. 2000. "A Fine Is a Price." *Journal of Legal Studies* 29 (1): 1–17.

Goldin, Claudia, and Robert Margo. 1992. "The Great Compression: The Wage Structure at Mid-Century." *Quarterly Journal of Economics* 57 (1): 1–34.

Green, Jay P., Brian Kisida, and Jonathan Mills. 2010. "Administrative Bloat at American Universities: The Real Reason for High Costs in Higher Education." Policy Report No. 239, The Goldwater Institute, August 17, 2010.

Hanks, Tom. 2015. "I Owe It All to Community College." *New York Times,* January 14, 2015. http://www.nytimes.com/2015/01/14/opinion/tom-hanks-on-his-two-years-at-chabot-college.html.

Hillman, Nicholas. 2016. "Why Performance Based College Funding Doesn't Work." *The Century Foundation,* May 25, 2016. https://tcf.org/content/report/why-performance-based-college-funding-doesnt-work/.

Hillman, Nicholas, David A. Tandberg, and Alisa H. Fryar. 2015. "Evaluating the Impacts of "New" Performance Funding in Higher Education." *Educational Evaluation and Policy Analysis* 20 (10): 1–19.

Hoxby, Caroline M. 1997. "How the Changing Market Structure of U.S. Higher Education Explains College Tuition." NBER Working Paper 6323 (December).

Hoxby, Caroline M. 2009. "The Changing Selectivity of American Colleges." *Journal of Economic Perspectives* 23 (Fall): 95–118.

Hoxby, Caroline M., and Christopher Avery. 2013. "The Missing 'One-Offs': The Hidden Supply of High-Achieving, Low-Income Students." *Brookings Papers on Economic Activity,* Spring, 1–65.

Hoxby, Caroline M., and Sarah Turner. 2013. "Informing Students About Their College Options: A Proposal for Broadening the Expanding College Opportunities Project." The Brookings Institution.

Hoxby, Caroline M., and Sarah Turner. 2015. "What High-Achieving Low-Income Students Know About College." *American Economic Review: Papers and Proceedings* 105 (5): 514–17.

Humphries, Brad R. 2006. "The Relationship Between Big-Time College Football and State Appropriations for Higher Education." *International Journal of Sport Finance* 1 (2): 119–28.

Hungerford, Thomas, and Gary Solon. 1987. "Sheepskin Effects in the Returns to Education." *Review of Economics and Statistics* 69 (February): 175–77.

Ikenberry, Stanely O., and Terry Hartle. 1998. *Too Little Knowledge Is a Dangerous Thing: What the Public Thinks and Knows About Paying for College.* Washington, DC: American Council on Education.

Jaschik, Scott. 2005. "Cutting Tuition, Increasing Revenue." *Chronicle of Higher Education.* https://www.insidehighered.com/news/2005/07/11/tuition.

Jones, John Bailey, and Fang Yang. 2016. "Skill-Biased Technical Change and the Cost of Higher Education." *Journal of Labor Economics.* 34 (April): 621–62.

Joyce, Ted, Sean Crockett, David A. Jaeger, Onur Altindag, and Stephen D. O'Connell. 2015. "Does Classroom Time Matter?" *Economics of Education Review* 46 (3): 64–77.

Kantrowitz, Mark. 2009. "Analysis of Why Some Students Do Not Apply for Financial Aid." http://www.finaid.org/educators/20090427CharacteristicsOf NonApplicants.pdf.

Kelderman, Eric. 2016. "Grim Budget Means More Pain for Louisiana Colleges." *Chronicle of Higher Education* LXII (March 11): A10.

Kelly, Christina Bsonsenga. 2013. "Argentina at the Top—For Its Dropout Rate!" *Inside Higher Ed*, August 5, 2013. https://www.insidehighered.com/blogs/world-view/argentina-top-%E2%80%94-its-dropout-rate.

Kelly, Patrick J., and Dennis P. Jones. 2005. "A New Look at the Institutional Component of Higher Education Finance: A Guide for Evaluating Performance Relative to Financial Resources." Boulder, CO: National Center for Higher Education Management Systems.

King, Andrew, and Baljir Baatartogtokh. 2015. "How Useful Is the Theory of Disruptive Innovation." *MIT Sloan Management Review*, Fall. http://sloanreview.mit.edu/article/how-useful-is-the-theory-of-disruptive-innovation/.

Laband, D. N., and B. F. Lentz. 2003. "New Evidence of Economies of Scale and Scope in Higher Education." *Southern Economic Journal* 70 (1): 172–83.

Lau, Christopher V. 2014. "The Incidence of Federal Subsidies in For-profit Higher Education." (working paper, Northwestern University, Evanston, Illinois, 2014).

Lenzner, Robert, and Stephen S. Johnson. 1997. "Seeing Things as They Really Are." *Forbes*, March 10, 2003, 122–28.

Leonhardt, David. 2014. "How the Government Exaggerates the Cost of College." *New York Times*, July 29, 2014. http://www.nytimes.com/2014/07/29/upshot/how-the-government-exaggerates-the-cost-of-college.html?_r=0.

Lewis, Darrel R., and Halil Dundar. 2001. "Costs and Productivity in Higher Education: Theory, Evidence, and Policy Implications." In *The Finance of Higher Education: Theory Research, Policy and Practice*, edited by Michael B. Paulsen and John C. Smart. New York: Agathon, 133–88.

Marano, Hara Estroff. 2002. "Crisis on Campus." *Psychology Today*, May 2, 2002. https://www.psychologytoday.com/articles/200305/crisis-the-campus.

Matthews, Dylan. 2013. "Introducing 'The Tuition Is Too Damn High.'" *Washington Post, Wonkblog*, August 26, 2013. http://www.washingtonpost.com/blogs/wonk-blog/wp/2013/08/26/introducing-the-tuition-is-too-damn-high/.

McPherson, Michael S., and Lawrence S. Bacow. 2015. "Online Higher Education: Beyond the Hype Cycle." *Journal of Economic Perspectives* 29 (Fall): 135–54.

NACUBO. 2015. "The NACUBO Tuition Discounting Study." National Association of College and University Business Officers, 2015.

NCES. 2015. "Digest of Education Statistics, 2015." https://nces.ed.gov/pubsearch/pubsinfo.asp?pubid=2016014.

Oreopoulos, Philip, and Uros Petronijevic. 2013. "Making College Worth It: A Review of Research on the Returns to Higher Education." NBER Working Paper 19053 (May).

Oreopoulos, Philip, and Kjell Salvanes. 2011. "Priceless: The Nonpecuniary Benefits of Schooling." *Journal of Economic Perspectives* 25 (Winter): 159–84.

Panzar, John C., and Robert D. Willig. 1981. "Economies of Scope." *American Economic Review* 71 (May): 268–72.

Parry, Mark. 2009. "Obama's Great Course Giveaway." *Chronicle of Higher Education*, August 3, 2009.

Perna, Laura, Alan Ruby, Robert Boruch, Nicole Wang, Janie Scull, Chad Evans, and Seher Ahmad. 2013. "The Life Cycle of a Million MOOC Users." University of Pennsylvania (December).

Pope, Devin G., and Jaren C. Pope. 2009. "The Impact of College Sports Success on the Quantity and Quality of Student Applications." *Southern Economic Journal* 75 (3): 750–80.

Prescott, Brian T., and Peace Bransberger. 2012. *Knocking at the College Door: Projections of High School Graduates.* 8th ed. Boulder, CO: Western Interstate Commission for Higher Education.

Press, Eyal, and Jennifer Washburn. 2001. "The Kept University." In *AAAS Science and Technology Policy Yearbook 2001*, edited by Albert H. Teich, Stephen D. Nelson, Celia McEnaney and Stephen J. Lita (Washington DC: American Association for the Advancement of Science), 293–318.

Quandt, Katie Rose. 2014. "College Has Gotten 12 Times More Expensive in One Generation." *Mother Jones*, September 3, 2014. http://www.motherjones.com/politics/2014/09/college-tuition-increased-1100-percent-since-1978.

Reid, Ship. 2015. "Closing of Historic Va. Women's College Signals Turmoil for Higher Education," *CBS News*, March 31, 2015. http://www.cbsnews.com/news/closing-of-sweet-briar-college-signals-turmoil-for-higher-education/.

Riddell, W. Craig. 2008. "Understanding Sheepskin Effects in the Returns to Education: The Role of Cognitive Skills." University of British Columbia Working Paper.

Ridley, Clarence E., and Herbert A. Simon. 1938. *Measuring Municipal Activities: A Survey of Suggested Criteria and Reporting Forms for Appraising Administration.* Chicago: International City Managers' Association.

Rueben, Kim, Sarah Gault, and Sandy Baum 2015. "Simplifying Student Aid: An Overview of Eight Plans." The Urban Institute.

Sanderson, Allen R., and Jojn J. Siegfried. 2015. "The Case for Paying College Athletes." *Journal of Economic Perspectives* 1 (Winter): 115–38.

Schachner, Nathan. 1962. *Mediaeval Universities.* New York: A. S. Barnes and Company.

Scott, John C. 2006. "The Mission of the University: Medieval to Postmodern Transformations." *Journal of Higher Education* 77 (January/February): 1–39.

Selingo, Jeffrey J. 2013. *College (Un)Bound: The Future of Higher Education and What It Means for Students.* New York: New Harvest.

Selingo, Jeffrey J. 2015. "The Value Equation: Measuring and Communicating the Return on Investment of a College Degree." *Chronicle of Higher Education*.

http://images.results.chronicle.com/Web/TheChronicleofHigherEducation/%7B684ffae1-dda4-46b3-a3b8-2eb8be2a6e56%7D_Student_Outcomes_Report_v7_Lynda_LOWRES.pdf.

Senate Bill 2954. https://www.gpo.gov/fdsys/pkg/BILLS-113s2954is/pdf/BILLS-113s2954is.pdf.

Shaffer, Mathew. 2011. "Back to the Future, with Peter Thiel." *National Review Online*, January 20, 2011. http://www.nationalreview.com/articles/257531/back-future-peter-thiel-interview.

Sheehy, Kelsey. 2012. "States, Districts Require Online Ed for High School Graduation." *US News and World Report*, October 24, 2012. http://www.usnews.com/education/blogs/high-school-notes/2012/10/24/states-districts-require-online-ed-for-high-school-graduation.

Shulevitch, Judith. 2015. "In College and Hiding from Scary Ideas." *New York Times*, March 21, 2015.

Shulman, James L., and William G. Bowen. 2001. *The Game of Life: College Sports and Educational Values*. Princeton, NJ: Princeton University Press.

Staton, Michael. 2014. "The Degree Is Doomed." January 8, 2014. http://blogs.hbr.org/2014/01/the-degree-is-doomed/.

Steinberg, Matthew P., and Lauren Sartain. 2015. "Does Teacher Evaluation Improve School Performance? Experimental Evidence from Chicago's Excellence in Teaching Project." *Education Finance and Policy* 10 (4): 535–72.

Taylor, Mark C. 2010. *Crisis on Campus*. New York: Alfred A. Knopf.

Taylor, Paul, Kim Parker, Richard Fry, and D'Vera Cohn. 2011. "Is College Worth It?" Pew Research Center, May 11, 2011. http://www.pewsocialtrends.org/files/2011/05/higher-ed-report.pdf.

Turner, Lesley. 2012. "The Incidence of Student Aid: Evidence from the Pell Program." http://econweb.umd.edu/~turner/LTurner_FedAid_Apr2012.pdf.

Turner, Lesley. 2014. "The Road to Pell Is Paved with Good Intentions: The Economic Incidence of Federal Student Grant Aid." http://econweb.umd.edu/~turner/Turner_FedAidIncidence.pdf.

Washburn, Jennifer. 2005. *University Inc. The Corporate Corruption of Higher Education*. New York: Basic Books.

Watson, John, Larry Pape, Amy Murin, Butch Gemin, and Lauren Vashaw. 2014. "Keeping Pace with K12 Digital Learning." Evergreen Education Group. http://www.kpk12.com/wp-content/uploads/EEG_KP2014-fnl-lr.pdf.

Webber, Douglas A. 2015. "Risk-Sharing and Student Loan Policy: Consequences for Students and Institutions." Temple University, May 22.

Worthington, Andrew C., and Hellen Higgs. 2008. "Economies of Scale and Scope in Australian Higher Education, 1998–2006." Available at SSRN: http://ssrn.com/abstract=1309384 or http://dx.doi.org/10.2139/ssrn.1309384.

Zemsky, Robert, William Wenger, and William Massy. 2005. *Remaking the American University: Market-Smart and Mission Centered*. New Brunswick, NJ: Rutgers University Press.

Zimmerman, Seth. 2014. "The Returns to College Admission for Academically Marginal Students." *Journal of Labor Economics* 32 (October): 711–54.

Zook, George Frederick. 1947. *Higher Education for American Democracy, a Report*. Washington, DC: US Government Printing Office.

Index